NORDSTROM

P9-CIW-417

Jews, Idols and Messiahs

For my dear wife, Miriam, to whose unfailing support and forbearance this book owes its appearance

JEWS, IDOLS AND MESSIAHS
The Challenge from History

LIONEL KOCHAN

Basil Blackwell

Copyright © Lionel Kochan 1990

First published 1990

Basil Blackwell Ltd
108 Cowley Road, Oxford, OX4 1JF, UK

Basil Blackwell, Inc.
3 Cambridge Center
Cambridge, Massachusetts 02142, USA

British Library Cataloguing in Publication Data

A CIP catalogue record for this book is available from the British Library.

Library of Congress Cataloging in Publication Data
Kochan, Lionel.
    Jews, idols, and messiahs : the challenge from history / Lionel Kochan.
        p.   cm.
    Includes bibliographical references.
    ISBN 0-631-15477-9
    1. Jews—Politics and government.   2. Jews—Berlin (Germany)–
History—18th century.   3. Jews—England—London—History.
4. Jewish messianic movements.   5. Berlin (Germany)—Ethnic
relations.   6. London (England)—Ethnic relations.   I. Title.
DS140.K598   1990
943.1′55004924—dc20   90–202
                                                                                                  CIP

Typeset in 10 on 12 pt Ehrhardt
by Photo·graphics, Honiton, Devon
Printed in Great Britain by TJ Press Ltd., Padstow, Cornwall

Contents

Acknowledgements

Parts of this book have been discussed at seminars in Oxford, Cambridge, London and Jerusalem. I am deeply grateful to all participants and to those other colleagues who have commented on the manuscript. The editors of *Modern Judaism*, *Pardès* (Paris) and *The Jewish Law Annual* have kindly permitted me to reprint material that originally appeared in their pages.

To Mr David Massil, of the Board of Deputies of British Jews, I express warm appreciation: his ready help in making available certain of the Board's Minute Books was invaluable.

I also acknowledge with gratitude the financial help generously extended at different times by the Leverhulme Trust and the British Academy.

L.K.

Introduction

'A Book is never finished; it is only laid aside.' On re-reading what I have written, this dictum of Paul Valéry strikes home more convincingly than ever before. When I began to write I hoped to elucidate two conflicting themes in Jewish history – the communal and the messianic – which are in fact one. I would like to think that despite admitted lacunae, I have staked out the origins and dimensions of the conflict. Further research will, I hope, enable me to amplify my argument.

The first, communal, theme takes shape as the attempt to establish Jewish communities in which, as particular circumstances allow, it will become possible to fulfil the requirements of the Torah, as understood at any particular time. This is what I try to convey by the 'politics' of the Torah, potentially a total prescriptive system. But this totality is normally denied so that no case is known of its complete implementation. In this situation of universal incompleteness, to choose the modern communities of Berlin and London to illustrate the communal theme cannot be more arbitrary than any other choice would be. It has, however, the advantage of displaying side by side a compulsory and a voluntary community.

The second, messianic, theme is the counterpart, the 'other side', to the communal. In a sense it is the very product of the first for its zeal to re-establish Jewish life in the Promised Land is generated by precisely the same hopes that animate the Torah. The messianic theme, however, is unable to co-exist with the limitations imposed by circumstances. It must therefore seek inspiration and legitimacy from entirely extraneous sources that the Torah itself has condemned – from the world of idolatry, in the broadest sense. Again, as in the case of the communities, a large variety of messianic movements presented itself as illustrations. Those I have selected – in Europe, from the thirteenth to the twentieth centuries – display some of this variety in their ability to draw inspiration from the stars, a charismatic individual, the nation-state and the soil.

If my presentation of these two themes is correct, then Jewish history can be construed as the arena of their conflict. But although, in this sense,

I do deal with history, my intention has certainly not been historical. Rather, if I have succeeded, I will have introduced the reader to the outline of a typology of conflict in which the issue at stake is a commitment to the repair of the world.

Part I

1

The Politics of the Torah

At Grips with Nature

In the context of the quest for salvation – however defined – human response may range 'from limited demand for *ad hoc* instant therapy to a programme for the reorganisation of the world'. Within these extremes the response to the quest will require perhaps conversion, or withdrawal from the world or even its actual destruction as a pre-condition to the state of ultimate perfection.[1] These responses are drawn from the experience of religious movements of protest but they are not irrelevant as a framework within which to evaluate a Jewish contribution to the debate.

This too has its origin in a sentiment of dissatisfaction at the imperfection of the world. Both the world and man are incomplete. The creation, though of divine origin, still stands in need of improvement, if it is to be made congenial to man. The Creator has, as it were, relinquished to his creation the further work necessary. The world has been created but more needs to be done.[2] These responsibilities man alone can discharge, and 'make straight that which [God] has made crooked'. A homely *midrash* adds: 'all the work of the six days of creation needs further work – the wheat grains must be ground, the thistles and the lupins made sweet to the taste'.[3]

This obligation, for such it is (as I hope to show below), necessitates at the outset a comprehension and acceptance of the real in its most literal, manifest and obvious sense, what Hegel would have called 'reconciliation with reality'. But it is for all that reconciliation with a difference in that this is not ultimate, but represents rather a starting point for the transcendence of the real. The Hegelian 'reconciliation with reality' has for its antithesis 'a world as it should be [which] does certainly exist but only in his [man's]

---

[1] B. Wilson, *Magic and the Millennium*, London, 1973, pp. 22ff.
[2] Gen. 2:3.
[3] MR Gen. 11:6. See also the discussion of this theme in R. Louis Jacobs, 'A.L. Heller's Shev Shema Tata', *Modern Judaism*, I (1981), No. 2, p. 199.

opining'.[4] Jewish thinking is also familiar, notably in the visions of the prophets and in the writings of messianic figures, with 'a world as it should be' – in, for example, the vision of Zechariah (14:9): 'And the Lord shall be king over all the earth: in that day shall the Lord be One and His name one.' This is a definition of cosmic harmony and coherence and as such would designate the antithesis to cognizing the real as imperfect and incomplete. There is, however, also a third view that accepts the real but only in the confident expectation of its susceptibility to change towards 'a world as it should be'.

This is the purport of the Sinaitic covenant and the concomitant entry of God into history through the medium of the Torah. 'The Torah', writes Maimonides, 'although it is not natural, enters into what is natural.'[5] Maimonides posits an order within nature which, because it is accessible and receptive to the Torah, can also be brought to fruition through the Torah. We can go even further: if man needs the Torah, the converse is equally true. Without a seat in reality the Torah would lack all *raison d'être* and the means to fulfil itself, and this would be tantamount to the absence of God from the world. A *midrash* represents God saying to the angels: 'had Israel not accepted the Torah, there would be no dwelling for Me and neither for you';[6] and this is understood to mean that the world, were it not for the Torah, would revert to its pre-creation state, namely non-existence.

What averts this fate is the attempt to supersede nature through the establishment of a discontinuity that insists, however, on accommodation to nature as a *point de départ*. The amplitude of this 'discontinuity' is evident from the classic statement of Maimonides that also illuminates the political import of the Torah: 'the Law of Moses our Master . . . has come to bring us both perfections – I mean the welfare of the states of people in their relations with one another through the abolition of reciprocal wrongdoing and through the acquisition of a noble and excellent character. In this way the preservation of the population of the country and their permanent existence in the same order become possible, so that every one of them achieves his first (bodily) perfection; I mean also the soundness of the beliefs and the giving of correct opinions, through which ultimate perfection is achieved.'[7]

The opposition between 'the Law of Moses our Master' and nature, and the latter's dependence on the former, can be further clarified through an

---

[4] G.W.F. Hegel, *Grundlinien der Philosophie des Rechts*, Hamburg ed. 1962, p. 16.
[5] Moses Maimonides, *The Guide for the Perplexed*, 2:40 (referred to later as *Guide*). I have used the translation by S. Pines, Chicago, 1963.
[6] *Pesikta Rabbati*, ed. M. Friedmann, Vienna, 1880, p. 20.
[7] *Guide*, 3:27.

admittedly cursory juxtaposition of the conflicting views of the modern philosopher of hope, Ernst Bloch, and the sixteenth-century R. Judah Loew b. Bezalel of Prague. Bloch's *The Principle of Hope* [8] is inspired by the notion of a world that yearns, hungers and hopes for the 'not yet'. This drive is conceived not as an entity external to the material world but as an entity comprehended in it that continuously seeks to satisfy itself through the transforming of the material world: 'the world process is itself a utopian function, with the material of the objectively possible as substance.'[9]

A cosmic optimism animated Bloch in that the process was guaranteed of fulfilment: 'that a drive directs itself at something, that presupposes the drive but also a capacity in that to which it directs itself, to satisfy it.'[10] It was also possible for Bloch to find in the accounts of utopian societies and in art and music not illusion but intimations of the 'not yet' in the form of 'a laboratory and also a festival of fulfilled possibilities'.[11] He looked to the materialist dialectic of Marxism to provide 'a link with the potentially possible'.[12]

R. Judah Loew b. Bezalel, however, took from the Talmud the view that nature presents itself to man not as aim-directed and creative but as amoral, ignorant and inert. An adulteress can conceive; a stolen grain of wheat grows as readily as one honestly acquired.[13] Nature's lowly status is further exemplified in its ignorance of the Sabbath. The only river whose flow ceases on the Sabbath is a river that does not exist, the legendary Sambatyon.[14] This is to say nothing of nature's need for rules, such as those governing agricultural production prohibiting the gathering of fruit within certain limits[15] or the sowing of diverse species in the same area, which must also be understood as a means to make nature congenial to man.[16]

---

[8] *Das Prinzip Hoffnung*, 2 vols, Frankfurt on Main, 1959.

[9] Ibid., p. 203; see also Arnold Metzger, 'Utopie und Transzendenz', and Fritz Velmar, 'Die Welt als Laboratorium Salutatis', both in S. Unseld (ed.), *Ernst Bloch zu ehren*, Frankfurt on Main, 1965, pp. 75ff., 125ff. H. Gekle, *Wunsch und Wirklichkeit*, Frankfurt on Main, 1986, p. 179, gives an analysis of Bloch's view of an animate nature.

[10] Bloch, *Prinzip*, p. 1,551.

[11] Ibid., p. 248.

[12] See the section 'Dialektik und Hoffnung' in E. Bloch, *Subjekt-Objekt*, enlarged edition, Frankfurt on Main, 1962, pp. 510–20.

[13] TB AZ 54b. Cf. also *Guide*, 3:43.

[14] TB San 65b.

[15] Lev. 19:23.

[16] Hence also the obligation on man not to abuse nature by indulging in such wanton destruction as blood-sports; see below p. 20 and A. Carmell, *Das Judentum und der Umweltschutz*, in *25 Jahre Jüdische Schule Zürich*, Jerusalem, 1980, pp. 87–107. Wealthy Jews who acquired country estates and engaged in hunting on

To Judah b. Bezalel, against this background, only the actions of man, more particularly those of the adherents of the Torah, could, as it were, bring to perfection a nature that was 'no more than matter', 'incomplete', 'in a state of privation'.[17] R. Judah in fact identified man's 'divine deeds', namely those in accord with the Torah, with 'unnatural deeds'.[18] If, for Bloch, hope is actualized as a force immanent in matter and nature, then, for Judah b. Bezalel, these are refractory entities that only the Torah can overcome and convert to their full potential. Thus the world is no *tabula rasa* but already exists with certain attributes that will condition, say, the rate of change. 'Men make their own history', writes Marx, 'but they do not make it just as they please; they do not make it in circumstances chosen by themselves, but in circumstances directly found, given and transmitted from the past. The tradition of all the dead generations weighs like an incubus on the brain of the living.'[19]

No more than nature is man a *tabula rasa*. What might be termed the 'reality principle' of the Torah locates man also within the dimension of time and here too the Torah seeks to impose its sway. From eternity God has created time.[20] The creation of the 'days' proceeds *pari passu* with the creation of the world itself.[21] This is as much man's abode as is space and he is as little abstracted from the one as from the other. Time is conceived not in terms of an unfolding sequence but is in some sense assimilated to spatial categories through a process of division.[22]

---

the model of their gentile neighbours incurred rabbinical censure (cf. the remarks of R. Zvi Hirsch Kaidanover quoted in A. Shoḥet, *Im Ḥilufei Tekufot*, Jerusalem, 1960, p. 40; and R. Ezekiel Landau's admonition to a Jewish landed magnate, bent on hunting, not to commit useless destruction and to cause unnecessary suffering to animals ('Noda bi'Yehuda', *Yore Deah*, Jerusalem (1969), No. 10).

[17] *Tiferet Yisrael*, repr., Jerusalem, 1970, pp. 10ff.

[18] *Derekh Ḥayyim*, repr. London, 1961, p. 182; see also Byron Sherwin, *Mystical Theology and Social Dissent*, London/Toronto, 1982, ch. 10 *passim*; B. Safran, 'Maharal and early Ḥassidism', in *Ḥassidism: Continuity or Innovation*, Cambridge, Mass., 1988, pp. 50ff.; and R. Schatz, 'Ha-Tfisa ha-mishpatit shel ha-Maharal', *Da'at* (1978–9), Nos 2–3, pp. 149–57. This is now available in an English translation, *JLA*, VI (1987), pp. 109–25.

[19] K. Marx, 'The eighteenth Brumaire of Louis Bonaparte', in *Marx-Engels Werke*, Berlin, 1960, vol. VIII, p. 115.

[20] A. Néher, 'Vision du temps et de l'histoire dans la culture juive', in *Les Cultures et le Temps*, Paris, 1975, pp. 171–92.

[21] Gen. 1:1ff.

[22] J.-J. Goux, *Les Iconoclastes*, Paris, 1978, p. 29.

The greatest of such divisions is the weekly sabbath.[23] This also serves as the agency whereby the Torah seeks to impose itself on nature – not only enforcing on man a regular period of, at the lowest, abstention from manipulative activity but also affording nature a regular period of relief from manipulation at the hands of man. Should a man lose count of time whilst travelling at sea or in the desert, he can still observe the sequence of sunset and sunrise and impose a sabbath derived from his own calculation.[24] The institution of the sabbatical year and the jubilee year further emphasize this relief for man and nature and its regularity – as 'a sabbath of solemn rest for the land'.[25] Furthermore, because of the rhythmic and regular recurrence of time conceived in this way, time is never 'lost' and any moment can contain both the past and present.[26]

Within this created order man certainly enjoys a superior status. The world is 'good' but not until man is created does it become 'very good'.[27] Man, 'crowned with glory and honour', enjoying 'dominion over the works of thy hands', is exalted by the psalmist as supreme amongst God's creatures.[28]

For all that, he is no being abstracted from history and is consequently limited. On the one hand he is free to choose 'the blessing and the curse';[29] on the other, the choice he makes is qualified by his own natural condition. What is in question is not sinfulness such as would vitiate any choice or course of action. The Deuteronomist wrote: 'blessed shalt thou be when thou comest in; and blessed shalt thou be when thou goest out' (Dt. 28:6). R. Johanan interpreted the passage to mean: 'just as you enter the world without sin, so shall you leave it without sin'.[30] Rather, the particular limitation of man is born of the fact that he is a historical creature, a natural product of the past with certain dispositions to act and think in a certain way and hence free to choose only within certain parameters. If, from 'the

---

[23] A. Safran, 'Jewish Time: Sabbatical Time', in J. Sacks (ed.), *Tradition and Transition: Essays presented to Sir Immanuel Jakobovits*, London, 1986, pp. 267–81; see also the responsum of R. Ḥayyim of Voloszin referred to in R. Louis Jacobs, *Theology in the Responsa*, London, 1975, p. 263.

[24] For an indication of the *modus operandi*, see Shulhan Arukh, *Orekh Ḥayyim*, 344:1.

[25] Ex. 23:10–11; Lev. 25:8 ff.

[26] See S. Handelman, *The Slayers of Moses*, Albany, New York, 1982, pp. 36ff.

[27] Gen. 1:31.

[28] Ps. 8:6–7.

[29] Dt. 30:1.

[30] TB BM 107a; cf. also W. Hirsch, *Rabbinic Psychology*, London, 1947, pp. 163, 187, 278; and N. Solomon, *Division and Reconciliation*, St. Paul's Lecture, London, 1980, pp. 5–6.

merits of the patriarchs'[31] he may hope to draw benefit, he may also expect his freedom of action to be undeservedly and inescapably circumscribed through the iniquities, errors, shortcomings etc. of his ancestors. This is part of a history-bound inheritance that impairs man's freedom. The past is present whether as constraint or release, and as part of this inheritance the transgressions of the fathers are visited on the children 'unto the third and unto the fourth generation'.[32]

It is true of course that both Jeremiah and Ezekiel rejected the dictum: 'the fathers have eaten sour grapes and the children's teeth are set on edge.' They spoke of individual retribution: 'every man shall die for his own iniquity.'[33] But this assurance is born of the collapse of the kingdom of Judah and the burden of the Babylonian exile and the consequent need to comfort the afflicted. Moreover, it is nothing but the divine promise of a future state of affairs, part of the commitment to 'a new covenant with the house of Israel and with the house of Judah', proclaimed by Jeremiah.[34] The prophet here envisages a realm of future freedom, 'in those days', as a refuge from the harsh and disturbing reality of the present realm of subordination to the past. Neither the Deuteronomist nor the prophet falsifies the present in the emphasis that each lends to a freedom of action that is historically circumscribed and burdened with the inheritance of the past. There is, for the present at least, no release from the natural and historical world.

This presentation stands out all the more clearly by comparison with the state of nature offered by Locke and Hobbes. Locke emphasizes men's 'state of perfect freedom to order their actions, and dispose of their possessions and persons as they think fit, within the bounds of the law of Nature, without asking leave or depending upon the will of any other man'. Men are not only free in this condition, but also in a state of equality 'wherein all the power and jurisdiction is reciprocal, no one having more than another, there being nothing more evident than that creatures of the same species and rank, promiscuously born to all the same advantages of nature, and the use of the same facilities, should also be equal one amongst another, without subordination or subjection'.[35] Equality is not absolute; age, virtue, birth, particular merit, may each or all demand 'a just precedency'. But 'in respect of jurisdiction or dominion one over another' these

---

[31] Figuratively expressed in the notion that the right horn of the ram sacrificed by Abraham in place of Isaac will also be the horn used to sound the ingathering of the exiles (*Pirkei de R. Eliezer*, Lvov, 1867, ch. 31, end).

[32] Ex. 34:7; Dt. 5:9.

[33] Jer. 31:29–30; Ezek. 18:2–4. See also the discussion in TB Mak. 24a.

[34] Jer. 31:31.

[35] Locke, *Two Treatises of Government*, London, 1978, Book II, ch. 2, p. 118.

distinctions will not conflict with equality.[36]

To Hobbes the natural state of man is marked by equality in body and mind:

> as that though there be found one man sometimes manifestly stronger in body, or of quicker mind than another; yet when all is reckoned together, the difference between man, and man, is not so considerable, as that one man can thereupon claim to himself any benefit, to which another may not pretend, as well as he. For as to the strength of body, the weakest has strength to kill the strongest, either by secret machination, or by confederacy with others, that are in the same danger with himself.
>
> And as to the faculties of the mind . . . I find yet a greater equality amongst men, than that of strength. For Prudence is but experience; which equal time equally bestows on all men, in those things they equally apply themselves unto.[37]

But this is unhistorical by comparison with the Biblical account of the beginnings of human society. In the Garden of Eden this knows only fleetingly of a primal state of abundance, freedom and tranquillity. No sooner does the expulsion take place than the Bible reveals its sensitivity not only to those factors (hereditary or other) that limit human freedom but also to a wide variety of inequalities in body and mind, not to mention those suffered by widows, orphans, the poor etc. It deals in fact with a historical reality that has little in common with the Lockeian and Hobbesian models of nature.

Preserving Order

This understanding of nature and of man's place within it, as mediated by the 'reality-principle', has one important political consequence: it relegates natural law and natural morality to a peripheral part in the politics of the Torah, if indeed they are not entirely absent, as argued by José Faur.[38] Natural law, in the sense of a law discoverable by human reason, would in any case be incompatible with revealed law.[39] When natural law does

---

[36] Ibid., p. 142.

[37] *Leviathan*, ed. W. G. Pogson Smith, Oxford, 1947, ch. xiii.

[38] J. Faur, 'Understanding the Covenant', *Tradition*, IX (1968), p. 41.

[39] 'It is not by chance', Melamed writes, 'that the term "natural law" does not appear explicitly in Jewish thought before Albo (fifteenth century) and when it does appear it is of minor importance by comparison with its definition in classical and

appear, as the product of human reason it is most apparent in relation to the wellbeing of society in its most simple sense, in the form of social harmony and the need for self-preservation. The *Sefer Ha-Ḥinukh – Book of Training* – attributed to a certain 'R. Aaron Halevy' of Barcelona in the thirteenth century,[40] argues very strongly that certain of the commandments are, or could be, the product of reason alone, having regard to the human need for an ordered society. If there were no justice amongst men, no sanctions against theft and oppression, then 'men would not form communities and would never stand side by side'. Life in common would collapse.[41] But of course the vast majority of the commandments are theonomous and not discoverable, though normally fathomable, by reason.

By extension, Maimonides ruled, in accord with the theory of natural law, that the king in a Jewish state or the court – depending on particular circumstances – had the power to suspend the normal process of law and apply extra-legal sanctions against those guilty of endangering the social order through homicide: 'if a person kills another and there is no clear evidence, or if no clear warning has been given him, or there is only one witness, or if one kills accidentally a person whom one hated, the king may, if the exigency of the hour demands it, put him to death to ensure the stability of the social order.'[42]

This was no vain threat, however exceptional, and the enormous historical importance of natural law showed itself in the middle ages, during periods of persecution in the German lands and also in Spain. The particular case

---

scholastic thinking. Medieval Jewish thought, based on the recognition of the primacy of the authority of revelation, found it difficult to accept literally the theory of natural law based on the acceptance of the autonomy of human reason which acknowledges the natural need to be organised in society to ensure the continuity of the species and the social order. Only those who acknowledge the autonomy of reason, limited as much as may be by comparison with the authority of revelation, can postulate the existence of natural law' ('Ḥok ha'teva ba'makhshava ha'medinit ha'yehudit', *Da'at*, No. 17, 1986, p. 64). J. David Bleich writes: 'nowhere in the vast corpus of rabbinic, legal or philosophical literature is there to be found a fully-developed doctrine of natural law' (*Judaism and Natural Law*, Proceedings of the Eighth World Congress of Jewish Studies, Division C, Jerusalem, 1982, p. 7).

[40] But see I. Ta-Shmah, 'The author of *Sefer Ha-Ḥinukh*', *Kiryat Sefer*, 55 (1980), No. 4, pp. 787–90.

[41] *Sefer Ha-Ḥinukh*, ed. R. Ḥayyim Dov Chavel, Jerusalem, 1977, commandments 46, 232, 233, 236, 237 (pp. 99, 309, 311, 313, 314).

[42] MT Laws of Kings, 3:19. I am greatly indebted for this argument to D. Sinclair, 'Maimonides and natural law theory', *L'Eylah*, (New Year 5747–1986), No. 22, pp. 35–40; cf. also Sir Immanuel Jakobovits, 'The morality of warfare', *L'Eylah*, (Autumn 5743–1983), No. 4, pp. 1–7; and N. S. Hecht and E. B. Quint, 'Exigency jurisdiction under Jewish law,' *Dinei Yisrael*, IX (1978–80), pp. 28–99.

in point is that of the Jew who informed on his fellows. The Jewish legal authorities of the day treated him as a traitor. 'Many times [informing] leads to mortal danger', wrote R. Meir b. Baruch of Rothenburg in the thirteenth century;[43] and to avert disaster the presumed informer could, R. Meir noted, be damaged, maimed or even executed so as to prevent him accomplishing his 'evil purposes'.[44] In the contemporary law code, known as the *Tur*, compiled by R. Jacob b. Asher of Toledo, the extra-judicial nature of the proceedings is clearly enunciated:

> every man is permitted to kill him [the informer] and it is not necessary to take testimony in his presence for it is known that he is seized of betrayal and slander, the gentiles bring him close on account of their benefit; and even if he wishes to bring witnesses and for his case to be examined and investigated, let him never be tried for he will save himself by informing; for even if he is not in danger he will inform on the one and the many . . . and endanger all Israel. Therefore it is customary in all parts of the Dispersion that when an informer is seized three times [of his crime] and has betrayed Israel or their property into gentile hands that a device and means are sought to remove him from the world to avert the crime [*migdar milta*] that others may be deterred and informers do not multiply in Israel and also to save those of Israel persecuted in gentile hands.[45]

Consistent with this view, R. Jacob was himself one of the signatories to the sentence of death passed on an informer.[46] Joseph (Josel) of Rosheim (sixteenth century) reports a case from Strasburg when one of two informers was hanged, apparently by the gentile authorities at the behest of the Strasburg community.[47]

[43] S. Assaf, *Batei Ha-Din Ve-Sidrehem*, Jerusalem, 1924, pp. 18/19, fn. 4; see also R. Solomon b. Adret of fourteenth-century Barcelona, who writes that an informer could be executed 'on suspicion alone' and in this context refers to Castile, Aragon and Catalonia (*She'elot u-tshuvot I*, repr. Bnei Brak, 1958, No. 181, and Adret's responsum edited by D. Kaufmann in his article 'Jewish Informers in the Middle Ages', *JQR*, VIII (1896), pp. 217–38. These were no empty threats: see the cases of punishment 'outside the law' cited by F. Baer (*History of the Jews in Christian Spain, II*, Engl. trans., Philadelphia, 1961, pp. 448ff.). This was normally grounded in the threat to the social order that informing represented.

[44] See also below p. 000.

[45] *Tur*, Ḥoshen Mishpat, No. 388, 13.

[46] Judah b. Asher, *Zikhron Yehuda*, Berlin, 1846, No. 75 (pp. 55a–55b); see also Rabbenu Asher, *She'elot u-tshuvot*, Venice, 1607, klal XVII, No. 1.

[47] *Joseph of Rosheim, Sefer Ha-Miknah*, ed. H. Fraenkel-Goldschmidt, Jerusalem, 1970, pp. 7 ff.

With the easing, though not the cessation, of persecution at the turn of the sixteenth century, when resort to gentile courts was no longer considered inseparable from informing, the penalty for such action was correspondingly relaxed. In 1603, at Frankfurt, the last rabbinic synod in Germany substituted for execution the severest form of ostracism.[48] Even so, the circumstances remain exceptional. The legislation is of an emergency character in the interests of social order and only to this limited extent does it partake of natural law.

Imitatio Dei

When the Torah contemplates its recipients what does it see? What can be added to man as 'the product of nature'? Much of the answer is contained in the famous midrashic homily of R. Joshua b. Levi. He depicts the dismay of the angels that 'the beautiful Torah' should be entrusted to 'men of flesh and blood'. Moses, at God's bidding, overcomes their objections in these terms:

> Did you, he asked of the angels, go down to Egypt? Were you enslaved by Pharaoh? What need have you for the Law? It is written, you shall have no other gods. Do you dwell among the uncircumcised who practise idolatry? It says, remember the Sabbath day. Do you do any work that you need a day of rest? It says, honour your father and mother. Have you any fathers or mothers? It says, do not murder, or commit adultery, do not steal; is there any envy, any evil temptation amongst you? . . . Then they praised God and became friends of Moses.[49]

This passage is a remarkable demonstration of the effort made by the Torah to grasp man in his true and existential context. Its Israelite recipients at Sinai were in no exceptional situation. Rather, here is a paradigm of certain salient aspects of man's condition: the effects of servitude, the effects of contact with an immoral environment, the need for rest from the compulsion to work, the problematics of family relationships, the drive to transgress. These are inseparable from life in general, not merely that of the Israelites in Egypt. They are all so many expressions of the natural order against which the Torah pits itself.

But this is not the whole truth. Enfeebled though the Israelites may be

[48] L. Finkelstein, *Jewish Self-Government in the Middle Ages*, 2nd printing, New York, 1964, ch. VIII, sec. 1.

[49] TB Shab. 88b–89a.

through their experience of servitude in Egypt (and in this respect, as in others, the sons cannot divest themselves of their fathers' inheritance), there also exist certain features of the natural order whereby the Torah can gain purchase on human recalcitrance and break the system of inertia and inheritance. By nature, Maimonides argued, following Aristotle, men are political beings, so that only through association with others can even their most elementary needs be fulfilled.[50] Even if it is also the case that the very diversity of individuals makes their co-operation in society problematic, this only renders the operation of the laws more urgent.[51]

It is at this point, therefore, that the laws enter into nature, working with man's natural sociability and directing that natural urge towards ends of which man may not himself be aware, though, in the form of an ordered and just society, they will unquestionably be to his benefit.[52] In this way just such a society comes to be grounded in an authentic and distinctive feature of reality. This is probably the nearest that the Torah, considered as a political document, comes to any social contract theory of human association. The covenant whereby God entrusts the Torah to the Israelites rules out the notion of human initiative, rejects the idea of human rights and is highly sensitive to human inequality. The effect of the covenant is to substitute for all these normal components of the social contract a counter-natural order mediated through a corpus of prescriptive norms. (These of course are interpreted and applied by man and thus qualify what would otherwise be a wholly theocentric universe.) Moreover, though these prescriptions certainly do have general implications, they are in fact and in reality addressed only to a specific body of people.[53]

How do the prescriptions fulfil their task? Montesquieu has a passage in which he hypothesizes: 'supposing there were no God, we should still be obliged to love justice; that is, exert ourselves to resemble that being of whom we have such a sublime notion and who, if he exists, would necessarily be just.'[54] There is here a degree of suggestibility in that the justice of God has yet to make itself felt. At the same time, the words oddly echo the multiple rabbinic exhortations to an *imitatio dei*.[55] It is the *modus operandi*,

[50] *Guide*, 3:51; 2:40.

[51] Ibid.

[52] See A. Funkenstein, 'Maimonides: Political theory and realistic messianism,' *Miscellanea Medievalia*, XI (1977), pp. 81–103, esp. pp. 92 ff.

[53] For a discussion of the possible relationship between the social contract and covenant ideas, see B. Jackson, 'Secular jurisprudence and the philosophy of Jewish law', *JLA* (VI), 1987, pp. 8 ff.

[54] Montesquieu, *Lettres Persanes*, ed. P. Vernière, Paris, 1960, No. 83.

[55] See also *Pesikta de-Rab Kahana*, Lyck, 1868, 15:339–40; for a theological interpretation, cf. N. Lamm, 'Notes on the concept of Imitatio Dei', in L. Landman (ed.), *R. Joseph Lookstein Memorial Volume*, New York, 1980, pp. 217–29.

however, that differentiates the two viewpoints. Whereas Montesquieu's call to 'resemble' God lacks a body of prescriptions, it is precisely the presence of such prescriptions that – if it is not indeed its *raison d'être* – distinguishes the Torah. This begins by grounding the very possibility of imitation in the notion of a certain equivalence between man and God; the former is created in the manner and after the likeness of the latter.[56] This common ground makes it possible to establish God as an action-model for man: 'Holy shall you be, for holy am I, the Lord your God.'[57] The imitating of God's attributes by way of *vita activa* is further emphasized in the interpretation of the passage: 'after the . . . Lord your God shall you walk and unto Him shall you cleave.'[58]

Objection: is not God compared to 'a devouring fire'?[59] Answer: 'it means to walk after the attributes of the Holy one, blessed be He. As He clothes the naked . . . so do you also clothe the naked . . . visited the sick . . . comforted mourners . . . so do you also comfort mourners . . . buried the dead . . . so do you also bury the dead.'[60] These are all activities which, by virtue of their non-fulfilment, are in fact part of the imperfections of the creation and of nature (see above p. 5), and which man is called on to make good. It is therefore not possible, within the terms of this obligation, to dissociate the descriptive judgement from its prescriptive accompaniments and consequences.[61]

Imitatio dei, in terms of this commitment, as for example in Abraham's attempt to avert the indiscriminate destruction of the innocent with the guilty at Sodom,[62] involves action in co-operation with God, in opposition to the natural, normal and imperfect course of events. Another example of such normality is that of the adulteress who should not, but can, conceive; and this is, according to the Talmudic sages, because 'the world follows its natural course'; and R. Simeon b. Lakish has God say: 'it is not enough for the wicked to make my coinage cheap but they trouble me and make me set my seal on it' (that is, create an embryo).[63]

For this reason the quest for a theodicy is replaced by a counter-natural system of action, that can, however, draw support from man's natural need

---

[56] Gen. 1:26.

[57] Lev. 19:2; cf. also *Guide* 3:54, and M. Lazarus, *Die Ethik des Judentums*, Frankfurt on Main, 1898, pp. 85ff.

[58] Dt. 13:5.

[59] Ibid., 4:24.

[60] TB Sota 14a.

[61] As does, for example, J. Plamenatz; see his 'The use of political theory', in A. Quinton (ed.), *Political Philosophy*, Oxford, 1968, p. 26.

[62] Gen. 18:23ff.

[63] TB AZ 54b.

for association. Such a system is tantamount to a mode of appropriate practice.

For the sake of simplicity I confine myself largely to those practices known collectively as the 613 commandments (*mitzvot*). This total derives from an obiter dictum of R. Simlai: 'Six hundred and thirteen commandments were given to Moses; three hundred and sixty-five negative commandments corresponding to the number of days in the solar year, and two hundred and forty-eight positive corresponding to the number of parts of the body.'[64] There are of course very different frameworks of understanding within which the commandments can be evaluated, and clusters of thought have gathered around their classification and interpretation.[65] The failure of R. Simlai to denominate the components of the total of 613 has generated fruitful controversy, of which the *locus classicus* is that between Maimonides and Nachmanides;[66] for example, does 'the first commandment' of the Decalogue rank as one of the 613? To Maimonides, that it does so is unquestioned;[67] but Nachmanides, following another tradition, denies it this status and writes:

> the composition of the 613 mitzvot consists only of His decrees, May He be exalted, which he required us to do or to refrain from doing, but belief in His existence which he made known to us through signs and demonstrations and the revelation of His presence before our eyes is the root and principle from which they were generated and is not to be included in their enumeration.[68]

On the view of Nachmanides, therefore, the existence of God is not in itself a commandment but the necessary and sufficient pre-condition of all commandments. Knowledge of the existence of God is also epistemologically distinct from knowledge of the commandments in that the former is certain whereas the latter, that which is known through human agency, is

---

[64] TB Mak. 23b. For other references in Talmudic and Midrashic literature, cf. the material listed in G. Appel, *A Philosophy of Mitzvot*, New York, 1975, pp. 203–4, nn. 2–3; see also Rabbiner Dr S. Katz, 'Von den 613 Gesetzen', *Jeschurun*, II (1915), pp. 381–402, 573–84.

[65] I. Heinemann, *Ta'amei Ha-Mitzvot be-sifrut Yisrael*, 2 vols, Jerusalem, 1954, 1956.

[66] C.D. Chavel (ed.), *Sefer Ha'Mitzvot Le'Ha'Rambam im Hassagot Ha'Ramban*, Jerusalem, 1981; see also M. Peritz, 'Das Buch der Gesetze', in J. Guttmann (ed.), *Moses ben Maimon*, Leipzig, 1908, I, pp. 439–74.

[67] Cf. the analysis of his views in L.E. Goodman, 'Maimonides' philosophy of law', *JLA*, I (1978), pp. 72–107.

[68] *Sefer Ha-Mitzvot*, p. 152.

susceptible to, and requires, interpretation.[69] *In toto*, following a variant mode of enumeration, Nachmanides excludes twenty-six positive and thirty-one negative commandments from Maimonides's list.[70]

Despite this uncertainty, it is clear, so far as objective is concerned, that R. Simlai intended to provide a regularly recurrent occasion for the fulfilment of a commandment in such a way that no act would be value-free and that this in its turn would also encourage man's *imitatio dei*, for in performing a commandment man is conducting himself in relation to his fellow-men in precisely the same way as does God towards the creation. The commandments therefore are all couched in terms of practice, in the spirit of behaviourist psychology, as a corpus of actions (or abstentions from action) which regard the disposition of the soul, or spirit or mind or whatever, as the product of action: 'opinions do not last', writes Maimonides, 'unless they are accompanied by actions that strengthen them, make them generally known and perpetuate them among the multitude.'[71]

The *Sefer Ha-Ḥinukh* is one of the most articulate statements to this effect, in regard both to the task of the commandments as a mode of therapeutic action and to the bearing of action on this consummation. The book's *point de départ* is this:

> know that man is affected in accordance with his actions, and his heart and all his thoughts always [follow] after the deeds with which he concerns himself whether for good or evil, and even a man of absolute evil in his heart, whose every instinct in his heart is all the day for evil, if his spirit is aroused and he exerts himself and concerns himself constantly with the Torah and the commandments – even though not for the sake of heaven – he will at once incline towards good and by the force of his acts will kill his evil instinct, for hearts are drawn after acts.

The converse also holds good: 'even if a man be of absolute righteousness and his heart upright and perfect, delighting in Torah and commandments, if he perhaps occupies himself with worthless matters – if, for example, a king forced him to enter an evil occupation and he were truly to be busy all day in the occupation, then he would in time turn away from the righteousness of his heart to become a man of absolute evil, for it is truly known that every man is affected by his actions.'[72]

---

[69] Ibid., p. 156.

[70] Ibid., appendix II, pp. 22–5.

[71] *Guide*, 2:31.

[72] *Sefer Ha-Ḥinukh*, commandment 20, p. 73. Cf. also commandments 40, 98, 99, 263, 265, 267, (pp. 95, 157, 158, 345, 349, 351) for representative statements of the same argument.

The rationale of this process is what the Ḥinukh terms 'a partnership of body and soul' of such a nature as to generate interaction between them.[73] The body is the vessel or receptacle of the soul or spirit. The latter cannot therefore effectively be addressed or influenced directly, but only through the agency of the body. Thus, in expounding the commandment not to eat the flesh of an animal torn by beasts, the Ḥinukh writes that at the root of this commandment lies the fact that

> the body is the instrument of the soul and with it performs its actions; without it its work would never be completed and therefore it is protected by the body for its own good ... the body is in the hands of the spirit like the tongs in the hands of a blacksmith with which he produces a tool for his purpose. Thus, if the tongs are strong and adapted to grasp the tools, the craftsman will make them well, but if the tongs are poor, the tools will never be shaped and agreeable. Similarly, if there is any defect in the body from any cause whatever, the work of the mind will be nullified in accordance with that defect and therefore a perfect Torah kept us distant from all matters that cause defect and in this way according to the plain meaning of the test the prohibition of all forbidden foods came to us through the Torah.[74]

This method enabled the Ḥinukh to associate each of the 613 commandments with a desirable attribute. Each has a reason – often more than one – couched in terms of benefit to man and to society.[75] To rest on the seventh day serves, for example, to recall the creation and thus to deny the eternity of matter. The commandment forbidding the sale of a Hebrew maidservant by an owner who has purchased her from her father inculcates the virtue of kindliness. Not to suffer a witch to live teaches the need for the world to continue on the path divinely impressed on it from the beginning of creation. The commandment to lend to a poor man to the limit of one's ability is even greater than the giving of charity, for it may avert the need for the latter and will implant the virtues of compassion and loving-kindness. The injunction not to consume the blood of an animal is attributed by the Ḥinukh to the fact that man would thereby acquire 'some of the attribute of cruelty' inherent in the animal's soul; furthermore, following Nachmanides, 'since it is known that what is eaten returns to the

---

[73] Ibid., commandment 152, p. 220.

[74] Commandment 79, p. 133.

[75] Though there are occasions, such as over details of the sacrifices, when the Ḥinukh confesses to a lack of comprehension (commandment 135, p. 202).

body of the eater so that if a man consumes blood, thickness and coarseness will enter his soul, in the way that an animal's soul is thick and coarse'. The commandment that prohibits the slaughter of sacrificial animals outside the Temple is understood by the Ḥinukh to include the unnecessary killing of any animal: 'for God in his great goodness delights in the welfare of His creatures and declares that he who offers [an animal] outside that chosen place, is reckoned to be shedding blood, meaning that God only allowed man the flesh of living creatures for atonement or for man's needs such as food or medicine or any matter of which man is in need, but to kill them without any benefit at all is destruction and is called bloodshed'. If a commandment prohibits intercourse between males it is because

> the Holy One Blessed Be He desires the world that He created to be peopled and therefore ordered men not to destroy their seed through intercourse with males for there is no fruit from it nor does it fulfil the commandment of marital intercourse; besides the purport of such frenzy is most repugnant and turbid in the eyes of the Lord and in the eyes of a rational being, and it is not fitting that man who was created to serve his creator should corrupt himself through such turbid acts.

Similarly, the commandment that prohibits bestiality derives, according to the Ḥinukh, not only from the immorality of the act but also from the wish of God that animals reproduce after their own kind, whereas those, such as mules, formed from the mingling of two species 'do not increase and multiply – likewise every tree blended from two species of tree will not succeed in yielding fruit after its kind, and all the more so man, who is the choicest of all species and it is not fitting that he should mingle with the animal species that is lower and inferior'.[76]

It is characteristic of the Ḥinukh's emphasis on action that in his exposition of the commandment 'not to covet', he quotes approvingly an interpretation that equates coveting with the actual taking of a step towards possession of the object coveted. Until that point is reached, the covetous

---

[76] Ibid., commandment 24, 58, 62, 66, 83, 148, 187, 209, 210 (pp. 75, 110, 112, 119, 139, 214, 266, 289, 290). For a modern presentation of much of this argument, see L. Goodman, 'The Biblical laws of diet and sex', in B. Jackson (ed.), *Jewish Law Association Studies II*, Atlanta, 1986, pp. 17–57. Goodman writes (p. 55): 'The theme is that of perfecting humanity in the individual by purifying and so sanctifying human motives and relations, fostering the emergence of a holy nation, one whose customs and symbolic institutions are expressive of and productive of an ethos of regard for humanity in self and others, respect for life and personality and the eschewing of dark passions and sordid, perverted or life-denying appetites.'

desire is not 'completed' and therefore the commandment has not been infringed.[77] There is only one exception to the rule that regulation extends only to speech or acts; that exception is the thought of idolatry which, for obvious reasons, is regarded as an act.[78] Throughout, it is taken for granted that no 'pure' thought exists but that this need not inhibit the imitation of God through an action prescribed by God, for the sequel will inevitably be a movement towards 'purity'. Eventually the effect will be to fashion the sort of person who habitually and in all circumstances will do 'what is upright and good'. The effect will be achieved through the combination of a whole programme of meritorious actions separated by no difference of principle, whether the act requires abstention from forbidden foods, the observance of the sabbath and other festivals, agricultural regulations, laws of war etc. The whole constitutes a concerted effort to mould man and nature.

One point deserving of particular emphasis is the determination to provide some sort of statutory support for what would otherwise be limited to exhortation. It would certainly be an exaggeration to argue that an ethical postulate can be matter for legislation. But it is also true that a postulate of this type can be embedded in a certain normative context that will encourage its implementation.

Commendable actions are made dependent on a system of machinery required to sustain these actions. This is the association made by R. Shimon Anatoli, who does indeed understand the ten commandments and other laws and statutes as 'necessary everywhere and at all times for the maintenance of life in common for all mankind'. But they alone are inadequate, so that Anatoli adds: 'therefore He joined the portion "These are the ordinances" (Ex. 20:21–4) to the ten commandments to teach that man's perfection is not attained through wisdom and truth alone until there are ordered laws amongst them in such a way that they can live with each other.' Anatoli then cites the laws governing the manumission of servants, damages to the person, to property, the responsibilities incumbent on a bailee: 'a way of life appropriate to man is not achieved save through the participation of others.'[79]

Anatoli's argument can be followed up further in relation to the commandment to 'love one's neighbour as oneself' (Lev. 19:18). This is exalted

---

[77] Commandment 38, p. 93.

[78] Commandment 225, p. 305. Elsewhere also it is argued that unworthy thoughts – though known to God – do not incur punishment so long as they are not translated into speech or action: cf. R. Abraham b. Ḥiyya, *Hegyon Ha'Nefesh*, ed. I. Friedmann, Leipzig, 1860, p. 13b. God is said not to take account of an evil thought accompanying an evil act that is not implemented (TB Kidd. 39b).

[79] R. Shimon b. Anatoli, *Malmad Ha-Talmidim*, Lyck, 1866, pp. 71b ff.

by Hillel, the greatest of the Pharisees, as 'the whole of the Law', but unless and until it has been exposed to 'commentary' that will establish a particular relationship between this abstract exhortation and the real it is incomplete and ineffective. Who, in fact, is this 'neighbour'[80]? What is 'love'?[81] Commentary, therefore, takes the two as yet indefinite terms, 'love' and 'neighbour', and locates them, for example, in the respective and reciprocal stances of parent and child, husband and wife, judge and criminal.[82]

This averts the hazard of an undifferentiated and indiscriminate imperative by taking the 'neighbour' and encountering him in a specific relationship – for example, most specific of all, as the man next door; not only that, but perhaps as the man next door at the moment when he wishes to sell his property. The general norm requires that if neighbour A wishes to sell his property, neighbour B has first option to purchase. But suppose, for example, that the willing vendor of a piece of property is approached by two prospective purchasers neither of whom is an immediate neighbour of the vendor and each of whom has ready cash; how is the conflict resolved? Maimonides ruled:

> If one is a fellow-townsman [of the vendor] and the other a country-dweller, the townsman has priority; a townsman and a scholar, the scholar has priority; a relative and a scholar, the scholar has priority; a neighbour and a relative, the neighbour has priority for this also is included in the principle 'and you shall do that which is good and upright'; if a man is quick to buy, his purchase stands and his fellow, who is entitled to priority, may not eject him, for neither of them is an immediate neighbour for in this respect the sages commanded only the way of the pious and it is a fine soul that acts thus.[83]

In this way, ultimately and ideally, man will learn to assimilate his own attributes to those of God. The sphere of contrary motive, hope, intent etc. is abolished in an undifferentiated act, pure of all extraneous matter. It is thus described by Rabban Gamliel: it is to 'make His will as your will, so that He may make your will as His; annul your will before His so that He

[80] TB Shab. 31a.

[81] See the discussion in E. Simon, 'The neighbour(*Re'a*) whom we shall love', in M. Fox (ed.), *Modern Jewish Ethics*, Ohio, 1975, pp. 29–56; also R. Loewe, 'Potentialities and limitations of universalism in the "Halakha"', in R. Loewe (ed.), *Studies in Rationalism, Judaism and Universalism*, London, 1966, pp. 115–50.

[82] Cf. Z. Falk, *Erkhei Mishpat Ve-Yahadut*, Jerusalem, 1980, p. 26.

[83] MT Acquisition; Laws of Neighbours 14:5.

may annul the will of others before your will.'[84] What is needed, Falk writes, is 'to negate the distinction between the voluntary performance [of a commandment] and the compulsion of the law'. He quotes this declaration by R. Elazar ben Azariah (Sifra, end K'doshim):

> Why shall a man not say, it is impossible to wear *shaatnez*, it is impossible to eat the flesh of a pig, it is impossible to commit adultery. But it is possible, and what shall I do if our father in heaven has forbidden it to me: we are taught, 'I have set you apart from the peoples, that you should be mine' (Lev. 26:20), thus he holds aloof from transgression and takes on himself the kingdom of heaven.[85]

In a challenging formulation R. Judah b. Bezalel of Prague combines the identification of the individual and the divine will with a version of *vita activa* so conceived as to unify idea and act. From 'we shall do and we shall obey',[86] he deduces the priority of action (even over knowledge): 'for Israel were created to serve their creator and therefore they make "We shall do" precede "We shall obey", for that which is the principle, for the sake of which they were created, takes precedence over that which is not the principle – the rationale. The principle is the act as the Lord desires.'[87] Further, from the view that 'Remember the sabbath day' and 'Keep the sabbath day'[88] constituted a single utterance,[89] the annihilation of any distinction between 'keep' and 'remember' is deduced. In other words, what is paradigmatically expressed here is the unity of the idea and the act. Those who keep the Sabbath *eo ipso* recall that the world is a divine creation *ex nihilo* and not a mere natural product. Those who remember the Sabbath *eo ipso* keep its prescribed ordinances. There is no distinction. To remember is to keep and to keep is to remember. The act becomes a thought and the thought an act. The greatest of all such paradigms is of course the creation itself, the emanation of a divine fiat.

In the same way as God's commandments are comprised in his actions[90] and in the same way as Moses is both lawgiver and statesman,[91] so too

---

[84] *Pirke Avoth*, II, 4. The aspiration to psychological unity and an integrated personality is also of course a familiar Biblical theme: 'love the Lord thy God with all thy heart, and with all thy soul, and with all thy might' (Dt. 6:5); 'make one my heart to fear your name' (Ps. 86:11).

[85] Falk, *Erkhei Mishpat* p. 32.

[86] Ex. 24:7.

[87] *Tiferet Yisrael*, ch. 29, p. 87; cf. also ch. 28, p. 113.

[88] Ex. 20:8; Dt. 5:12.

[89] *Tiferet Yisrael*, ch. 44, p. 135.

[90] *Guide*, 1:54.

[91] Ibid., II, 38.

does the Torah exemplify the coincidence of prescription and action; that is, it fulfils its purpose when it is implemented purely for its own sake; there is no distinction between the intent to which an action in fulfilment of a norm is directed and the action in itself; the one complements the other. And if it is not implemented for its own sake, then the intent will follow from the implementation.

This creates a thought-act complete in itself, in that both components are perfectly matched and blended, leaving, as it were, no space vacant for divergent thoughts. The norms generate a totality in action and a vehicle whereby the aspiration to betterment can be expressed and discontent with the existent relieved. Hope is provided with a means to substantiate itself. It need not languish at the level of sentiment. Kant described longing as 'the empty wish to be able to annihilate the time between the desire and the attainment of what is desired'.[92] But this interval need not be empty where the longing is equipped with a means to physical expression – where it is in fact and in effect transformed into physical expression – and where the very object of the longing is itself designated *ab initio* by an inculcated discontent with the existent. The two combined can bring about a repair of the perceived deficiency. This is precisely the point adumbrated in the Talmud: if 'hope deferred makes the heart sick' (Prov. 13:12), then the answer, according to R. Hiyya b. Abba, is to 'study Torah', in effect tantamount to the practice of the Torah.[93]

Only in liberal Jewish thought are idea and act dissociated. Kaufmann Kohler writes, for example: 'But it is never the act but the conviction in which the whole weight is placed. The pure heart alone is valid (*gilt*) before the holy God – that is the kernel of Jewish theology.'[94] Buber's failure to ground the 'I-thou' relationship in any normative context is another example of dissociation in favour of sentiment. His thought 'is detached from the whole world of the *halakha*', writes one critic.[95] It is therefore limited to exhortation and fails to translate its prescriptions or moral requirements into any specific scheme of action. This is synonymous with saying that it fails to engage with, and lacks purchase on, reality.

---

[92] *Anthropologie in pragmatischer Hinsicht*, Bk 3, para. 73.

[93] TB Ber. 32b.

[94] K. Kohler, *Grundriss einer systematischen Theologie des Judentums auf geschichtlicher Grundlage*, Leipzig, 1910, p. 2.

[95] J. Levinger in the symposium on Jewish philosophy, reported in M. Ḥalamish and M. Schwarz (eds), *Hitgalut, Emuna, Tvuna*, Ramat-Gan, 1976, p. 151. Even a broadly sympathetic critic writes of Buber's 'antinomianism' (Arthur A. Cohen, 'Martin Buber and Judaism', *LBYB*, XXV (1980), pp. 287–300); see also D. Novak, *Law and Theology*, 2nd series, New York, 1976, p. 15.

Bettering the Good

This whole system is predicated on, and requires, a collective or some form of organized political entity. The Ḥinukh therefore (Commandment 493) makes the appointment of a king mandatory, 'for without this the settlement of the people will not be sustained at peace'.[96] And this is an indispensable component of the engagement with reality that will encourage man's natural sociability and curb his individualism. The Torah is not concerned with individuals *per se* – only in their capacity as members of a collective, in the trust that it can make possible, at its lowest, the common life of such members. The 'men of flesh and blood' whom the Torah addresses are also a collective of flesh and blood – the people of Israel.

It is further indicative of the reality principle of the Torah that not only is it entrusted to a certain body of men for its implementation, but also that a more or less specific territory is designated and promised for this purpose. People and land must go together. There would be no point in determining the rules of agricultural cultivation were there no land to cultivate. Some commentators (such as R. Obadiah Sforno in the late fifteenth/early sixteenth centuries) emphasize that the divine covenant with Abraham already included 'a place when they would be a people of sufficient size for a political collective and in it they would be united in His hand to serve Him with one body'.[97] It is only in the Promised Land that the totality of the laws can be put into practice. Only there, consequently, can the ideal state be conceived.

But this should not be envisaged in terms of a condition of static perfection – rather in terms of an effort in optimum circumstances. The corollary is an effort in circumstances that are less than optimal. But whatever the attendant political circumstances may be – whether these impose constraints or not, and if so to what extent – the problem, both in the Promised Land and in the dispersion, remains the same. Geography, in this respect, is irrelevant.

The ideal state is not the mimetic intellectual construction mentioned by Socrates – 'perhaps in heaven there is laid up a pattern for it'[98] – but rather, in the Jewish case, the real and the ideal effectively overlap and are interfused. It would be happier therefore to speak of the partially ideal and the completely ideal. The two levels lie along the same continuum. There is no absolute ontological separation between them. 'Three things', the

---

[96] This is based on Dt. 17:15; but see below p. 28 for some of the controversy over a 'monarchic' interpretation of this passage.

[97] 'Hakdamat R. Obadiah Sforno', *Sefer Bereshit*, end.

[98] *The Republic*, IX, 592.

Talmud suggests, 'are an anticipation of the world to come: Sabbath, sunshine and sexual intercourse.'[99] It is not ideal and reality that confront each other but different degrees of ideality; the world that is to be made better is already good. Certainly, infinitely varied modes of accommodation have to be devised in order to preserve and transcend what is only partially ideal, but ideally these remain congruent with what is required for the completely ideal.

Socrates may now be quoted to greater effect, when he argues that whether the ideal state exists or not is immaterial; in either case the man of understanding will adopt the practices of such a state.[100] In the Jewish case, *mutatis mutandis*, where only the partially ideal is accessible, it is still obligatory to observe those norms that it does allow of and thereby to advance what is still incomplete.

When Maimonides, for example, codifies into normative conduct the Talmudic discussion concerning those instruments of war which can be worn or carried on the Sabbath, he distinguishes two types: those that are an adornment (shield, helmet) – which he permits – and those others that do not adorn (lance, bow) – which he prohibits.[101] In this way encouragement is given to the peace that is to characterize the messianic age. Not only is some part of the peaceful future brought to the violent contemporary world, but in itself the purport of so doing helps to accelerate that development.

It is because of this situation, where the claims of the partially ideal are paramount, that Jewish literature knows of no ideal state – only, of course, in the generalized descriptions of the prophets; and these in any case cannot be taken literally, at least in the view of such commentators as Maimonides.[102] Moreover, paradise, the ideal, does not welcome visitors and is dangerous to those who venture there. Of the four men who entered 'the garden' only one returned whole: 'Ben Azzai looked and died . . . Ben Zoma looked and went mad . . . Aher mutilated the shoots [that is, became a heretic]. R. Akiba departed in peace.'[103]

In such a situation, where the ideal is unknown and in any case inaccess-

----

[99] TB Ber. 57b; see also D. Hartman, *A Living Covenant*, New York/London, 1985, pp. 225ff. Maimonides, on the other hand, argues that the world to come exists in the present and is so called only because it 'comes to man' after the life of this world (MT Laws of repentance 8:8); for a further indication of Maimonides's views see p. 167 below.

[100] *The Republic*, IX, 591–2; cf. the Kantian imperative: 'always in actuality to regard ourselves as the designated citizens of a divine (ethical) state' (Schriften zur Ethik und Religionsphilosophie', *Werke*, Wiesbaden, 1956, IV, p. 802).

[101] MT Laws of the Sabbath 19:1.

[102] See below p. 165.

[103] TB Hag. 14b; cf. also *Sifrei on Deuteronomy*, New York, 1969, Piska 356.

ible, only one generalization seems possible: that the collective suffers from no danger of reification. To quote Bamberger: 'traditional Judaism does not concern itself with the conflicting claims and interests of the individual and state as political entities. It does not know the state as a mystic, eternal, spiritual substance, any more than it knows the joint stock corporation as a legal person. It knows only kings, exilarchs, rabbis, judges, *parnassim* and householders.'[104] It is characteristic of the Biblical standpoint that it should associate its first reference to a state with Nimrod and the sin of the Tower of Babel.[105]

Politics into Law

The political world is envisaged primarily not in terms of constitutional arrangements but in terms of the welfare of persons, or groups of persons, in conflict or co-operation with each other, and their co-operation is to be furthered, and their conflicts resolved, through the Torah.

This does not, however, rule out a political standpoint that is goal-directed and therefore rational, in the sense that it is governed by the operations of the laws. At one extreme stands Maimonides's Mishneh Torah, which provides for the exercise of all those powers that a state normally exercises – judicial, military, administrative etc.[106] It is characterized by its range of applicability in that it provides for optimum conditions as well as those that are less so, namely those in which sovereignty is limited.[107] Other rabbinic versions discuss the role of monarchy, judiciary, magistrates, executive, political authority and obligation, the prophetic institution etc.[108] Another group of political thinkers, from the fifteenth to the seventeenth centuries, mainly from Italy (such as Johanan Alemanno), interpreted the political institutions of the Torah in the light of their admiration for Florence and Venice, and vice versa. Alemanno, influenced by Renaissance Platonism, saw the Platonic ideal of the philosopher-king in the embodiment of Lorenzo di Medici but the prototype of such a king

---

[104] B.J. Bamberger, 'Individual rights and the demands of the state: A position of classical Judaism', *CCAR*, liv (1944), p. 209.

[105] Gen. 10:8–10; see also the discussion of this point by J. Banner in E.-J. Finbert (ed.), *Aspects du Génie d'Israel*, Paris, 1950, pp. 95–104.

[106] For a recent analysis of Maimonides's political views, see G. Blidstein, *Ikronot medini'im le'mishnat ha'Rambam*, University of Bar Ilan, 1983.

[107] For examples cf. pp. 30, 34.

[108] See M. Sicker, *The Judaic State – A Study in Rabbinic Political Theory*, New York, 1988, passim.

is the Biblical Solomon.[109] Don Isaac Abrabanel was exceptional in his rejection of man as a natural political animal, regarding government and the city as a mere concession to 'the evil instinct'. He was also a determined opponent of monarchy, and his ideal constitution was formed of a leader, such as Moses, and his successors, the Judges; an aristocratic element (the Sanhedrin); and a democratic element of locally and popularly elected judges. Patently, the inspiration of the Venetian Republic was dominant.[110]

The problem posed by Socrates, therefore, is no longer that of conduct as determined by the known ideal but conduct in the light of an ideal that is unknown save for its broadest outlines. It is no longer a question of adopting the practices of a known but of an unknown entity; or, in our terminology, of reconciling the claims of the partially ideal with those of the completely ideal. This is achieved by the transmutation of political philosophy into the operation of the Torah.

Ultimately, it is intended to resolve all political conflicts into conflicts of conduct (that is, into law), or, as Maimonides claimed, to render the study of political philosophy superfluous, for this is already contained within the Torah.[111] In other words, political conflicts are collapsed into the legal-normative mode, where the laws become 'the executive arm' of political philosophy.[112]

An example of such 'transmutation' or 'collapse' may be found in the case before R. Moses Minz in Würzburg in the fifteenth century. At issue are the respective rights of the majority and the minority. A divided Jewish community confronted a renewal of anti-Jewish decrees, which it at first unanimously agreed to counteract through the establishment of a court empowered to take such measures as seemed imperative. Subsequently some of those who had agreed to this action withdrew their agreement.

---

[109] These themes are examined in A. Melamed, 'Jewish Political Thought in the Renaissance', PhD dissertation, Tel Aviv University, 1976; see also A. Melamed, 'The Hebrew "Laudatio" of Yohanan Alemanno;, in *The Jews of Italy*, Jerusalem, 1988 (Engl. Sec.), pp. 1–34; and E.I.J. Rosenthal, 'Some observations on Yohanan Alemanno's political ideas', in S. Stein and R. Loewe (eds), *Studies in Jewish Religious and Intellectual History presented to Alexander Altmann*, Alabama, 1979, pp. 247–61.

[110] B. Netanyahu, *'Don Isaac Abravanel'*, Philadelphia, 1968, ch. 3. Abrabanel lived in Venice after 1503, as adviser to the Senate.

[111] See I. Efros, 'Maimonides' treatise on logic', *PAAJR*, viii (1937–8), pp. 19, 63ff., L. Strauss, 'Quelques remarques sur la science politique de Maimonide et de Farabi', *REJ*, 100 (1936), pp. 1–37; L. Strauss, Maimonides' statement on political science', in L. Strauss, *What is Political Philosophy?*, Westport, 1973, pp. 155–69.

[112] Z. Harvey, 'Ben pilosofiya medinit le-halakha be-mishnat ha-Rambam', *Iyyun*, 29 (1980), pp. 208–9.

This disunity R. Minz condemned. He referred to Biblical precedent (Ex. 23:2 and Is. 41:6 – 'they helped everyone his neighbour'), and to the Talmud (BM 105a) denying the right of one partner to dissolve a partnership without the consent of the other partner: 'how much the more is one not permitted to dissolve the partnership against the clear wish of the other partner(s). If this applies in a case of a partnership of two individuals, it applies all the more where an individual is trying to stand against the wishes of a majority of the community.' Citing more recent cases, where the corporate authority of the community had been upheld in fiscal matters, Minz concluded that also in the present case 'the majority may use whatever coercion they wish to' in order to compel the individuals to comply with the decision of the Jewish court.[113]

In this way the conflict of majority versus minority is transposed into the mutual obligations of partners. This is in line with a tradition from Talmudic times onwards which prefers to regard the community as a partnership (even if involuntary) of individuals and not as an independent legal entity.[114]

In terms of the partially ideal, therefore, where the politics of the Torah are concerned, the authority of the laws inevitably and necessarily emphasizes the decision-making power of the court, in the overt political realm, as the principal locus of Jewish sovereignty. It was a seat of power, with strong defensive characteristics. To protect and preserve the integrity of the court had a political connotation commensurate with its role as the adjudicator of disputes. If 'the sceptre shall not depart from Judah',[115] then the court, with its power to impose and implement judgement, served as the central organ of self-government. The hand that wielded Judah's sceptre was perceived to be political, by both the Jewish and gentile worlds – hence the incessant disputes over their respective areas of jurisdiction. Nothing is more characteristic of the charters that determined the relationship of Jew and gentile than the latter's recognition, in one degree or other, of the Jewish court.[116] For its part, recognition on the Jewish side also comprised

[113] R. Moses Minz, *She'elot u-Tshuvot*, Lemberg, 1851, No. 63.

[114] See M. Schapira, 'Ha'Musag "Tsibur" ba'Mishpat ha'ivri', *Dinei Yisrael*, I (1970), pp. 75–94. Other valuable material is contained in Sh. Albeck, *Dinei Mammonot ba'Talmud*, Tel Aviv, 1976, pp. 506–16; M.P. Golding, 'The juridical basis of communal associations in medieval rabbinic legal thought', *JSS*, xxviii (1966), No. 2, pp. 67–78; S. Morrell, 'The constitutional limits of communal government in rabbinic law', *JSS*, xxxiii (1971), Nos. 2–3, pp. 87–119.

[115] Gen. 49:10.

[116] See, for example, the charters governing Jewish settlement in Speyer and Worms at the end of the eleventh century (J. Aronius, *Regesten zur Geschichte der Juden*, Berlin, 1902, Nos 168, 170–1; also G. Kisch, *The Jews in Medieval Germany*, 2nd edn, New York, 1970, pp. 101–3; M. Frank, *Kehillot Ashkenaz u-vatei dineihen*, Tel Aviv, 1937, pp. 35ff. See below for examples from Berlin and London in modern times.

the acknowledgement of the legitimacy of the gentile state and the commitment to loyalty.[117] This did not extend by any means to an acknowledgement of the legitimacy of all the legislation of such a state, especially where this was discriminatory in character.[118] But the general attitude holds good.

This is, of course, an argument couched in political terms, making resort to the gentile court almost an act of treachery. But it is inseparable from the 'religious' argument; in the words of Maimonides: 'all who appear before the judges of the gentiles in their courts – even though their laws are as the laws of Israel – is evil and it is as though he blasphemes and insults and raises his hand against the Torah of Moses our master.' Even when force majeure makes it impracticable for the Jewish litigant to secure justice from 'a powerful and violent' gentile adversary, Maimonides does not authorize the former to resort to a gentile court until he has first secured permission from the Jewish court.[119]

In an actual case that came before him in his capacity as respondent (though no details are available), Maimonides gave an identical ruling, and authorized the plaintiff, although it was 'not fitting' to do so, to summon the defendant before a gentile court, 'if he is unable to have recourse to Jewish law'.[120] Even in such a situation there is still an attempt to reserve to the Jewish court some *locus standi* in the conduct of the litigants. Provision for this is contained in a number of communal ordinances from the twelfth to the fifteenth centuries. The Jewish authorities and their court must insist on their power to grant or refuse permission to the aggrieved Jew compelled to summon his Jewish adversary before a gentile court.[121] For R. Meir of Rothenburg, a Jew who took his case before a gentile court deserved to be 'put in the stocks and pilloried'. Such action was a source of 'mortal danger'.[122]

[117] W. Wurzburger, 'Digmei Tafkid ba'manhigut ha'ruhanit', in Ella Belfer (ed.), *Manhigut Ruhanit b'Yisrael*, Jerusalem, 1982, p. 25.

[118] For a treatment of this theme (in terms purely of religious teaching), see S. Shilo, *Dina d'Malkhuta Dina*, Jerusalem, 1974; also I. Lampronti, *Pahad Yitzhak*, Venice, 1753, II, 93b–94a for references to some of the source material.

[119] MT Laws of the Sanhedrin, 26, 7; see also the sources quoted in Caro's commentary on the *Tur* (Ḥoshen Mishpat, Laws of Judges, 26).

[120] J. Blau (ed.), *Tshuvot Ha'Rambam*, 3 vols, Jerusalem, 1958–61, I, No. 27.

[121] L. Finkelstein, *Jewish Self-Government*, p. 195; M. Frank, *Kehillot Ashkenaz u-vatei dineihen*, p. 121.

[122] *Sefer She'arei Tshuvot*, ed. M. Bloch, 2 vols, Berlin, 1891, II, No. 978; see also the case when two Jews apparently informed on each other before a gentile court (*She'elot u-tshuvot Maharam b. Baruch*, Lvov, 1860, Nos 247–8). In many such cases, not only are the authority of the Torah, good order and public security at stake – there is also a financial motive in the desire to prevent the alienation to the

Moses Minz in the fifteenth century castigated a litigant, not so much for taking his case to a gentile court as for doing so without the prior approval of the local Jewish authorities.[123] In all such cases there is the fear of informing.

Who Rules?

But the political leadership of the Torah, mediated through the court, is not exercised in a vacuum. The time has now come to follow further the Talmudic adage: 'go outside and see what men do.' The leadership role of the Torah has always to be exercised in a political context and through specific men and media. In short, who rules?

I shall limit myself principally to the medieval period in the German lands. But the problem is of course ancient: when Moses faced it he was instructed by his father-in-law to seek out able, God-fearing, truthful men and men who hated unjust gain.[124] Moses, as the commentators point out, could in fact find leaders with only two of these qualities – 'wise men and full of knowledge'.[125] For Maimonides the problematic of the ideal leader was encapsulated in his ability to parallel God's own concern for the world He has created. 'The relationship of the philosopher to the state is the same as that of God to the universe', writes Berman;[126] and Maimonides founds this view on his interpretation of Jacob's dream (Gen. 28:10ff.): 'how well put is the phrase *ascending and descending* in which *ascent* comes before *descent*. For after the *ascent* and the attaining of certain rungs of the ladder that may be known comes the descent with whatever decree the prophet has been informed of – with a view to governing and teaching the people of the earth.'[127]

---

gentile authorities of capital generated within the *kehillah*. Even fines levied within the *kehillah* might be diverted to the gentile authorities. King Ruprecht (1400–10) is estimated to have collected 20,000–30,000 florins from Jewish amerciements (M. Stern, *König Ruprecht von der Pfalz in seinen Beziehungen zu den Juden*, Kiel, 1898, p.lvii).

[123] *She'elot u-Tshuvot*, no. 44; R. Jacob Weil imposed an additional fine on a litigant who summoned his opponent before a gentile court (*She'elot u-Teshuvot*, Hanau, 1610, no. 147).

[124] Ex. 18:21.

[125] Dt. 1:15.

[126] 'Maimonides on leadership', in D. Elazar (ed.), *Kinship and Consent*, Ramat-Gan/London, 1981, p. 117.

[127] *Guide*, 1:15; cf. the discussion of this interpretation in S. Klein-Braslavy, 'Perushei ha-'Rambam le-'halom ha-sulam shel Ya'akov', in *Sefer Ha-shanah*, Bar-Ilan, vols 22–3, 1988, pp. 344ff.

Classical Judaism sought an answer in the concept of the 'three crowns': those of Torah; of priesthood; and of kingship. Ultimately this division of authority reaches back to the threefold role of king, priests and levites, and prophet outlined in chapters 17 and 18 of Deuteronomy. Each has 'a distinct focus of interest . . . as separate mediating devices between God and His people . . . [and] each is entitled to exercise a constitutional check on the others'.[128] Obviously, with the destruction of the Temple 'the crown of priesthood' retains only a vestigial relevance.

The other two categories of rulership were transmuted into lay and rabbinical leadership. More precisely, lay leadership – 'the crown of kingship' – fell to the wealthy; and 'the crown of the Torah' fell to the rabbis. In his commentary on Ezekiel 34:2 the sixteenth-century Italian cabbalist, Mordecai Dato, wrote of 'the two shepherds of the Diaspora – the wealthy and the sages'.[129] The two bodies shared a breadth of power, though normally the wealthy were dominant in the secular realm. It would be otiose to document the incidence of oligarchic rule.[130]

This was certainly not because any inherent virtue or capacity for leadership was attributed to the wealthy but rather because, in the medieval period and after, wealth as such took an instrumental role as the raw material from which bribes, *douceurs* and gifts of all kinds could be derived, at a time of physical persecution and arbitrary financial exactions. If, at the end of the twelfth century, the Rhineland rabbi R. Joel Halevy emphasizes the need for cash wherewith to bribe gentiles, 'who multiply decrees against us . . . it is all in order that we may live for we do not know what tax the king will demand'[131] – then the ascendancy of the wealthy must be promoted; they alone are in a position to offer bribes. The same socio-economic phenomenon has been noted in medieval France.[132] It was a duty incumbent on the wealthy to help their fellow-Jews; they are, as it were, only trustees for

---

[128] Stuart A. Cohen, 'The concept of the three Ketarim ("Crowns"): Its place in Jewish political thought and its implications for a study of Jewish constitutional history', *AJSR*, ix (1984), no. 1, pp. 34–5; cf. also S. Trigano, 'Le fait politique juif moderne', *Pardès*, VI (1987).

[129] Quoted by R. Bonfil, *Ha-rabbanut be-Italiya bi-tekufat ha-renaissance*, Jerusalem, 1979, p. 31.

[130] But this does not necessarily signify that rabbinical views were silenced; cf. below pp. 68–9, 105.

[131] 'Or Zarua', Pt III, *Piskei Baba Metzia*, Jerusalem, 1887, ch. 5, No. 208, p. 59. S.W. Baron (*Social and Religious History of the Jews*, Philadelphia, JPSA, XII, 1967, p. 198), quotes a number of other rabbis to the same effect.

[132] R. Chazan, *Medieval Jewry in Northern France*, Baltimore/London, 1973, p. 187.

'the property of Israel'. Even so, their activities in this regard clearly had an individualistic relevance.

This must necessarily affect the composition of the community leadership, as indicated in the contemporary *Book of the Pious (Sefer Ḥassidim)*: 'if you see a man who has nothing and his words are not heeded and there is a rich and good man who is heeded and you wish to appoint him [that is, the former] as leader, do not listen to them, but [and] say, make that rich man a leader'.[133] This is no unqualified endorsement of wealth: the rich man must be 'good' and also ready to consult with the sage, who will in this way determine the voice of wealth. The rich will speak to 'the man of the city' but the words will be those of the sage.[134] Even so, the drift of power is unmistakeable. The ascendancy of the wealthy assumed constitutional form in the transition towards collegiate government. In R. Joel Halevy's time it was already customary to elect a communal council of 'seven good men of the city'.[135] Halevy elsewhere specifies that a communal leader need not be a learned man, though certainly a man of 'goodly deeds'.[136]

These not necessarily learned men are in fact the wealthy, and it is about this time that the *Book of the Pious* equates communal leader and man of wealth. The latter's gradual emergence was also encouraged by the demand that those elected to communal office grant interest-free loans to local rulers, such as ten marks annually to the archbishop of Trier.[137] Also in the thirteenth century, R. Meir b. Baruch of Rothenburg, in writing to R. Abraham Halevi, takes it for granted that leaders will only be drawn from the taxpaying class: 'If there is friction amongst your community and they cannot reach agreement in the selection of leaders with the concurrence of all – this one says this and this one that – and there is no justice, truth or peace in the city nor in the dependent lands – what shall they do? It seems to me', wrote R. Meir, 'that you must assemble tax-paying heads of households who will take an oath to give his opinion for the sake of heaven and the betterment of the city and they all follow the majority to choose leaders, cantors, etc.'[138] At the end of the sixteenth century, R. Judah Loew b. Bezalel of Prague found it truly providential that there were men 'who were close to the kingdom . . . elders appropriate to each kingdom and to

---

[133] Ed. J. Wistinetzki, Berlin, 1891, no. 1340.

[134] Ibid., no. 1341.

[135] *Sefer Rabiah*, 3 vols, repr., New York, 1983, II, no. 590, pp. 316–17.

[136] Ibid., III, no. 850, pp. 599–600.

[137] For both points, see Y. Handelsman, 'Tmunot be-hanhagat kehillot Yisrael be-Ashkenaz bi'ymei ha-benayim', PhD dissertation, University of Tel Aviv, 1980, p. 118.

[138] *Sefer She'arei Tshuvot*, ed. M. Bloch, no. 865.

its inner essence' through whom Israel would be saved.[139] From this it was only a short step to argue, as did R. Joseph Stadthagen in the late seventeenth/early eighteenth centuries (he being himself close to the Hanover court Jew, Leffman Behrens), that those who were 'close to the court' and those lesser men 'at the gates of power', occupying themselves with the welfare of Israel amongst 'judges and officials', deserved special respect. They should, as circumstances required, be allowed a degree of latitude in their obedience to the laws.[140] Much earlier, Maimonides had already ruled: 'an Israelite who is close to the kingdom and must appear before their rulers and is unseemly because he does not resemble them is permitted to dress like them and to shave in their manner.'[141]

The ascendancy of the wealthy also had internal justification. The organized Jewish community – the *kehillah* – was a financial institution as much as anything else, having the power to raise taxes and disburse funds for religious purposes etc. In this light it was perceived as anomalous that the propertyless should have at their disposal the assets of the propertied. This is the pre-supposition of a case that came before R. Israel Isserlein in the fifteenth century: a certain community was subjected to an unexpected impost and decided to appoint five independent assessors, charging them with responsibility for assessing the tax burden of each individual member. Two wealthy and powerful brothers demanded the right to appoint two of the five. Isserlein agreed to this demand on the grounds that it would give the brothers the assurance that the assessment was in order 'and they would no longer seek to use their power to raise obstacles'. Moreover, the brothers' two appointees would in any case constitute a minority amongst the five. But Isserlein also imposed a condition – 'only if the men of wealth choose persons of trust, but if they appoint untrustworthy men of cunning devices, then certainly not'.[142] In another case, reported by R. Menachem Mendel Krochmal, in the seventeenth century, the notables in a certain community sought to establish a custom whereby only those 'who paid high taxes or were learned in the Torah should have the right to vote ... since most public matters require the expenditure of money; therefore how could the opinion of the poor be equal to that of the wealthy? Similarly, how could the opinion of the ignorant be equal to that of the scholar?' Of course, the ignorant man lacked the benefit of wealth. The poor naturally objected and Krochmal supported them, arguing forcibly that the few taxes paid by the

---

[139] *Netzach Yisrael*, repr. London, 1960, ch. x, p. 63.

[140] R. Joseph Stadthagen, *Divrei Zikaron*, Amsterdam, 1705, pp. 68b–70a.

[141] MT Laws of Idolatry, 11:2.

[142] R. Israel Isserlein, *Trumat Ha'Deshen*, repr., Bnei Brak, 1971, no. 344; for similar situations, see A. Schreiber, *Jewish Law and Decision-making*, Philadelphia, 1979, p. 316, fn. 114.

poor were accounted in each case as equivalent to the major taxes paid by the rich. Second, to eject the unlearned from the communal consensus would generate hatred, alienate them from the community and lead to their withdrawal – 'and in this way dissensions in Israel would multiply, heaven forfend'. Krochmal strongly urged the mediation of a sage to reconcile the warring parties.[143] In another case, where a small minority of a certain community (five families out of fifty) paid three-fifths of the communal taxes and therefore sought to appoint their own candidates as communal officials, Krochmal again sought to bring rich and poor into political harmony: 'even though the few rich are considered the majority because they supply most of the funds ... the majority who are poor cannot impose decrees on them at their own discretion in matters of money. But in any case the minority of wealthy also cannot impose decrees on the majority at their discretion even in money matters.' The wealthy and the majority must be of one mind.[144] But irrespective of such sentiments and the decision rendered in any particular case, the fact is that rabbinic opinion had to accept the dominant role of the wealthy and work within their framework. The wealthy became identified with the *kehillah* as a juridical entity or, as R. Yair Bacharach of Worms put it in the late seventeenth century, since 'the existence of every *kehillah* depends more on money than on numbers ... the minority of the wealthy are called the majority'.[145] In sum, rabbinical teaching, fortified by the financial pressure of the needs of the *kehillah*, accepted, for eminently pragmatic reasons, the governance of wealth.

In the twelfth and thirteenth centuries when the wealthy began their ascent there was no obstacle to a symbiosis between the new men and rabbinical guidance. This was a time when rabbis were not yet professionalized, the position of communal rabbi did not yet exist and rabbis received no material payment for their services. They derived their income from the same sources – mainly trade, pawnbroking and moneylending – as did their 'lay' compeers. Until the thirteenth century there was homogeneity between parnassim and rabbis.[146] That is why the *Book of the Pious* could claim that the sage 'will utter his wisdom to the righteous man of wealth and the man of wealth will speak to the men of the city and his words will be heard'.[147]

But in the fourteenth century, and particularly so after the Black Death,

---

[143] R. Menachem Mendel Krochmal, *Tsemach Tsedek*, Lemberg, 1861, no. 2. This case and the views of other rabbis confronted with similar questions are discussed in M. Elon, 'On power and authority', in D. Elazar (ed.), *Kinship and Consent*, Ramat Gan/Philadelphia, 1981, pp. 196ff.

[144] Krochmal, *Tsemach Tsedek*, no. 1.

[145] *Ḥavot Yair*, Frankfurt on Main, 1689, no. 157.

[146] M. Breuer, *Rabbanut Ashkenaz biymei ha'benayim*, Jerusalem, 1976, pp. 22–3.

[147] See above, p. 33.

1348–50, the relative power of the wealthy and the sages moved in favour of the former to the detriment of the latter. Already a century earlier the leadership of the *kehillah* as a political institution was beginning to separate itself from the rabbinical court.[148] By the fifteenth century it is without comment that R. Israel Isserlein writes: 'the good men of a community, when they are in session to supervise the actions of the community and individuals and are equivalent to a court'.[149]

Certainly, in the life of the *kehillah* the rabbi retained an indisputable role, but it was no longer a central, governing role, as hitherto. Rather, it was limited to monitoring communal ordinances[150] and to deciding matters of personal status (for example, officiating at marriages and divorces) and doubtful questions of ritual.[151] But these boundaries did not everywhere apply; for instance, in 1434 R. Zalman Katz of Nuremberg, R. Nathan Epstein of Frankfurt and R. Jacob Weil of Augsburg negotiated with the authorities the coronation tax imposed by the newly elected Emperor Sigismond on the communities of the empire.[152] But these cases were certainly exceptional.

Rabbinical withdrawal from a public-political role in communal affairs was no doubt correlated with a decline in the rabbi's economic status. He ceased to be self-employed but became a communal employee. Again, the picture is not uniform. In the late fourteenth and fifteenth centuries notable rabbis (R. Meir Halevy of Vienna, R. Elijah of Prague, R. Seligmann of Ulm, R. David Sprinz of Nuremberg, R. Meisterlein of Neustadt) continued to support themselves from the proceeds of moneylending or various forms of trade,[153] and to refrain, in the traditional phrase, from using the Torah as 'a spade to dig with'.

None the less there is transition towards a paid and professional rabbinate – at first in the form of the fees derived from officiating at religious

---

[148] Handelsman, 'Tmunot be-hanhagat kehillot Yisrael' pp. 198ff.

[149] *Trumat Ha-Deshen*, Pesakim u-ketavim, no. 214.

[150] For a general picture of this activity see M. Elon, 'Le-Mahutan shel takanot ha-kahal ba-mishpat ha-ivri', in G. Tedeschi (ed.), *Mehkarei mishpat le-zekher Abraham Rosenthal*, Jerusalem, 1964, pp. 1–54.

[151] I.J. Yuval, *Ḥakhamim be-doram*, Jerusalem, 1989, p. 338. The point is also made that the ordinances drawn up by R. Moses Minz in 1469 for the community in Bamberg concerned themselves with religious matters alone (Breuer, *Rabbanut Ashkenaz*, p. 25).

[152] Yuval, *Ḥakhamim be-doram*, pp. 23–4.

[153] M. Frank, *Kehillot Ashkenaz*, p. 24; S. Shpitzer, 'Ha-rabbanut ve-ha-rabbanim be-drom Germaniya ve-Austriya be-reshit ha-meah ha-15', *Sefer Ha-Shanah*, Bar-Ilan, nos 7–8 (1970), p. 270; S. Eidelberg, *Jewish Life in Austria in the 15th Century*, Philadelphia, 1962, p. 109.

ceremonies (betrothals, weddings, funerals) or from acting as scribe and teacher.[154] R. Jacob Molin (b. Mainz c.1360) earned a large part of his income from matchmaking.[155]

The practice of accepting fees for the performance of religious functions was repugnant to certain teachers, all the more so as it was part of the movement towards 'ordaining' rabbis. 'The crown of the Torah and its authority', R. Israel Isserlein wrote, 'lies before and is available to all who wish to become worthy of it and if there is concern for livelihood through the reward that falls to the pockets of leaders on account of divorces, the remarriage of childless widows and the administering of oaths to women and the blessing of betrothals, marriages etc., is there anything worth while in receiving this reward? We are ashamed and only with effort do we find justification for most such cases.'[156]

But in certain communities – Schweidnitz, 1370, and Erfurt, 1373 – there are already strong suggestions that ad hoc payments were a preliminary to the engagement of salaried rabbis.[157] In any case, a century later it is clear that the economic independence of rabbis had yielded to a position of dependence on the communities. They were chosen by the latter, as the responsa of Weil, Bruna and others make explicit.[158] It was also not unknown for laymen to nominate the third member to a rabbinic court of assessors.[159] Rabbinical dependence on the communal leadership was an outspoken theme in the writings of R. Judah b. Bezalel of Prague (late sixteenth – early seventeenth centuries). He complained bitterly that judges and rabbis 'were all dependent on the leaders and individual members of the community in that each or every third year they appoint him to his position'. Rabbis feared for their re-appointment; there was mutual distrust between rabbis and their communities: 'and it is fitting to say that a judge in this position is unfit to judge'.[160] This was 'a feature of the generation', declared Judah b. Bezalel. Doubtless he had Bohemia and Moravia in mind, but it is likely that his remarks had wider application.

In certain communities, the situation was such that men of wealth and

---

[154] Isserlein, *Trumat Ha-Deshen*, Pesakim u-ketavim, no. 128.

[155] *Sefer Maharil*, Shklov, 1796, p. 55a.

[156] Isserlein, *Trumat Ha'Deshen*, Pesakim u-ketavim, no. 128; cf. also Y. A. Dinari, *Ḥakhmei Ashkenaz be-shilhei y'mei-ha'benayim*, Jerusalem, 1984, p. 61; M. Breuer, 'Ha-Semikha ha-ashkenazit', *Zion*, 32–3 (1967–8), pp. 15–46.

[157] Frank, *Kehillot Ashkenaz*, p. 26, fnn. 8, 9.

[158] See the material cited in S. Assaf, *B'Ohalei Ya'akov*, repr., Jerusalem, 1943, p. 32; also R. Jacob Weil, *She'elot u-Tshuvot*, Hanau, 1610, no. 146.

[159] M. Breuer, 'Ma'amad ha-rabbanut be-hanhagatan shel kehillot Ashkenaz ba-me'ah ha-15', *Zion*, 40–1 (1975–6), pp. 61–3.

[160] *Netivot Olam*, repr. London, 1961, ch. 2.

political influence were able to intimidate or silence the rabbinical judge, or at least oblige him to trim his views. Such rabbis as Perez, Minz, Weil and Isserlein studiously refrained on a number of occasions from becoming involved in using their judicial prerogatives.[161] Weil reports in one of his responsa that he had been told by a reliable source that a certain R. Shlomo (of Halle) 'does not wish to venture his head in this dispute in any respect because of the hostility of Abram Ezra who is known for his violence and his business affairs and the bishop of Merseberg is sympathetic to him with the bishop of Magdeburg and the bishop of Magdeburg rules over the Jews in Halle'.[162] Weil himself wrote in general terms of the contemporary rabbinate that they would 'be at risk' if they were to protest at all the misdeeds committed.[163] For these and cognate reasons Isserlein and Bruna were reluctant to use their powers of expulsion.[164]

The fifteenth century was in any case a period of intensified suffering and persecution for the Jews of medieval Germany. They were subjected to a vast campaign of incitement and accusations of ritual murder which culminated in the mass expulsion of Jews from towns and cities with the exception of Worms, Prague and Frankfurt on Main.[165] The consequence was a breakdown in communal discipline: to quote R. Weil: 'the communal elders oppress and crush the people with force. They do not act for the sake of heaven but they intend their own benefit. They remove the yoke from themselves and place it round the neck of the afflicted.'[166] It seems that an attitude of *sauve qui peut* developed amongst the communities.

In such circumstances the notion that the partially ideal and the completely ideal lie along the same continuum is stretched almost to breaking point. But it is not lost. The very intensity of protest testifies to its persist-

---

[161] E. Zimmer, *Harmony and Discord*, New York, 1970, pp. 70–1.

[162] Weil, *Responsa*, nos 148, 149; Isserlein, *Trumat Ha-Deshen*, Pesakim u-ketavim, No. 175; cf. also B. Rosensweig, *Ashkenazi Jewry in Transition*, Ontario, 1975, p. 98.

[163] Weil, *Responsa*, no. 157.

[164] Zimmer, *Harmony and Discord*, p. 96. In London also, at the beginning of the nineteenth century, there is evidence of the differential application of rabbinical sanctions and punishments (see below p. 92).

[165] This process is described in B.-Z. Degani, 'Da'at ha-kahal ha-anti-Yehudit ke'gorem le-gerusham shel ha-yehudim mei-arei Germaniya be-shelhei y'mei ha-beinayim 1440–1530', PhD dissertation, Hebrew University, Jerusalem, 1982. The prevalence of ritual murder trials at this time (for example, Endingen, 1470; Regensburg, 1470–6; Freiburg, 1504) is described in R. Po-chia Hsia, *The Myth of Ritual Murder: Jews and Magic in Reformation Germany*, Yale University Press, 1988.

[166] Weil, *Responsa*, no. 173. Isserlein, *Trumat Ha-Deshen*, Pesakim u-ketavim (nos 174, 214), gives examples of corruption and *force majeure*. Cf. also Zimmer, *Harmony and Discord*, p. 21.

ence. None of the claims made by the Torah has been abandoned, though some are certainly in eclipse.

For all that, and despite its deficiencies, the structure of the 'two crowns' remains intact, in the German lands at least, until the end of the eighteenth century. It functions as that form of community rule which governs all sides of community life. Lukacs has precisely conveyed the condition of success: 'only when man is able to grasp the present as becoming, by recognising in it those tendencies from whose dialectical conflict he is able to *create* the future, does the present, the present as becoming, become *his* present.'[167] It is not necessary to accept the notion of a 'dialectical conflict' to transpose without difficulty this mode of action into the action of the Torah. I have already tried to show how the commandments, for example, grasp nature, as it were, 'grasp the present as becoming', and annihilate longing through action.[168]

In pursuit of this aim communities have been established as means to redeem man from nature, where sons will no longer suffer for the sins of their fathers nor the innocent with the guilty, and the partially ideal will be brought closer to the completely ideal. I now try to show this process at work in the modern Jewish communities of Berlin and London. 'The Torah is not in heaven',[169] but it is in Berlin and London, as much and as little as anywhere else.

---

[167] G. Lukacs, *Geschichte und Klassenbewusstsein*, Berlin, 1923, p. 223.
[168] See above p. 24.
[169] TB BM 59b.

2

A Tale of Two Cities: Berlin, 1670–1800

Preamble

The Torah is not in heaven and it is also not for angels, who have known none of the trials to which men are exposed. It must therefore be made to serve the particular circumstances of particular men. It would otherwise lead a shadowy existence, in an enforced, artificial isolation from that very reality where it belongs and which it seeks to master. In terms of governance I have already tried to show that the Torah in medieval Ashkenaz adapts for its own purposes the two 'crowns' of the kingdom and the rabbinate, to each of which falls a more or less defined area of jurisdiction. Berlin Jewry (like London Jewry) inherits this structure. But my investigation into the ways of the Torah now goes deeper and seeks answers to questions of central concern. How do the Jews of Berlin organize their relations with the Brandenburg state? What provision do they make for education and study and worship? How do they compose their internal differences? How do they cope with change? How do they meet the needs of the poor and humble? Where, in short, is the court, the circumciser, the charity collector, the butcher, the notary, the teacher etc. that the Talmud finds essential to life in the city?[1] There are attempts at function and fulfilment in all these areas. It is no part of my argument that the Jews of Berlin met these demands in an exemplary manner. Indeed, they did not – as the following pages make clear. The Torah remains distinguishable from this particular community, but not entirely so. Here is 'a holy community in Israel'.

The Formation of a Community

In 1571 the elector of Brandenburg, Joachim II, expelled the Jews 'for all time' from his territory. A century later Frederick William, the great elector, invited a select group of fifty Jewish families to settle in Brandenburg.

---

[1] See below p. 46.

Behind this change of policy stood the Thirty Years War, 1618–48, and certain favourable consequences that it incidentally entailed for the Jews of the German lands.[2]

Jews had fought in the warring armies (in Wallenstein's forces, for example, and in the defence of Prague against the Swedes in 1648).[3] But they were not actually enrolled and their participation had no influence on the favourable turn of post-war events. Rather, the conflict itself imposed a cessation of persecution; also, the unremitting need for supplies, and the loot that armies generated, gave varied opportunities for enrichment. Grimmelhausen's famous novel of the war, *Simplicissimus*, has Jewish traders buying booty in one camp and selling it in the enemy's, and Jews supplying horses to the army.[4]

By the same token the devastation wrought by the wars throughout Germany created a need for repair and reconstruction in the second half of the seventeenth century. This coincided with an enhanced Christian appreciation of Jewish mercantile ability, an opinion widely cherished in Western and Central Europe at this time.[5] Notably in the German states, this factor encouraged rulers to engage Jews to serve at their courts in an economic, financial and sometimes diplomatic capacity.[6]

But for the mass of Jews life was dominated by the upheaval that war left in its wake. The mass expulsions of the sixteenth century had certainly ceased; they gave way to localized expulsions – from Vienna (1670); from Berlin and parts of Brandenburg (1718 and after); from Prague (1744). The memoirs that Glückel of Hameln began to write in 1689 give a vivid picture of the physical insecurity and sense of alarm that constantly accompanied the life of the Jews in the German lands.

Reconstruction took place under the auspices of a new type of state. It was absolutist, bureaucratic, mercantilistic and territorially based, with only a loose attachment to the empire. The demands made of their court Jews by the hundreds of different rulers of such states inevitably varied, but finance was certainly dominant – whether for the upkeep of the army and the court or for investment in the economy. The ruination of the Christian

---

[2] For a general picture of this aspect of the war, see Jonathan Israel, 'Central European Jewry during the Thirty Years' War', *Central European History*, xvi (1983), no. 1, pp. 3–30.

[3] See F. Priebatsch, 'Die Judenpolitik des fürstlichen Absolutismus im 17. und 18. Jahrhundert', *Festschrift für D. Schäfer*, Jena, 1915, p. 614.

[4] See the references cited in W.J. Cahnmann, *German Jewry – its History and Sociology*, New Jersey, 1989, p. 45.

[5] Cf. Sh. Ettinger, 'The beginnings of the change in the attitude of European society towards the Jews', *Scripta Hierosolymitana*, VII (1961), pp. 193–219.

[6] The standard work here is S. Stern, *The Court Jew*, Philadelphia, 1950.

banks during the years of war, combined with the inability or unwillingness of the Estates to furnish the required funds, created an opportunity for those Jews who had benefited from the years of war to provide the funds demanded.[7] Judaism was certainly not one of the religions recognized by the Peace of Westphalia in 1648, yet the movement towards *raison d'état* and a secular conception of politics helped to dull Christian reluctance to sanction the proximity of Jews to the public life of states.

Brandenburg-Prussia was unquestionably amongst the more highly developed German states in terms of its machinery and administration. But here too, in the aftermath of war, recourse was had to the support that Jews might render to the electorate. As early as 1650, in the bishopric of Halberstadt, part of the territories acquired by Brandenburg under the Peace of Westphalia, the great elector issued letters of protection initially to ten Jewish families granting them trading and residential rights. By 1661 their number had risen to fifteen; by 1665 to forty-one; and by 1669 to fifty-five, totalling 284 individuals lodged in twenty-five houses.[8]

In Berlin virtually a new Jewish settlement came into existence in 1671 when, 'for the furtherance of trade and traffic', the fifty Jewish families were admitted to Brandenburg. They formed part of the Jewish community of Vienna, expelled in 1670. Negotiations between three of the Jewish leaders from Vienna – Herschel Lazarus, Benedict Veit and Abraham Ries – and the Prussian resident in Vienna led to the issue of an edict of admission in 1671, fashioned in part on the Halberstadt model of 1650. The edict governed the status of the fifty Jewish families in a number of material details. It permitted them to settle in any convenient area. They might also rent, buy or build residences; it required 'all [the elector's] subjects and servants . . . to allow the said Jews to pass freely and securely everywhere in the whole of our Electorate and other lands, to attend the public fairs, depots and places of trade, to offer all their wares for sale publicly, and to give them facilities without let or hindrance for honourable trade and such traffic as is not forbidden, and not to molest them'. It exempted the Jews from the body tax and imposed on them the same duties and excise taxes as on other subjects, but also required eight reichsthaler annually per family in protection money and one golden gulden 'whenever one of them [that is, the Jews] marries'. In civil cases the Jews were subject to the jurisdiction of the local burgomaster; criminal cases had to be brought

---

[7] For some of the connections between those Jews (such as the Gomperz and Lehmann families) who came to prominence in 1618–48 and their later role as court Jews, see H. Schnee, *Die Hoffinanz und der moderne Staat*, 6 vols, Berlin, 1953–67, I, 79; II, 170; III, 178ff.

[8] E. Wolbe, *Geschichte der Juden in Berlin und in der Mark Brandenburg*, Berlin, 1937, pp. 94–5.

before the elector personally. The edict disallowed a synagogue, permitting worship only in private dwellings, but it did authorize the employment of a (ritual) slaughterer and schoolteacher and 'against payment of an equitable fee', it enjoined local magistrates to assign land for a Jewish cemetery. The edict had a validity of twenty years.[9]

In 1685, after the revocation of the edict of Nantes, a group of Huguenots was also admitted to Brandenburg as a means to stimulating the local economy and replenishing its population.[10] Later came Protestants from Switzerland, Bohemia and the Palatinate. The conditions governing the admission of the Huguenots were markedly more favourable than those extended to the Jews. The former imposed no time limit, permitted full freedom of religious life and internal jurisdiction, provided travel facilities from France, made subsidies available for manufacturers and for six years exempted the Huguenots from 'all public charges'.[11]

The Jews were not only handicapped religiously, economically etc., they were also highly unwelcome to the Estates and guilds.[12] In 1669 a mob systematically destroyed the synagogue in Halberstadt, in the absence of any intervention by the local authorities.[13] In 1672 the elector had to rebuff a petition from the Estates that the Jews be expelled. The trading activities of the Jews were 'not harmful but beneficial', he maintained.[14] In 1673, barely two years after the resettlement, Christian merchants in the town of Brandenburg were already accusing the Jews of dealing in stolen property, evading tolls and 'exhausting the land and its people with constant deceit'.[15] The quasi-benevolence of the great elector and his sympathetic officials had to contend with widespread popular hostility.

Part of this hostility was undoubtedly expressed in the multitude and variety of taxes, tolls and levies imposed on the Jews, particularly in the latter part of the eighteenth century. The original edict of 1671 had been

[9] For the text of the edict, see Selma Stern, *Der Preussische Staat und die Juden*, 7 vols, Tübingen, 1962–75, I, pt. 2, no. 12. This work is referred to below as Stern, *Der Preussische Staat*, followed by volume, part and document (or page) number. The edict is analysed by S. Jersch-Wenzel in P. Freimark (ed.), *Juden in Preussen – Juden in Hamburg*, Hamburg, 1983, pp. 11ff. For the process of resettlement, see Moritz Stern, 'Die Niederlassung der Juden in Berlin im Jahre 1671', *ZGJD*, II (1930), no. 2, pp. 131–49.

[10] See S. Jersch-Wenzel, *Juden und 'Franzosen' in der Wirtschaft des Raumes Berlin/Brandenburg zur Zeit des Merkantilismus*, Berlin, 1978.

[11] Ibid., pp. 33ff., gives a detailed comparison of the respective legal status of Jews and Huguenots.

[12] Stern, *Der Preussische Staat*, I/2, p. 11, n. 2.

[13] Ibid., no. 121.

[14] Ibid., no. 24.

[15] Ibid., no. 28.

comparatively liberal in this respect. Subsequent imposts, both direct and indirect, regular and extraordinary, made good this 'deficiency'. Jewish merchants had to pay double the excise duties levied on their Christian competitors; the community had to supply the funds to raise and supply a foot regiment of 1,200 men; birth and divorce taxes were added to the original marriage tax; in 1713 they had to pay 1,500 thaler to buy permission not to be forced to wear red hats; there were taxes when Jewish elders were elected; and there were taxes to compensate for the Jews' exemption from military service.

These exactions obviously reflect the increase in the Jewish population, despite popular enmity and the fearsome tax burden. The increase applied both to Berlin in particular and to Brandenburg-Prussia in general. As distinct from other German states, the Jews here were primarily an urban and mercantile element. In 1705, in fact, they were forbidden to live in the countryside and to engage in agriculture. Later, Frederick the Great refused even to sanction the lease of a mill to a Jew. He argued that only on account of trade and industry were Jews tolerated in Prussia.[16] So the population growth is an urban phenomenon. The four or five families in Landsberg in 1671 rose to twenty-one in 1690 and to 417 persons by 1717.[17] At Halberstadt the Jewish population, at 639 individuals in 1699, had approximately doubled since 1670.[18] Between 1728 and 1749 the total of families paying protection tax increased from 1,191 to 2,093 (the latter not including East Friesland and Silesia).[19] In all, the number of Jews has been calculated at some 25,000 in 1700, and at 70,000 by mid-century, from a total of 12,500 families.[20]

Berlin itself was the main centre of Jewish settlement in 1671 – nine of the fifty original families settled there. (The other centre was Frankfurt on the Oder, to which Jewish settlers were attracted by the fair.) By 1688 the nine had grown to about forty and to 117 by 1700. The number continued to increase – though intermittently, owing to government policy; in 1737 some 500 Jews were expelled from the city. By 1750 Berlin Jewry totalled

[16] B. König, *Annalen der Juden in den preussischen Staaten (1790)*, 1912, p. 297, quoted H.M. Graupe, *Die Entstehung des modernen Judentums*, Hamburg, 1969, p. 119; see also Stern, *Der Preussische Staat*, I/2, no. 290.

[17] O. Lassally,'Zur Geschichte der Juden in Landsberg an der Warthe', *MGWJ*, 80 (1936), pp. 407, 410.

[18] Stern, *Der Preussische Staat*, I/1, p. 103.

[19] Shohet, *Im Hilufei Tekufot*, p. 16; see pp. 267–8, no. 4, for details of population changes in the individual Prussian territories.

[20] Ibid., pp. 18–19; J. Toury, 'Der Eintritt der Juden ins deutsche Bürgertum', in H. Liebeschütz and A. Paucker (eds), *Das Judentum in der deutschen Umwelt*, Tübingen, 1977, p. 139.

2,188 persons (1.93 per cent of the total population) and by 1770, 3,842 (2.88 per cent).[21]

This made Berlin one of the largest Jewish communities in all the German lands. It was also one of the wealthiest. The original settlers of 1671 were required to be 'people of substance',[22] and in 1674 after the settlement, twelve of them assured the great elector that this would remain so: they promised to take action against 'incapable persons' seeking to secure unlicensed residential status in Berlin.[23] The state's policy of favouring the wealthy and excluding the poor – in which the wealthy co-operated – and the extension to Jews of state-sponsored manufacturing opportunities, particularly in the nascent textile industries after 1730, created a stratum of oligarchs, often related by ties of blood and marriage. In 1705 the Berlin Jews already paid excise taxes (internal duties and tolls) of 117,437 thaler, whereas Christian traders in all paid a total of 43,865 thaler;[24] and this despite the limitation of Jews to markets, fairs and itinerant peddling. In 1737 only ten of the 120 individually licensed and tolerated Berlin Jews had assets of less than 1,000 (reichs-) thaler; all the others had assets of between 2,000 and 20,000 thaler.[25]

A census of the employed Jews in Berlin at mid-century shows that 43.5 per cent were engaged in the money trade, in merchandizing and as employees; 6.9 per cent as craftsmen, factory workers, hostel-keepers and innkeepers; 35 per cent as domestic servants and day labourers; and 9.5 per cent as synagogue officials, teachers and students of the Talmud.[26] At any one time, the Berlin *kehillah* also housed a varying number of the vagrant, transient and indigent – the so-called 'beggar-Jews'. This class existed on the margins of settled Jewish society. It was recruited from the families of those whose breadwinners failed to return from the Thirty Years War, from bankrupt merchants, from survivors of the Khmelnitzki massacres in the Ukraine (1648/9) who had fled to Germany, etc. Always living from hand to mouth, at times the beggar-Jews also became assimilated to the German underworld.[27]

---

[21] H. Seeliger, 'Origins and growth of the Berlin Jewish Community', *LBYB*, III (1958), pp. 159ff.; H. Silbergleit, *Die Bevölkerungs – und Berufsverhältnisse der Juden im deutschen Reich I*, Berlin, 1930, p. 2.

[22] Stern, *Der Preussische Staat*, I/2, no. 11.

[23] Ibid., no. 31.

[24] I. Elbogen-E. Sterling, *Die Geschichte der Juden in Deutschland*, Frankfurt on Main, 1966, p. 142; Jersch-Wenzel, *Juden und 'Franzosen'*, pp. 53–4. By this time the Jews had to pay twice the taxes of Christians (Stern, *Der Preussische Staat*, I/1, p. 41).

[25] L. Geiger, *Geschichte der Juden in Berlin*, 2 vols, Berlin, 1871, p. 43.

[26] Toury, 'Der Eintritt der Juden', table II, p. 145.

[27] See R. Glanz, *Geschichte des niederen jüdischen Volkes in Deutschland*, New York, 1968, passim; M. Shulvass, *From East to West*, Detroit, 1971, pp. 31ff.; M. Friedman,

'A scholar', declares the Talmud, 'should not live in a city where the following ten things are not to be found: a court of justice that imposes flagellation and decrees penalties; a charity fund collected by two and distributed by three; a synagogue; public baths; a public toilet; a circumciser; a surgeon; a notary; a slaughterer; and a schoolmaster.'[28] Berlin Jewry from its earliest beginnings set about the establishment of certain of these institutions. The foundation document of 1671 did indeed treat the Jews as a group but made no provision for their collective life. This life was their own creation. In 1672 the immigrants acquired a cemetery and in 1675 formed a society for the burial of the dead and for the care of the poor.[29] By the end of the century four separate congregations were worshipping in private houses, given the refusal of the 'Austrian' newcomers to submit to the authority of the electorate's state rabbi ('Landrabbiner') Salomon Kajjem Kaddish, from whose jurisdiction they were later exempted.[30] It seems that his jurisdiction extended from the religious into that of civil disputes amongst Jews to an extent that went beyond the bounds established by the government.[31] But it is also true that 'political' motives were at work, insofar as Kaddisch was associated with the great elector's court Jew, Israel Aaron, to whom the 'Austrians' were highly unwelcome as possible rivals in commerce.[32] In 1695 every head of household was permitted with his dependants to hold religious services in his residence.[33] Not until 1714 was a central synagogue erected in Berlin (on payment of 3,000 thaler for royal permission) and ceremonially inaugurated in the presence of the new king, Frederick William I, and his court. The occasion was also marked by a speech from Herschel Benjamin Frankel, an elder of the community, and by the betrothal of a daughter of the court embroiderer Aaron Isaak.[34] The establishment of the synagogue followed several years

---

Mikhtavei Hamlatza le-kabtzanim – '*ktavim*', *Michael II*, Tel Aviv, 1973, pp. 34–51; Priebatsch, Die Judenpolitik, p. 585; M. Köhler, *Juden in Halberstadt*, Berlin, 1927, pp. 79–81.

[28] TB San., 17b.

[29] Geiger, *Geschichte der Juden*, p. 6. The latter date is here given as 1676. But J. Meisl, in his *Pinkas kehillat Berlin*, Jerusalem, 1962, p.xiii, fn. 5, shows that the correct date must be 30 December 1675.

[30] M. Stern, 'Salomon Kajjem Kaddisch, der erste kurbrandenburgische Landrabbiner', *Jeschurun*, VI (1919), 373–87; Stern, *Der Preussische Staat*, I/2, nos 19, 20.

[31] Meisl, *Pinkas kehillat Berlin*, p. xiv.

[32] M. Stern, *Salomon Kajjem Kaddisch*, pp. 376ff.

[33] Geiger, *Geschichte der Juden*, I, p. 21.

[34] Ibid., p. 23.

of dispute amongst the elders of the community, which only a state commission of enquiry could resolve.[35] One consideration present to the commission was certainly the desire of the authorities to facilitate their supervision of the Jews, which the limitation to a single place of worship would make possible.[36] It is also clear that at least by the early 1690s – earlier, very probably – the nascent community had evolved facilities for the care and relief of the Jewish poor. From 1703 Berlin Jewry maintained just outside the city walls a *hekdesh* – a combined hospice-hospital-shelter – administered by the society for the visitation of the sick (Bikur Holim).[37] The community also created a society to attend to the ceremony of circumcision (1715) and to provide poor brides with a dowry (1721).[38]

The continuing expansion in the scope and variety of communal activities is apparent from a glance at the officially sanctioned establishment of communal servants in 1713 and again in 1750. The first provided for three synagogue cantors, eight unmarried schoolteachers, two slaughterers, two grave-diggers, one scribe, two *schulkloppers*, two male medical attendants and two nurses for the sick and women in childbirth. By 1750 an even wider range of communal employees were provided for: a rabbi; four assistant judges, a chief and assistant cantor, four *schulkloppers*, three butchers, three slaughterers, one secretary to the meat market, three bakers, one restaurant-keeper, one male and one female bath-attendant, two hospital attendants, one physician, two gate-keepers and one assistant, two Hebrew printers, six grave-diggers, one cemetery guard, one communal scribe, eight hospital attendants, two teachers for girls (both of whom had to be married) and two employees in the synagogue school.[39] A change from the one slaughterer and one teacher of the 1670s!

Brandenburg and the Jews

The great elector, however, still less his successors, had not invited Jews to the Prussian domains in order to establish an outpost of the Torah. 'Trade and traffic' was the Hohenzollern objective, extracting the maximum of revenue from the minimum number of Jews, a minimum consistent with

---

[35] Stern, *Der Preussische Staat*, I/2, no. 327.

[36] Ibid.; see also no. 216.

[37] J. R. Marcus, *Communal Sick-care in the German Ghetto*, Cincinnati, 1947, p. 280; Meisl, *Pinkas kehillat Berlin*, p.lvii.

[38] Geiger, *Geschichte der Juden*, p. 158.

[39] Stern, *Der Preussische Staat*, II/2, no. 4; J.R. Marcus, *The Jew in the Medieval World: A Source Book, 315–1791*, New York, 1965, p. 86. (*Schulkloppers* were responsible for summoning congregants to services, meetings, etc.)

accommodation to the hostility of entrenched Christian interest-groups such as guild members and merchants. This in itself required some degree of supervision over the Jews lest they engage in forbidden areas of the economy, evade taxes etc. To a large extent the Jews themselves were charged with the task of supervising each other and this required the state to intervene in the internal affairs of the Jewish community, to ensure that this served as a compliant instrument of its policies. This, in its turn, also required the state to involve itself in the jurisdiction of the Torah, as exercised by the rabbinical court. Finally, the element of sheer prejudice must be allowed for, amounting at times to antisemitism *avant la lettre*. Frederick the Great, to whom Jews were avaricious, superstitious and barbarous, shared to the full in the prejudices of his mentor, Voltaire.[40]

In actual fact, no lasting solution to the resultant friction between the jurisdiction of the state and that of the Jews was found. The edict of 1671 had assigned civil cases to the local burgomaster and criminal cases to the elector.[41] But this division soon showed itself altogether too imprecise to match a changing reality, if for no other reason than that there were contending forces both in the state and in the community. The confusion was such that in 1714 and again in 1730 Frederick William I abolished the judicial autonomy of the Jews – in 1730 as a means to his increasing centralization of state power. This also involved removing landowners' right of jurisdiction over their peasants, the abolition of the guild courts and restrictions on municipal self-government.[42] By the mid-eighteenth century this process of supervision and intervention had indeed succeeded in turning the Jewish community into a department of the Prussian state.

As early as 1681, the *Hausvogt* – police-chief – of Berlin was ordered to ensure that civil and criminal matters involving both Jews amongst themselves and Jews and Christians should be referred to the *Kammergericht* – court of appeal.[43] In 1684 this subordinate relationship went further when an electoral decree to Berlin Jewry, *inter alia*, ordered the court-factor, Jost Liebmann, and mint-master, Bendix Levi, 'to attend Jewish courts and all assemblies to observe their proceedings and punishments' and to inform the appropriate authorities, including the *Hausvogt*, 'of all happenings'. Their particular task was to divide the community into rich, middling and poor Jews for the purpose of collecting the protection money due to the

---

[40] For their respective attitudes, see *Judentum im Zeitalter der Aufklärung*, Wolfen-büttel, 1977, pp. 79ff., 113ff.

[41] See above, pp. 42–3.

[42] This is described in Shohet, *Im Ḥilufei Tekufot*, p. 86.

[43] Stern, *Der Preussische Staat*, I/2, no. 46.

state, to report thefts, to maintain a register of objects pawned and to prevent the open display of goods.[44]

At the end of the seventeenth and in the early years of the eighteenth century the state moved towards a closer and more systematic supervision of the community. This followed some years of dispute among the Jewish elders so that no, or only disputed, elections took place.[45] When the dissident Jews brought their grievance to the authorities, the latter took the opportunity to order new elections. These took place in September 1698 in the presence of R. Simon Berend (son of the factor, Jost Liebmann) and the *Hausvogt*. Four elders and three overseers of the poor were elected, who took office alongside the senior elder, Wolf Perlheffter, nominated by the elector.[46] But Perlheffter only obtained his position by promising to make an annual payment of 100 reichsthaler during his tenure of office.[47] In his report the *Hausvogt* noted that the elders and the rabbi requested the Elector to ensure that 'the elders should preside over the whole community as is customary in other places where Jews dwell'.[48] A number of decrees in 1700 did in fact further strengthen the authority of the elders *vis-à-vis* the community. The decrees empowered the elders to collect the annual protection money of 3,000 thaler for which all Jews were collectively liable; to apportion taxes amongst the licensed members of the three income groups; to check and be responsible, together with the *Hausvogt*, for the issue of letters of protection; to supervise outsiders and prevent the entry of unauthorized Jews; and to decide, together with the rabbi, minor disputes and civil cases.[49] The state undertook to protect the elders from unjustified complaints; and 'incitement' against them was to be punished.[50]

In 1708 the establishment of a Jews' Commission and in 1750 Frederick the Great's issue of a revised Jewish Regulation (Juden Reglement) further strengthened and centralized state authority *vis-à-vis* the *kehillah*.[51] The commission was required to ensure that the number of licensed Jewish families in Berlin would never exceed 100; that any foreign Jew admitted must possess a capital of 4,000–6,000 reichsthaler; that all disputes both amongst Jews and between Jews and Christians involving sums of 100 thaler

[44] Ibid., no. 51; cf. also no. 50.
[45] Ibid., I/2, nos. 233, 234.
[46] Ibid., I/2, nos 237, 241.
[47] Ibid., nos 236, 237.
[48] Ibid., no. 241.
[49] Ibid., no. 246.
[50] Ibid., no. 247.
[51] D. Cohen, 'Ha-Yehasim sheben irguneihem shel Yehudei ha-provinziyot ha-prussiyot', *Sixth World Congress of Jewish Studies*, Jerusalem, 1976, II, pp. 149–57 (Heb. Sec.).

or less be settled by the commission; and disputes involving larger sums be submitted to the *Kammergericht*.[52]

In the same way as the state intervened in the public and material affairs of the *kehillah*, so too did it impinge on the activities of the rabbi and his court. (This division is somewhat rough and ready but for the moment let it suffice – see below p. 53). The same general picture emerges, whereby the state moves more or less consistently towards a limitation of rabbinical power.

In 1672 R. Chaim (R. Solomon Kajjem Kaddisch), hitherto rabbi in the Neumark, was appointed rabbi in the whole of the electoral Mark of Brandenburg with powers to resolve 'all disputes arising out of Jewish ceremonies, rites and customs'; and he was authorized, if necessary, to call on the assistance of the local authorities to enforce his decisions. This followed a plea to the great elector by his court Jew, Israel Aaron.[53] The 'Austrians' in Berlin contested Kaddisch's appointment, arguing that they 'far surpassed him in knowledge', and within a few months they were released from his jurisdiction.[54] In 1687, R. Simon Berend succeeded Kaddisch, with similar powers. He had his seat at Frankfurt on the Oder 1687–92 and then moved to Berlin, visiting Frankfurt three times annually for the fair.[55] His authority came under attack from two directions: first, from the Jews themselves who on occasion preferred to take their disputes to the Christian courts;[56] and also from the state, which overturned one of Berend's decisions. The case concerned Lewin Wolf, an alleged gambler who, together with his wife, was expelled from the community on grounds of having made his sister-in-law pregnant. Her marriage then ended in divorce. Wolf was not considered competent to give evidence before the rabbinical court. He complained that he had been unfairly treated and made the victim of communal hostility. Wolf took his plea to the *Landvogt* – provincial governor – who secured his readmission to the community.[57] From 1705 on, no member could be subjected to expulsion until and unless the case had been referred to the appropriate department of state and the latter had obtained royal assent to the punishment.[58] As early as 1696, the

---

[52] Stern, *Der Preussische Staat*, no. 293.

[53] 'Cain' or 'Kain', as given in certain documents, is an error (See E. Landshut, *Toldot Anshei Ha-Shem u-f'eulatam be-adat Berlin*, Berlin, 1884, p. 1; M. Stern, 'Salomon Kajjem Kaddisch'; Stern, *Der Preussische Staat*, I/2, no. 19.

[54] Stern, *Der Preussische Staat*, I/2, p. 26, fn. 1; see also above p. 46.

[55] Landshut, *Toldot Anshei Shem*, p. 4; Stern, *Der Preussische Staat*, I/2, no. 56.

[56] Stern, *Der Preussische Staat*, I/2, no. 224.

[57] Ibid., nos. 232, 235. (Dice-players, moneylenders etc. are not considered reliable witnesses in court under rabbinical law – see M. San. 3:3.)

[58] Ibid., no. 276; cf. also no. 325.

state also prohibited marriages where the parties fell within the permitted degrees of relationship according to Jewish law, but fell without those of the civil law.[59]

Clearly, there was, as Selma Stern writes, 'unclarity and confusion' in the legal position of the Jews, whether considered from the Jewish or the state's standpoint.[60] Partly in order to remedy this situation, Frederick the Great introduced in 1750 a Revised Jewish Regulation. This represented a major definition of governmental policy, which remained substantially in force until 1812. It was in the making from the late 1740s and this interval gave interested parties the opportunity to seek to influence the government. The Christian leather dealers in Berlin complained that their Jewish rivals had supplied badly cured leather to the cavalry for bridles and saddlery, which would 'not last in the field and withstand hard wear'.[61] The Berlin merchants' guild complained that Jewish traders were selling forbidden goods and engaging in smuggling etc.[62]

Submissions from Prussian Jewry centred on two aspects: the need for relief from the economic constraints under which they suffered and the value they attached to legal autonomy. To be more specific, the Jews' submissions concentrated on hindrances to their trading rights, the request for a joint consultative commission, permission for a second child to enjoy the same advantageous legal position as the first, the rejection of collective liability for trafficking in stolen goods and for fraudulent bankruptcies, and freedom from the body tax throughout all the Prussian territories.[63] From the viewpoint of the Jewish elders the most objectionable provision of the proposed regulation arose from a paragraph which imposed collective liability on all the members of a Jewish family should any one of its members (for example, a pawnbroker or moneylender on pledges) be found in possession of goods that were stolen or illegally acquired, and be unable to compensate the true owner to the full extent of the loss; and furthermore, if the family could not make this compensation, 'then the entire Jewry of the town is officially to be held liable for cash payment in compensation'.[64] A memorandum in December, 1748 in the name of all the Jews in Berlin and the Prussian provinces, argued that such a provision would not only make the innocent suffer with the guilty but also damage their credit standing – and thus, although this was not explicitly stated, also the interest

[59] Ibid., no. 221.
[60] Ibid., III/1, p. 114.
[61] Ibid., III/2–1, no. 63.
[62] Ibid., no. 68.
[63] Ibid., nos 65, 75, 78, 91.
[64] Marcus, *The Jew in the Medieval World*, pp. 92–3.

of the Prussian economy.[65] Collective liability also continued to apply to the payment of taxes.

As for legal autonomy, communities throughout Prussia sought to sway the king in its favour. In Cleves and Halberstadt they urged the government to preserve their religion and its associated laws, 'on which their whole weal and woe depended'.[66] The elders of the Berlin community and of all provincial communities submitted a similar plea to Cocceji, Frederick's chancellor: disputes between Jews should be decided in accordance with 'the Mosaic laws', on the grounds that Jewish litigants were by-passing the Jewish court and turning at once to the civil courts.[67] The memorandum denounced 'certain ruthless and obdurate persons amongst us who merely in order to avoid a judgement according to the Mosaic laws and to withdraw themselves from a decision of the rabbi and his assessors immediately bring their claims of Jew against Jew to a civil or secular forum'. These were 'untimely leaps into a secular jurisdiction'.[68]

Frederick remained inflexible on all counts. The great bulk of the regulation defined six categories of Jews in terms of their utility to the state, and the conditions and terms of the economic activities in which each group

---

[65] Stern, *Der Preussische Staat*, III/2–1, no. 78. The topic of collective liability for theft, vexatious and fraudulent bankruptcy etc. remained an incessant source of friction between the *kehillah* and the state. A noteworthy example came in 1769 when three Jews – Aaron Moses, Liebmann Solomon and Behrend Perlhoffter – were found guilty of participation in a large-scale robbery. Despite the most vigorous protests of the Berlin elders, in which they enjoyed the support of the Directory General but were opposed by the Justice Department, Frederick refused to countenance any change in the principle of collective liability (ibid., nos 386, 387, 390, 393, 394, 426, 427). The arguments put by the elders to the king skilfully blended economic *raison d'état* with a reminder of Berlin Jewry's position in the state: 'What foreigner would make a contract with us, entrust goods to us, give money, pass on commissions, or make credit available? At the time of the publication of the General Privilege (1750), our credit was by far not so strong as today [1769] and we lacked the means for great trading connections, for our community was weak and its trade confined. But since then very many of our members received privileges for considerable sums. The community has greatly increased and its activity, previously consisting of petty trade, has broadened out into factories, manufactures, money-changing operations and extensive foreign trade. Credit has greatly increased in proportion to trade and now we have connections in all parts of the world' (ibid., III/1, p. 181; see also III/2–1, nos 558, 561, 563, 565, 567, 568).

[66] Ibid., III/1, p. 120.

[67] Ibid., III/2–1, no.97.

[68] This memorandum is referred to in ibid., III/2–1, no. 97, and quoted in part by S. Rawidowicz in his introduction to *Moses Mendelssohn: Gesammelte Schriften*, Berlin, 1930, ii, pp. cxxxiv–cxxxv.

might legally engage.[69] It also codified the duties of the elders who now, from the middle of the eighteenth century, had to maintain a register of all Jews in Berlin, supervise and regulate the activities of visiting and transient Jews, keep lists of births, circumcisions, marriages and deaths, control the legal economic activities of the community's members, apprehend their illegal activities, record the sale and purchase of property, organize and supervise elections to the numerous communal bodies and – perhaps most burdensome of all – draw up tax lists and assess, apportion and collect the taxes and multifarious payments due both to the state and to communal bodies.[70] All that the Jews could secure was to delay the promulgation of the regulation for six years.[71] This was an indirect acknowledgement of its possible implications for their creditworthiness.

The regulation also made no concession to the plea for legal autonomy – may in fact have reduced the already exiguous authority of the rabbi to no more than the power of arbitration. The regulation (by paragraph xxxi) empowered the rabbinical court to resolve only those conflicts arising out of 'Jewish ceremonies and religious customs'. It was not empowered to excommunicate offenders or impose a fine of more than five reichsthaler without the foreknowledge of the magistrate. The rabbi and elders had no 'real jurisdiction' in civil cases: these were to be referred to the competent civil authorities. The regulation did permit the rabbi and his learned assessors to take 'some sort of judicial cognisance' in matters between Jew and Jew such as marriage contracts, wills, inheritances, inventories and appointment of guardians, 'which must be settled by them solely in accord with the Mosaic laws' – but this was only by way of arbitration.[72] This did not satisfy Cocceji, Frederick's chancellor and proponent of legal uniformity. He used an argument earlier presented by Spinoza in his *Theological-Political Treatise* (chapter XIX) and later echoed by Mendelssohn. Not only, said Cocceji, had the 'Republic of the Jews' and consequently its civil law ceased to exist more than 1,600 years earlier; also, Mosaic law made no reference to such matters of contemporary dispute as inventories, guardianships or inheritances.[73] Frederick comforted Cocceji: 'no one will be harmed by it [paragraph xxxi] for it is really only arbitration against which anyone can

[69] For text, see I. Freund, *Die Emanzipation der Juden in Berlin*, 2 vols, Berlin, 1912, II, no. 4; there is a fairly free English translation in Marcus, *The Jew in the Medieval World*, pp. 86ff.

[70] Meisl, *Pinkas kehillat Berlin*, pp. 36, 59.

[71] Stern, *Der Preussische Staat*, III/2–1, no. 113.

[72] Freund, *Die Emanzipation*, no. 31, p. 53.

[73] Stern, *Der Preussische Staat*, III/2–1, no. 106; for a brief sketch of the political views of Spinoza and Mendelssohn, see pp. 70ff. In 1750 Cocceji attended a session of the rabbinical court in Cleves and found it exceeding its powers (ibid., no. 98).

lodge an appeal with the judicial authorities.'[74]

The debate over rabbinical power at the fair at Frankfurt on the Oder in 1775–6 shows the continuing concern with which the state regarded any exercise of rabbinical jurisdiction. The Jewish merchants from Poland, who took a prominent part in Poland's foreign trade, requested the services of the Berlin chief rabbi, Hirsch Levin, to judge their disputes, aided by the Frankfurt rabbi and Polish rabbis as assessors. The Berlin chief rabbi refused. The matter did not end there, for the Prussian Directory General welcomed the merchants' request, arguing, pragmatically, that 'the flourishing of the Frankfurt fair depends largely on the Polish Jews'. But the Prussian Fiscal-General opposed the request, as did the Kammergericht and the Frankfurt magistracy: 'to exempt [some part of the merchant body], whatever confession they belong to, from the ordinary jurisdiction of the state and to grant them a legal adjudication independent of the highest authority in the state, is so peculiar an idea, precisely contradicting all maxims of state administration, that in our opinion it could only have been invented by Jewish heads.'[75] In the end the proposal came to nothing – the state rejected 'such a fateful innovation'.[76]

The Jews and Brandenburg

The limits imposed on rabbinical jurisdiction, the subordination of the election of elders and rabbinical appointments to governmental approval and the manifold interventions of the state in Jewish affairs have led one historian to argue that 'the autonomy of the communities was reduced in the main to the function of tax collectors.'[77] But to define autonomy in terms of tax-collecting, when the collectors had virtually no control over the amount to be collected and could only determine the precise contribution of

[74] Ibid., no. 107.

[75] The various interchanges are summarized in Stern, *Der Preussische Staat*, III/1, pp. 121–2; cf. also, III/2–1, no. 454 and particularly no. 466. (Hirsch Levin is also sometimes referred to as Hirschel Loebl and Hirsch Lewin. For the sake of simplicity I have ignored all variations and used the first appellation. In London, where Levin earlier officiated as chief rabbi of the Great Synagogue [see below p. 121], he was known normally as Hart Lyon. Again I have ignored all variation and in the London context used this English version of the name.)

[76] Geiger, *Geschichte der Juden*, II, 125. Landshut, however, the historian of the Berlin rabbinate, declares that it remained customary for a rabbi from Berlin to visit the fair to attend to the religious needs of the Jewish merchants until the death of Levin in 1800 (*Toldot Anshei Shem*, p. 4).

[77] S. Jersch-Wenzel, 'The Jews as a "classic" minority in eighteenth and nineteenth century Prussia', *LBYB*, XXVII (1982), p. 41.

each taxpayer, is itself a curious concept. The judgement as a whole illustrates the perils of assessment without access to the sources.

If, however, those sources that relate to the working of the Jewish community of Berlin are taken account of, then the question becomes a different one: the undeniable absence of autonomy in a number of important respects is seen as so many concessions that governance by and through the Torah must perforce make to the gentile state in the circumstances of the dispersion.

Two conflicting systems of law and government confront each other and at their interface a *modus vivendi* is worked out. On the Jewish side this is determined by the maxim 'the law of the land is the law', which, however, also sets limits to the concessions that can in fact be made to 'the law of the land', in accordance with circumstances.[78] The consequent flexibility of these 'limits' – for circumstances are always changing – is illustrated by an extreme example: could a gentile ruler appoint a rabbinical judge? R. Moses Isserles (Poland, sixteenth century) would accept such an appointment provided the rabbi in question were qualified and acceptable to the community; R. Moses Schreiber (Ḥatam Sofer, Moravia, nineteenth century) would, in certain circumstances, dispense with the second of these conditions.[79] In fact, on one celebrated occasion, in 1729, the Berlin community rejected a rabbi appointed by King Frederick I.[80]

The concept that 'the law of the land is the law' dates back at least to third-century Babylon, so that by the seventeenth and eighteenth centuries an enormous body of case law and doctrine had accumulated, elucidating the relations of Jew and gentile. It was this constantly evolving branch of jurisprudence that denoted the parameters of communal Jewish activity in Berlin, encouraged the establishment of certain institutions, left others perforce in abeyance and preserved a nucleus of self-rule that far exceeded the role of tax-collection on behalf of the Prussian state, important though this was. Berlin Jewry was not simply an object of Prussian policy but also a subject of Jewish history that found it possible to structure an existence, shaped by the state, but also able to withstand the state and transmit a set of institutions to later generations. By the same token, Berlin Jewry was itself the heir to earlier medieval communities in the German lands that had asserted a degree of autonomy in conditions far more adverse than those of the seventeenth and eighteenth centuries. Accommodation to the state must always be sought, but the Torah and its exponents proved sufficiently flexible and strong to survive and even flourish.

[78] See S. Shilo, *Dina d'Malkhuta Dina*, Jerusalem, 1974; and the review by Z.W. Falk in *Dinei Yisrael VI*, Tel Aviv, 1975, pp. 317–20.

[79] See the references cited in Shilo *Dina d'Malkhuta Dina*, pp. 430ff.

[80] See below, p. 61.

As elsewhere, in the past and present, power was exercised by those who bore the 'crown of the kingdom' and 'the crown of the Torah'. So far as the former is concerned this meant oligarchy. This was not of course exclusive to Berlin, but was reproduced throughout virtually all the German states, and beyond.[81] In Berlin a system of indirect elections to the governing board of the *kehillah* gave an enhanced weighting to the wealthy as compared with those Jews of middling means and the poor. This does not at all mean that the election results were always accepted without demur. There were intra-*kehillah* feuds and factions at the end of the seventeenth century and again in 1750, 1759 and 1762.[82] The struggle for power inside the *kehillah* mirrored to some extent rivalry amongst different financial groups, each seeking lucrative leases to operate and supply the royal mints. Herz Moses Gompertz, Daniel Itzig and Moses Isaac were pitted against Ephraim and sons, in a contest that sometimes cut across family ties through marriage.[83] However, the electoral system was able to accommodate these frictions and did not change substantially over the century. Normally, the governing body of the *kehillah* consisted of thirty men – nine elders and twenty-one officials responsible for the separate branches of the *kehillah's* activities. They were elected by seven electors – four from the wealthy, two from those of middling means and one from the poor.[84] Included amongst the elders elected in this way was one (sometimes two) 'senior elder' appointed by the state, who was not required to be one of the elected elders and had no primacy as against any of his colleagues. In Frederick the Great's time such senior elders were Nathan Veitel Heine Ephraim (1750–75), Jacob Moses (1775–92) and Daniel Itzig (1775–99).[85] Jacob Moses was also a banker and had earlier served the community as overseer of the society for providing poor brides with a dowry (1757), overseer of the poor (1759) and elected elder (1768).[86] In accordance with the centralizing policy of Prussia, Frederick's appointment of Itzig and Moses in 1775 gave them jurisdiction not only over Berlin Jewry but also over all other Jewish communities in Prussia.[87] This political authority was complemented by family alliances

[81] Shohet, *Im Ḥilufei Tekufot*, pp. 115ff.; for London, cf. ch. 3.

[82] See above, p. 46, and the summary in Stern, *Der Preussische Staat*, III/1, pp. 268ff.

[83] Jersch-Wenzel, *Juden und 'Franzosen'*, p. 185; see also D. Michaelis, 'The Ephraim family', *LBYB*, XXI (1976), pp. 201–28.

[84] For details, see Meisl, *Pinkas kehillat Berlin*, ch. 2, iii; and Geiger, *Geschichte der Juden*, p. 159.

[85] Meisl, *Pinkas kehillat Berlin*, no. 289.

[86] M. Stern, 'Der Oberlandesälteste Jacob Moses', *Mitteilungen des Gesamtarchivs der deutschen Juden*, vi (1926), pp. 14–40.

[87] See the discussion of this point in D. Cohen, 'Ha-Yeḥasim sheben irguneihem', p. 157.

outside Prussia. There was in the making a German-Jewish counterpart to the Anglo-Jewish 'Cousinhood' – a 'Vetterschaft', shall I say. Thus, Daniel Itzig and his wife Miriam had sixteen children. Of the five daughters two married the banking partners in Vienna – Baron Nathan von Arnstein and Baron Eskeles; another married the Königsberg banker David Friedländer; and a fourth the court jeweller Levi Salomon.[88]

The board of the Berlin *kehillah* directly, or indirectly through subordinated or associated bodies, bore responsibility for the conduct of all communal officials and the institutions where they functioned – synagogue, school, cemetery, slaughterhouse, *hekdesh* (a combined hospice-hospital-shelter), house of study. By way of these institutions the Torah, as mediated by the elders and their fellow members, sought to impress itself on a circumscribed reality. A mere dip into the *Pinkas* (record book) of the community is instructive. The elders organized elections, both to their own ranks and to subordinate bodies; they fixed the wages of community employees and servants (such as the rabbi, beadle, scribe and gatekeeper); in the interests of social control they prohibited private gatherings or worship, and the making of gifts to the authorities without the permission of the *kehillah*; social discipline required at times the imposition of limits on entertaining and sumptuary legislation; responsibility for meat supply was contracted out, and this required negotiations with the lessee and the supervision of the slaughterers – important matters not only because of the religious issues involved, but also because the tax on meat formed an important part of the community's income; special meal was distributed for the Passover festival; the monopoly for the production of sugar for the festival was made over to the Society for the Succouring of the Poor (*Hafsakat Evyonim*); special tax regulations were introduced in the case of widows, orphans and the unmarried. Other fiscal matters included the levying of a special tax on the occasion of the Russian occupation of Berlin in 1760, raising loans from the Berlin nobility to cover the Jews' share of occupation costs, and the release of 'Moses Dessau' (Moses Mendelssohn) from all taxes; the elders of the community agreed to make two annual payments, through an emissary, to the poor of the 'Holy City of Hebron'; the community took shares in the East India and Levant Company and a bolting cloth factory; they also arranged payment so that merchants from Berlin attending the twice-yearly fairs at Frankfurt on the Oder would enjoy the facilities of the local synagogue; and they approved a contract between two doctors, Markus Hertz and Benjamin Bloch, to care for the poor.[89]

---

[88] E. Werner, 'New light on the family of Felix Mendelssohn', *HUCA*, XXVI (1955), p. 545.

[89] For all the above, see Meisl, *Pinkas kehillat Berlin*, nos 1, 36; 9, 75; 10; 96; 64, 233; 15, 21, 34; 4; 240; 126; 201, 209; 44; 237; 249; 289.

In September 1743, the community undertook a new initiative when it authorized two elders, Bendit Katz and Löb Halberstadt, to collect funds for a house of study – Bet Ha-Midrash. Hitherto, there had been no fixed place for study and it had been conducted by rabbis in private residences, in return for board and lodging. Already in the 1720s R. Mordecai Tokeles had sought to remedy this by seeking funds from private subscribers to build a permanent centre.[90] Some twenty years later this effort moved towards fruition when, in October 1743, the elders elected Dayan Jeremiah from Halberstadt as third teacher at the projected institution, alongside Rabbis Naftali Herz Wolf and Joel Sachs, with a salary of 150 reichsthaler, to be paid quarterly. In January 1744 the community diverted to the Bet Ha-Midrash a legacy of 800 reichsthaler originally bequeathed by Elchanan Sofer for the purposes of Talmudic study. Hitherto the interest arising from the investment of this sum (12 reichsthaler per quarter) pending the establishment of a Bet Ha-Midrash in Berlin had been made available to support scholars in Posen or Lissa. Construction of the three-storey building was begun in 1744 and completed in the following January.[91] The second scholarly institution was a *Lehranstalt*, conducted on the lines of a *yeshivah*, supported by the income derived from a trust fund established by Veitel Heine Ephraim in 1774.[92] It was here that the noted scholar, Israel Samoscz from Galicia, earned his living as a teacher.[93]

The arrangements for the poor had a character of their own. How did the community meet Isaiah's demand (1:16–17): 'Seek judgement, relieve the oppressed, judge the orphan, plead for the widow'? Here, although the state took cognisance of *all* Jewish activities, both inside and outside the *kehillah*, the position of the poor involved the interests of the state more immediately through its impact on the wellbeing of the rich geese that laid the golden eggs. It was this sort of consideration that led Frederick the Great in 1772 to expel all Jews with assets worth less than 1,000 thaler from the newly annexed Netze district of Poland. Jacob Moses, an elder of the Berlin *kehillah*, was able to mitigate this action to some extent.[94] In general the *kehillah* co-operated with the state in excluding vagabonds and beggars. But it was also committed by the Torah and by self-interest to providing them with a modicum of care. It could not wash its hands of them entirely – all the less so as impressionistic and anecdotal evidence

[90] Landshut, *Toldot Anshei Shem*, p. 22.

[91] Meisl, *Pinkas kehillat Berlin*, nos 39, 40, 115–19; M. Stern, 'Das Vereinsbuch des Berliner Beth Hamidrasch, 1743–1783', *JJLG*, xxii (1931–2), pp. 404ff.

[92] Michaelis, 'The Ephraim family', p. 215; for other bequests to scholarly and charitable foundations, see Meisl, *Pinkas kehillat Berlin*, p. lviii.

[93] A. Altmann, *Moses Mendelssohn*, London, 1973, pp. 21–2.

[94] M. Stern, 'Der Oberlandesälteste Jacob Moses', p. 28.

suggests that the number of beggar-Jews began to increase from the end of the seventeenth century, and a class of hereditary beggars emerged.[95] They were shunted with their families from town to town, their life was 'a veritable Dance of Death', one student writes.[96] Assimilation into the underworld of German society was one consequence. Spiegelberg, one of Schiller's 'Räuber', was a Jew.

To meet this situation Berlin Jewry maintained from 1703 a *hekdesh* administered by the Society for the Care of the Sick (Bikur Holim).[97] It lay outside the city walls and, about 1750, according to its statutes, provided for regular visits by a member of the society, and offered a bed, clean linen, medical care, food and prescriptions. This institution served both the indigent and those who could pay for treatment. Women lying-in received one reichsthaler per week for food; later in the century a pedlar's wife had to pay for her own food. The society supported the mother for four weeks and on her departure provided her with linen and travel money. In the case of a male child the society arranged the circumcision ceremony and celebration.[98] In 1753 the *kehillah* made a loan to the Bikur Holim society of 3,000 reichsthaler for the construction of a new *hekdesh*.[99]

Was the reception in fact in accordance with the statutes of the society? When Solomon Maimon, the prodigy from Lithuania and later a foremost exponent of the new philosophy of Kant, arrived at the Rosenthal gate he was in a destitute state. But here, he thought,

> I would put an end to my misery ... because, as all are aware, no beggar-Jew is allowed in this town of royal residence, the Jewish community has had a house built by the Rosenthal Gate where the poor are taken in, questioned by the Jewish elders about their purpose in Berlin and then, when this is ascertained, either, if they are sick or seeking position, taken into the city or sent on further. So I too was taken to this house which was filled partly with the sick and partly with a miserable rabble.... Finally towards evening the Jewish elders came. Each of the people present was called forward and questioned about his purpose. My turn came and I said quite candidly that I wanted to stay in Berlin to study medicine there. The elders turned down my request without further ado, gave me a pittance and went off ... I was particularly grieved by the conduct of the overseer of

[95] Glanz, *Geschichte des niederen jüdischen Volkes*, pp. 133ff.

[96] Marcus, *Communal Sick-care*, p. 177.

[97] Marcus, *Communal Sick-care*, p. 280; Meisl, *Pinkas kehillat Berlin*, introduction, p. lvii.

[98] The above is based on Marcus, *Communal Sick-care*, p. 185ff.

[99] Meisl, *Pinkas kehillat Berlin*, no. 169.

the poorhouse who at the command of his superiors insisted on my speedy departure and did not rest until he saw me outside the gate.[100]

The statutes of the society, moreover, required the overseers of the poor to ensure that they removed 'the sick as soon as they can without danger or when it is seen that there is no cure for his affliction'.[101]

Maimon's next visit to Berlin was by post-chaise and he had no difficulty in entering the city. But until a distinguished Jewish family, impressed by his intellect, secured Maimon's residential rights, the Jewish police had all but hounded him out of Berlin.[102] The prohibition on settlement – *herem ha-yishuv* – retained its medieval validity.[103] This was no exceptional case. 'The rich oppress the poor', one Jewish vagrant told a missionary. 'Even if a Jew has a hundred thousand gulden, he sees off the poor man with no more than a pfennig ... The rich Jews prefer to go round in magnificent clothes rather than give the poor a pittance.'[104]

The Rabbi and his Court

'The crown of the Torah', as borne by the rabbi in the modern community of Berlin, was also a legacy of the medieval past: that is to say, he was engaged by the *parnassim* and played no part in the external life of the community. Later, the trend changed significantly: in the 1780s R. Ezekiel Landau of Prague, in defence of Jewish marriage law, confronted the Habsburg emperor, Joseph II; R. David Sinzheim of Strasbourg confronted Napoleon in somewhat similar circumstances, 1806–7; and in England, in the second half of the nineteenth century, chief rabbi Nathan Marcus Adler was unquestionably influential in helping to shape political intervention by the Board of Deputies of British Jews.[105] But this was not the case in Brandenburg-Prussia and elsewhere in Germany.

There was also a general tendency towards the family integration of lay

---

[100] S. Maimon, *Geschichte des eigenen Lebens*, Schocken edn, Berlin, 1935, pp. 127–9.

[101] Meisl, *Pinkas kehillat Berlin*, no. 10, para. 4.

[102] S. Maimon, *Geschichte*, pp. 141–2.

[103] See also Shohet, *Im Ḥilufei Tekufot*, p. 120.

[104] Quoted ibid., p. 272, fn. 64.

[105] See below pp. 105ff. It is also relevant to note that in the 1840s German rabbis were in the forefront of the campaign to avert the exclusion of Jews from compulsory military service, as proposed by Frederick William IV (R. Liberles, 'Was there a Jewish movement for emancipation in Germany?', *LBYB*, XXXI (1986), pp. 38ff).

leaders and rabbis, and even nepotism.[106] In Brandenburg and Berlin from the late seventeenth and well into the eighteenth century, court Jews installed their relations as rabbis. R. Benjamin Wolff Liebmann, brother of the court Jew Jost Liebmann and based at Landsberg on the Warthe, held office as rabbi of Electoral and Mark Brandenburg.[107] In 1709, Liebmann's son-in-law, R. Arend Benjamin Wolff, was appointed by Frederick as rabbi of certain specified areas in Mark Brandenburg and Further Pomerania.[108] In 1743 R. David Hirschel Fränkel, the learned mentor of Moses Mendelssohn and brother-in-law of Veitel Heine Ephraim, was appointed second rabbi in Berlin, and later chief rabbi. Ephraim had to pay to the community 150 reichsthaler a year during Fränkel's period in office.[109] This mode of appointment was not necessarily unfortunate: R. Fränkel had earlier studied with R. Michael Ḥassid in Berlin and enjoyed the highest repute as scholar and person.[110] It was not his fault that he was also related to one of the wealthiest Jews in Frederick the Great's entourage. But such a *modus operandi* was already irreconcilable with the independence required of a rabbi exercising even that limited measure of judicial authority permitted to him in Frederician Prussia.

It may not be altogether perverse to suggest that, had the rabbinate been in the royal gift, it might have enjoyed a greater degree of independence. But this was never the case, of course. On the contrary, this was one area where the elders brooked no interference. Was this because of their concern for religious autonomy? Or because of concern that the rabbi be subordinate to *them* ? The latter seems more likely. In any case, in 1729 when King Frederick I on his own initiative appointed R. Moses Aaron from Leipnik (Bohemia) to office in Berlin – the appointment was officially recorded in the communal annals[111] – there was a most violent reaction. Selma Stern talks of 'passive resistance . . . disputes . . . open disobedience, exchange of blows in the synagogue and in the streets'.[112] The royal appointee lasted

---

[106] See the remarks on this point in D. Cohen, 'Die Entwicklung der Landesrabbinate in den deutschen Territorien bis zur Emanzipation', in A. Haverkamp (ed.), *Zur Geschichte der Juden in Deutschland des späten Mittelalters und der frühen Neuzeit*, Stuttgart, 1981, p. 241; Shohet, *Im Ḥilufei Tekufot*, pp. 93ff.

[107] Stern, *Der Preussische Staat*, I/2, no. 45.

[108] Ibid., no. 300 (wrongly numbered 'no. 310').

[109] See Stern, *Der Preussische Staat*, III/1–2, nos 27, 129; Schnee, *Die Hoffinanz*, I, p. 156; Meisl, *Pinkas kehillat Berlin*, nos 111, 112, 130.

[110] Landshut, *Toldot Anshei Shem*, pp. 35ff.; see also M. Freudenthal's sketch of Fränkel's career in M. Brann and F. Rosenthal (eds) *Gedenkbuch David Kaufmann*, Breslau, 1900, pp. 569–98.

[111] Meisl, *Pinkas kehillat Berlin*, no. 46.

[112] Stern, *The Court Jew*, p. 195.

less than a year and was forced to move to Frankfurt on the Oder.[113] The elders were eventually allowed to appoint their own candidate, R. Esaias Hirsch from Poland, though only on payment of 1500 thaler.

When the Berlin elders did exercise their power to make appointments to rabbinical office, they normally submitted a name to the king, together with a letter of recommendation in general terms outlining the candidate's qualifications for office, his record and his acceptability.[114] The rabbi's contract specified a short-term appointment (though this was normally renewed) and a lowly salary. R. Mordechai Toklas (1725) had a three-year contract and an annual salary of 150 reichsthaler.[115] R. Jacob Joshua Falk of Cracow (1731) had a four-year contract and a basic salary of four reichsthaler per week. He was, however, also provided with a residence. Falk's principal functions were to teach, and to judge all disputes in civil law arising inside the *kehillah*.[116] In 1734 he was forced to leave Berlin for Metz, after having run foul of Veitel Ephraim in a dispute between Ephraim and one of his competitors, according to a reminiscence recorded by Landshut.[117] These men were distinguished for their Talmudic scholarship and erudition. Their predecessor in 1714–28, R. Michael Ḥassid (brother-in-law of R. Arndt Benjamin Wolff), was renowned for his mystical writings, though he was for a time a secret Sabbatean.[118] It is likely that in all these instances, there was additional ad hoc remuneration by way of judgement fees, payment for officiating at weddings and divorces, and gifts from community members celebrating some special occasion.[119]

The rabbi had duties to both the state and the *kehillah*. He counter-signed, with the elders, the monthly return to the government detailing any

---

[113] The documents in Stern, *Der Preussische Staat*, II/2, nos. 217–27, give a vivid picture of the dispute from every point of view; cf. also Shohet, *Im Ḥilufei Tekufot*, p. 296, no. 77.

[114] See, e.g., the submission on behalf of R. Hirsch Levin in 1773. Frederick the Great gave his approval in about ten days (Stern, *Der Preussische Staat*, III/2–1, no. 425).

[115] Meisl, *Pinkas kehillat Berlin*, no. 31. This salary, and that of Falk was roughly equivalent to that received by a young jurist or least well-paid teacher in a Prussian Latin school (see W.H. Bruford, *Germany in the Eighteenth Century*, pb. edn, Cambridge, 1965, p. 332).

[116] The contract is reprinted in Landshut, *Toldot Anshei Shem*, pp. 27–8.

[117] Ibid., pp. 29–30, 35, fn. 5; M. Horovitz, *Frankfurter Rabbiner* Jerusalem, 1969, p. 127.

[118] Landshut, *Toldot Anshei Shem*, pp. 11ff.; see also M. Freudenthal, 'R. Michel Chasid und die Sabbatianer', *MGWJ*, 76, NS 40 (1932), pp. 370–85.

[119] See the analysis of standard rabbinic contracts of the eighteenth century by J. Katz, 'L'toldot ha'rabbanut be-motzei y'mei ha'beynayim', in A.-Z. Melamed (ed.), *Sefer Zikaron l'Binyamin de Vries*, Jerusalem, 1969, pp. 281–94, esp. p. 284.

changes in the personal status of the Jews and also the statement of the individual Jews' assets as required by the regulation of 1750.[120] Inside the community the rabbi took no part in any of the frequent dealings with the government. This the elders and the *parnassim* reserved to themselves. On the other hand he participated in the discussions on the allocation of seats in the synagogue, organization of religious festivities, exclusion of a member from certain positions of honour, taxation of widows and the unmarried, measures against counterfeiting and against libel or slander (*Pasquille*) and electoral regulations; the rabbinical court decided in its own right the raising of the tax on kosher meat and the scale of betrothal and burial fees for the childless and unmarried. Two instances are recorded in the *Pinkas* where the court intervened in financial matters: in the first, in 1742, Rabbi Toklas and his assessor, R. Naftali Herz Wolf, determined the taxes to be paid by the heirs to the estate of Zalman Baruk; in the second, in 1748, R. David Fränkel, sitting with Wolf and Joel Sachs, determined the mode of repayment of a loan of 300 reichsthaler made by the *kehillah* to a deceased member, Meir Rintal, and now due for repayment from his estate.[121]

The rabbi's principal functions were bounded by the court and the house of study. The court normally sat on the afternoons of Monday to Thursday and reached its decisions by a majority vote of the presiding rabbi and his assessors. The presence of the chief rabbi might be limited to one sitting a week, his position on the bench being taken at other times by the second rabbi. Of course, both the jurisdiction and the penalties that might be imposed were severely circumscribed by paragraph xxxi of the Reglement of 1750: to repeat, the court could not impose a fine of more than the modest sum of five thaler or decree expulsion without the assent of the Prussian authorities; and only matters relating to marriage contracts and their validity in bankruptcy, the appointment of guardians, inventories and disputes amongst legatees could be adjudicated. And all this was only in the nature of arbitration.[122]

The last chief rabbi in Berlin was Hirsch Levin. He came to Berlin in 1772 by way of London, Halberstadt and Mannheim.[123] In Berlin his duties were to study and teach the Torah and to administer the Torah in religious matters and civil disputes. His salary was fifty thaler a month, which was, however, supplemented by contributions from other congregations and by judgement fees etc.[124] Levin was wont to say that in London he had money

---

[120] Freund, *Die Emanzipation*, II, pp. 26, 32.

[121] See the references in Meisl, *Pinkas kehillat Berlin*, pp. lxxii–lxxiii, fn. 152.

[122] See above, p. 53.

[123] See the sketch of Levin's career in M. Stern, 'Die Anfänge von Hirschel Loebels Berliner Rabbinat', *Jeschurun*, xvii (1930), pp. 129–47, 212–34, 363–91.

[124] See the analysis of the contract in C. Duschinsky, *The Rabbinate of the Great*

but no Jews; in Mannheim, Jews but no money; in Berlin, no money and no Jews. But this is surely an exaggeration, for his scholarship was held in high repute and his *yeshivah* in Berlin was well attended.[125]

Moreover, he had in Mendelssohn a fellow-spirit in their common appreciation of secular studies. Levin, in opposition to certain other contemporary rabbis, welcomed Mendelssohn's German translation of the Bible, not only for its own sake but also in the hope that it would remedy the lamentable ignorance of German amongst fellow Jews.[126] Levin's broad culture also aroused admiration in certain German literary circles. It is illustrative of his interests that Mendelssohn presented Levin with a Hebrew translation of some of Aristotle's works, on the occasion of the festival of Purim.[127]

The overall burden was heavy and in May 1798 Levin, now aged 77, asked Frederick William III to arrange with the elders some alleviation of his tasks: his office required, he informed the king, 'in addition to the most precise performance of all religious prescriptions, an ever-alert eye for maintaining the purity of faith among the nation dwelling here, settlement of all related questions and doubts, concern for the dissemination of Talmudic learning, and lastly the most extensive involvement in a large number of juridical cases among the nation, such as inheritances, divorces, etc.'[128]

Towards Re-formation

Autonomy is a relative concept, and that degree of autonomy permitted to Berlin Jewry by the Prussian state clearly did not inhibit the establishment of an organized community. The Torah had to yield up certain of its prerogatives but it did not succumb. Under the rule of elders and rabbis, a viable structure of communal life came into existence that covered a wide range of essential religious needs. Certainly this was not accomplished

---

Synagogue, London, 1756–1842, repr., London, 1971, pp. 36ff.; Meisl, *Pinkas kehillat Berlin*, no. 266.

[125] Duschinsky, *Rabbinate of the Great Synagogue*, p. 37; Landshut, *Toldot Anshei Shem*, pp. 81–2. It also seems possible to assume that in 1787 he refused an offer to become chief rabbi in the important community of Metz and head of its *yeshivah*. (Cf. A. Hertzberg, *The French Enlightenment and the Jews*, New York/London, 1968, p. 169).

[126] Ibid. There is a translation of the relevant passages of Levin's approbation in Altmann, *Moses Mendelssohn*, pp. 379–80.

[127] Landshut, *Toldot Anshei Shem*, pp. 82–3.

[128] M. Stern, 'Meyer Simon Weyl, Der letzte Kurbrandenburgische Landrabbiner', *Jeschurun*, xiii (1926), pp. 290–1.

without abuse, ambiguity, tension and conflict, but the Jews created a situation that combined adherence to the Torah with acquiescence in the demands of the state. The laws of the land remained the law, but so did the laws of the Torah.

Yet all was not well with Prussian Jewry towards the end of the eighteenth century. 'How deplorable is it, dear friend', wrote the translator of the Hebrew prayers into German (first edition, Königsberg, 1786), 'that if we are to hold fast to the prescribed and traditional prayers, which are uttered in a language of which we understand not a word, almost all the women and most of the men of our nation will be unable to savour this delight.'[129] Mendelssohn's translation of the Pentateuch into German (though printed in Hebrew characters) was in part intended to remedy the loss of Hebrew.[130]

This incipient breakdown in tradition had its counterpart at the communal level. As early as the 1760s symptoms of disaffection made themselves obvious in the refusal of elected *kehillah* officials to assume office and to prefer, as did Solomon Halpen in 1765, the alternative of a fine.[131] In 1775 the rabbis and elders of all the Jewish communities in Prussia complained of the lack of respect shown to them by certain members. In response all departments of state were ordered to authorize the rabbis and elders to impose a fine of from one to five thaler on all such delinquents; in 1778 Daniel Itzig and Jacob Moses, both bankers and senior elders in Berlin, reported that certain individuals were refusing to pay their annual contributions due to the charity-chest, hospital, aliens fund for foreign Jews, upkeep of the rabbi and cantor 'and other communal needs'. Heirs of protected Jews, the report added, were also refusing to take on their proportional obligations of charitable dues which the deceased had discharged during his lifetime and which his successors had, as it were, inherited. The Directory-General at once responded with an emphatic rejection of all such efforts to evade communal obligations.[132]

The most glaring symptom of communal disaffection concerned the resort to 'gentile courts'. This was no new phenomenon, of course. Rabbis repeatedly condemned it throughout the eighteenth century, and even earlier.[133] But it never died out. It took on such grotesque dimensions, in

---

[129] Quoted from Isaac Abraham Euchel's dedication to his translation of the liturgy, Königsberg, 1786, pp. 4a–b.

[130] W. Weinberg, 'Language questions relating to Moses Mendelssohn's Pentateuch translation', *HUCA*, LV (1984), pp. 197–242. This article fully documents the alarming decline in knowledge of Hebrew.

[131] Meisl, *Pinkas kehillat Berlin*, no. 234; see also ibid., p. xlviii.

[132] Stern, *Der Preussische Staat*, III/2–1, no. 491; ibid., III/1, p. 288.

[133] See the views of noted rabbis quoted in Shohet, *Im Hilufei Tekufot*, ch. 4, and G. Graff, *Separation of Church and State*, Alabama, 1985, pp. 186–7, n. 101; also M. Elon (ed.), *The Principles of Jewish law*, Jerusalem, 1975, p. 34; for the gravity of the whole matter, see above, p. 29.

fact, that a compendium of Jewish law had to be provided for the guidance of Christian judges when Jewish litigants sued each other in *their* courts.

The document in question is *Die Ritualgesetze der Juden*, prepared by Mendelssohn at the request of chief rabbi Hirsch Levin. This is best described as a compilation of guidelines relating to Jewish law in relation to inheritance, guardianships, bequests, wills and the property rights acquired by each party to a marriage contract. The document had its origin in a suit brought in 1769 by the rabbi and elders of the Königsberg community against one of its members, Lazar Kohn. In 1770, Frederick the Great ultimately ordered the Berlin leaders to supply the *Kammergericht* with a statement of Jewish ritual law to enable such courts to adjudicate between Jewish litigants[134]. This demand was clearly most unwelcome to the Berlin community: not only did they exploit every pretext in order to delay the completion and submission of the document – which was in fact almost six and a half years in the making (January 1770–May 1776) – but the preamble also made it clear that the guidelines could hardly serve the purposes of a judge who, applying Jewish law to a particular case, did not know Hebrew, had not studied the Talmud and codes and could not therefore, where necessary, draw on the sources of the laws.[135] But in 1784 the two senior elders, Daniel Itzig and Jacob Moses, changed their tune and now, in the name of all the Prussian communities, requested the government to give 'the Ritual Laws' binding force 'in order to achieve uniformity in legal decisions and thereby, as far as possible, to remove the existing uncertainty of judges and litigants' in cases of Jew against Jew.[136]

The problem of jurisdiction lasted into the early nineteenth century. In 1802 Elias Jacob Moses, a banker from Friedberg in the Neumark, and in 1803 the Berlin banker Ruben Samuel Gumperz, sought permission from Goldbeck, the Prussian chancellor, to make wills in accordance with the laws of the land, even if, in the words of Gumperz, this 'should run counter to the Jewish ritual laws'. Goldbeck, replying to Moses, informed him that he did indeed have the right to make his will in a Christian court in accordance with the general law. Testamentary dispositions in relation to his heirs, however, must be so formulated as to conform to the prescriptions of the Jewish ritual laws.[137]

---

[134] For all above, see Rawidowicz, *Moses Mendelssohn*, vii/i, pp. cvi–cx. A very similar request, though in opposition to Jewish wishes, was made by the Parlement of Metz earlier in the eighteenth century. See S. Schwarzfuchs, 'Les nations Juives de France', *Dix-Huitième Siècle* , (1981), pp. 131–2.

[135] Introduction to 'Ritualgesetze', in Rawidowicz, *Moses Mendelssohn*, p. 121.

[136] Rawidowicz, *Moses Mendelssohn*, p. cxxix.

[137] Ibid., p. cxxxc.

In a European Perspective

The disaffection inside the Berlin community and the increasing reluctance of communal leaders to defend their autonomy converged with the policy of the state. In 1792 the Directory General planned altogether to remove all remaining rabbinical jurisdiction, 'wherewith [the Jews] are maintained in a compulsion that hinders their improvement'.[138] This was not proceeded with at the time.

Two decades elapsed before rabbinical jurisdiction was abolished, and with it any semblance of the traditional *kehillah* – in Prussia, that is. Elsewhere the pace was different, but the movement was sufficiently uniform to require a broader treatment of the whole.

The Prussian initiative, though abortive, nonetheless epitomized and presaged similar developments both inside and outside Prussia – notably in the Habsburg empire and in revolutionary and Napoleonic France. In the guise of tolerance and emancipation, the assimilation of the Jews to the local legal systems became an object of policy. The obverse to this was the abolition of the *kehillah* and such legal jurisdiction as the Jewish court still possessed; barely less manifest was the threat to all the institutions of the *kehillah*, through which the Torah was mediated.

In 1781/2 Joseph II, the Habsburg emperor, introduced a number of patents of toleration that went some considerable way towards equalizing the situation of his Jewish and Christian subjects in respect of education, employment, occupation and taxation. He also made the Jews liable to conscription, as were his other subjects. This was acceptable under the formula 'the law of the land is the law',[139] for there was no question of anti-Jewish discrimination. But the case in relation to Joseph's Marriage Patent of 1783 was not so clear cut. It was designed to impose a uniform law of marriage on all the subjects of the empire; in the Jewish case, by requiring that only a state-authorized district rabbi conduct the wedding ceremony. Marriages not concluded in conformity with the terms of the

---

[138] Freund, *Die Emanzipation*, II, p. 77.

[139] See the responsa quoted in Y.-Z. Kahana, *Mehkarim be-sifrut ha-tshuvot*, Jerusalem, 1973, pp. 167ff. Some sections of Habsburg Jewry (e.g. in Trieste) welcomed military service as a testimony to the emperor's confidence in his Jewish subjects (S.K. Padover, *The Revolutionary Emperor*, 2nd edn, London, 1967, pp. 184–5). Jews in England had been serving in the Royal Navy since the mid-eighteenth century. During the Napoleonic wars, rabbi Hirschell reminded Jewish volunteers that so far as circumstances allowed, they were still subject to religious norms (G.L. Green, *The Royal Navy and Anglo-Jewry, 1740–1820*, London, 1989, p. 80).

patent would be considered null and void.[140]

In France, the assimilation of the Jews to the civil law was at its most extreme and took the form of their complete emancipation. The notables and rabbis from the French empire whom Napoleon summoned to Paris in 1806 declared: 'the rabbis exercise no manner of police jurisdiction among the Jews nor do they enjoy judicial powers.'[141] In the French satellite kingdom of Westphalia the decree of 1808 that granted the Jews all civil rights also expressly required the abolition of rabbinical jurisdiction.[142] Prussia eventually followed suit and the edict of emancipation (1812) declared 'On no account may rabbis and Jewish elders presume to exercise either jurisdiction or guardian-like governance (*vormundschaftliche Leitung*) and guidance.'[143]

None of these measures failed to arouse rabbinical protest. Not only did rabbis fear loss of status; they could not but view with concern the destruction of a traditional religious polity – all the more so because of the impetus that government policy everywhere gave to religious reform and because there was an evident connection between the imposition of legal uniformity and assimilation. To most rabbis they were virtually synonymous concepts. R. Wolf Boskowitz of Hungary (1740–1818), a leading Talmudic scholar and student of the natural sciences, wrote: 'If the nations desired us to assimilate with them only externally, then we would have some excuse for shedding the heavy yoke of exile and becoming like them. But this is not the case . . . their true desire is not for us to change our garments and the like, but they desire our souls and our religion, for they wish us to be like them in our inner selves and not only outwardly.'[144]

Rabbis in the Habsburg and French empires, as distinct from Prussia, led the counter-attack. In Austria so great was the opposition to the Marriage Patent of 1783 that the emperor sought the opinion of R. Ezekiel Landau, chief rabbi of Prague. Landau had given a cautious welcome to

---

[140] Graff, *Separation of Church and State*, p. 46; for the general context of Joseph's policy, see J. Karriel, 'Die Toleranzpolitik Kaiser Josephs II', in W. Grab (ed.), *Deutsche Aufklärung und Judenemanzipation*, Tel Aviv, 1980, pp. 155–77.

[141] Answer to the eighth question, *Transactions of the Parisian Sanhedrin*, trans. D. Tama, New York/London, 1985, pp. 194–5.

[142] For this period in the history of Westphalian Jewry, cf. J.R. Marcus, *Israel Jacobson*, Cincinnati, 1972, pp. 56ff.

[143] Freund, *Emanzipation*, II, p. 458, para. 30.

[144] Quoted M. Breuer, 'Emancipation and the rabbis', *Niv Hadmidrashia*, 13–14 (5738/9–1978/9), p. 28. This is an extremely valuable analysis of rabbinical views of the early part of the nineteenth century. Also useful for the interplay of Jewish and Christian opinion is H.D. Schmidt, 'The terms of emancipation, 1781–1812', *LBYB*, I (1956), pp. 28–47.

the Toleration Patents of 1781/2.[145] But his response to the Marriage Patent, in the form of a tract entitled *Jewish Marriage according to the Law of Moses and the Talmud*, has been summarized as follows: 'the kaiser's Jewish subjects would try to comply with the law of the state, but Jewish law would remain paramount: *kiddushim* (consecration to marriage) effectuated by Jewish legal process, though contrary to civil requirements, would not be considered null.'[146] This was unavailing and the Marriage Patent was reaffirmed in 1786. In France R. David Sinzheim of Strasburg, the elected president of Napoleon's 'Sanhedrin' of rabbis (1807), had greater success. Sinzheim was able to guide his rabbinical colleagues and the lay notables of the French empire into a formula that salvaged the integrity of Jewish marriage law: 'although the religion of Moses has not forbidden the Jews from inter-marrying with nations not of their religion, yet, as marriage, according to the Talmud, requires religious ceremonies called *Kiduschim* with the benediction used in such cases, no marriage can be *religiously* valid unless these ceremonies have been performed. This could not be done towards persons who would not both of them consider these ceremonies as sacred; and in that case the married couple could separate without the *religious* divorce; they would then be considered as married *civilly* but not *religiously*.'[147] Subsequently, even under the consistorial system of communal organization that Napoleon imposed on French Jewry, Jewish marriage and divorce retained their validity. Sinzheim argued that in whatever had been agreed by the Sanhedrin, the Jews had only drawn the consequences of their own law.[148]

Moses Mendelssohn and the New Community

In Prussia also the thrust and purport of the transition towards emancipation did not signify the end of the *kehillah*, though it certainly underwent a radical change in character. The herald of this development was Moses Mendelssohn. In Berlin he witnessed the early stages of the conflict over legal uniformity, disaffection in the *kehillah* and the centrifugal sentiments of the wealthy. He shared to the full in R. Ezekiel Landau's suspicions of

---

[145] See R. Kestenberg-Gladstein, *Neuere Geschichte der Juden in den böhmischen Ländern, I*, Tübingen, 1969, pp. 85–93.

[146] Graff, *Separation of Church and State*, p. 47.

[147] Answer to the third question, *Transactions*, trans. Tama, p. 155; cf. also L. Landman, *Jewish Law in the Diaspora: Confrontation and Accommodation*, Philadelphia, 1968, pp. 137ff.

[148] S. Schwarzfuchs, *Napoleon, the Jews and the Sanhedrin*, London, 1979, p. 95.

Habsburg policy, because of its assimilationist purport.[149] But he was also sensitive to the hardship and suffering of the Jewish poor, about which he wrote movingly.[150] An end to the enforced segregation of the Jews, the opportunity to enter previously prohibited occupations and the removal of arbitrary and oppressive taxation could not but redound to their benefit. Mendelssohn, however, was also a devoted and pious Jew and could not contemplate without alarm the prospect of wholesale assimilation as the price of such relaxation.

To reconcile these conflicts he propounded a revolutionary new concept of the *kehillah* that also took full account of the secularizing tendencies of the late eighteenth century – a concept of the *kehillah* as a purely voluntary body. In a sense Mendelssohn made a distinction between the state and civil society. The Jew could adhere to the former as secular citizen but in the latter he remained a Jew. In terms of Jewish law he anticipated the later Franco-Jewish application of the principle that 'the law of the land is the law' to sanction a division between Jewish civil and religious law.[151] Unquestionably, this took the former principle to its uttermost limit. Even so, together with the voluntary emphasis, it informed the dual message of his treatise *Jerusalem or on Religious Power and Judaism* (1783).[152] This must therefore be primarily understood not as an exercise in political theory but as a response to a specific political situation.

Jerusalem falls into two parts, following the division indicated by the subtitle. In 'Religious power' Mendelssohn makes mention neither of Judaism nor of Christianity and argues in favour of a religiously neutral state, where 'neither church nor state has a right to subject men's principles and convictions to any coercion whatsoever. Neither church nor state is authorized to connect privileges and rights, claims on persons and title to things, with principles and convictions, and to weaken through outside interference the influence of the power of truth upon the cognitive faculty.'[153] But if the state was to be secularized, that is dechristianized, then sauce for the Christian goose was also sauce for the Jewish gander; and in the second part of the treatise, 'Judaism', Mendelssohn used for his own purposes the argument put forward by Spinoza in the seventeenth century and earlier in the eighteenth by Cocceji.[154] That is to say, he argued that when the

---

[149] See his letters to Herz Homberg of 1783 and 1784, in *Gesammelte Schriften*, V, Leipzig, 1844, pp. 671, 677.

[150] Ibid., III, p. 366.

[151] See C. Touati, 'Grand Sanhédrin et droit rabbinique', in B. Blumenkranz and A. Soboul (eds), Le Grand Sanhédrin de Napoléon, Toulouse, 1979, pp. 27–48.

[152] I have used the translation by A. Arkush, Hanover/London, 1983.

[153] Ibid., p. 70.

[154] See above, p. 53.

Temple was destroyed, 'the civil bonds of the nation were dissolved; religious offences were no longer crimes against the state; and the religion, as religion, knows of no punishment, no other penalty than the one the remorseful sinner *voluntarily* imposes on himself.' What Mendelssohn called 'the Mosaic constitution' now no longer existed.[155]

Spinoza had interpreted the collapse of the state in a far more radical sense – that not only the state but the election of Israel by God had also lost its validity.[156] Mendelssohn, making a division between civil and religious law, could, however, accept the demise of the 'Mosaic constitution' yet continue to proclaim the unaltered status of the 'personal command-ments'.[157] This development made it possible for Jewry to accommodate itself to what Mendelssohn called 'civil union';[158] that is, enjoy rights equal to those of other subjects of the state, giving to God, and also to Caesar, their respective dues.[159]

Furthermore, Judaism possessed no dogmas, or articles of faith, Men-delssohn argued, pointing to the medieval philosophical controversies waged amongst Maimonides, Crescas and Albo, and the Kabbalists.[160] All that had been revealed at Sinai were 'commandments and ordinances'.[161] The Jews therefore had never had any beliefs or dogmas that required coercive machinery for their enforcement, and thus, by the same token, were already in a position to enter the religiously neutral state.

This line of reasoning utterly undermined the *raison d'être* of the contem-porary *kehillah*, which, in however truncated a form, existed precisely in order to provide a normative-political structure that encompassed far more than the sphere of 'personal commandments'. In this light, Mendelssohn's teaching was radical and destructive. But this did not imply on his part the slightest renunciation of allegiance, for his teaching was also conservative in the extreme: 'And even today', he exhorted his fellow-Jews, 'no wiser advice than this can be given to the House of Jacob. Adapt yourselves to the morals and the constitution of the land to which you have been removed; but hold fast to the religion of your fathers too . . . I cannot see how those born into the House of Jacob can in any conscientious manner disencumber

---

[155] Ibid., pp. 130–1.

[156] Cf. S. Pines, 'The Jewish religion after the destruction of Temple and state: the views of Bodin and Spinoza', in S. Stein and R. Loewe (eds), *Studies in Jewish Religious and Intellectual History*, Alabama, 1979, pp. 215–34.

[157] *Jerusalem*, p. 134.

[158] Ibid., p. 135.

[159] Ibid., p. 133.

[160] Ibid., pp. 100–101.

[161] Ibid., p. 98.

themselves of the law.'[162] He refined still further the conditions of Jewish participation in a 'civil union' – this had to be compatible with gentile acquiescence in a certain degree of legal differentiation:

> should you believe that you cannot love us in return as brothers and unite with us as citizens as long as we are outwardly distinguished from you by the ceremonial law, do not eat with you, do not marry you . . . if civil union can not be obtained under any other condition than our departing from the laws which we still consider binding on us, then we are sincerely sorry to find it necessary to declare that we must rather do without civil union.[163]

There is a deep inconsistency here which Maimon was one of the first to point out. How could Mendelssohn, on the grounds that the church had no rights in civil matters, protest at the action of Raphael Cohen, chief rabbi in Hamburg, when he excommunicated Samuel Marcus, a Jew who openly transgressed the law? On the one hand, Mendelssohn proclaimed the permanency of 'the Jewish ecclesiastical state'; on the other he denied it rights in civil matters. 'What is a state without rights?', Maimon demanded.[164] As it turned out, the inconsistency was inconsequential and no necessity for any renunciation of 'civil union' arose. Mendelssohn's hope proved itself brilliantly percipient: it did prove possible to enjoy emancipation without tears – at least without many.

To some small extent this process followed from the efforts made by the elders of Prussian Jewry, led by David Friedländer of Königsberg, to free themselves from the *kehillah* and its burdens. These efforts characterized the slightly more relaxed period after the death of Frederick the Great in 1786. In 1787 the body tax was abolished; in 1788 the porcelain export tax was commuted into a single payment of 40,000 reichsthaler; in 1792 collective liability for state and communal taxes was removed (though not for thefts and bankruptcies). The authorities would go no further – at least not until the defeat of Prussia at Jena in 1805 forced the re-organization of the state. In 1812 this came to embrace Jewish emancipation in terms of an edict that equalized the status of Jews with that of other citizens, thus abolishing special taxes and residential and occupational restrictions (the admission of Jews to the officers' corps, to public administrative offices and the judiciary was left open for further consideration). This was unquestionably a turning-point. It betokened, however, no loss of continuity – all the less so as emancipation was accompanied by the continuing obligation to

---

[162] Ibid., p. 133.
[163] Ibid., p. 135.
[164] Maimon, *Geschichte des eigenen Lebens*, p. 157.

contribute to communal expenses and by the inability to secede from communal bodies.[165]

Elsewhere in the German states the course of emancipation was tortuous, especially so in the Catholic states of the south, including the Habsburg empire; even in Prussia the edict of 1812 was subsequently limited. In the Prussian province of Posen, newly acquired at the Congress of Vienna (1815) where two-thirds of Prussian Jewry lived, only in 1833 did the offer of individual patents of naturalization make emancipation possible.[166]

It may well be that Rosenzweig was right when he accused Mendelssohn of leaving German Jewry 'defenceless' in face of the dangers of the nineteenth century – none of Mendelssohn's descendants belonged to the community, he pointed out.[167] Certainly, Mendelssohn's message was hardly inspiring. Yet it is also true that continuity was not lost. A new '*kehillah*' came into existence that assumed many of the functions of the old and/or transformed them in accordance with the new conditions. The synagogue became a corporation under public law. In this context, together with the elimination of the rabbinical court, and the diminished role of the *yeshivah*, not only did the synagogue move to the centre of Jewish life but the rabbi underwent an equally startling change: he became a preacher, pastor and teacher, for whom a secular education was all but essential. Certain states (Baden, Bavaria, Kurhessen, Württemberg) made academic qualifications a positive requirement for rabbinical posts. By 1847, sixty-seven German rabbis and preachers had acquired university degrees (about 20 per cent of the entire German rabbinate).[168]

Other institutions underwent a similar degree of change. The Jews' Free School established in Berlin in 1778 by Mendelssohn and his associates was remodelled and extended in 1826.[169] In 1812 schools of this type in Berlin were educating 215 of the school-age population of 900 – mainly from poorer families.[170] The Association for the Science of Judaism,

---

[165] R. Liberles, 'Emancipation and the structure of the Jewish community in the nineteenth century', *LBYB*, XXXI (1986), p. 61.

[166] For detailed analyses of these developments, see R. Rürup, 'Jewish emancipation and bourgeois society', *LBYB*, XV (1969), pp. 67–91.

[167] *Vorspruch zu einer Mendelssohnfeier, Kleinere Schriften*, Berlin, 1937, p. 53.

[168] M. Silber, 'The historical experience of German Jewry', in J. Katz (ed.), *Toward Modernity, The European Jewish Model*, New Brunswick, 1987, p. 131; see also I. Schorsch, 'The emergence of the modern rabbinate', in W. Mosse, A. Paucker and R. Rürup (eds), *Revolution and Evolution – 1848 in German-Jewish History*, Tübingen, 1981, pp. 205–47.

[169] See the history of the school in J. Gutmann, *Festschrift zur Feier des hundertjährigen Bestehens der Knabenschule der jüdischen Gemeinde in Berlin*, Berlin, 1926.

[170] M. Eliav, *Ha-Ḥinukh ha-yehudi be-Germaniya biymei ha-haskalah ve-ha-emanzipaziyah*, Jerusalem, 1961, p. 174.

founded in Berlin in 1819, was short-lived but initiated one of the most influential scholastic movements in Jewish history. In 1812 a society for the promotion of industry (handicrafts and agriculture) amongst young Jews was founded and admitted thirty boys for vocational training. A home for the aged (1829), a commission to support and provide work for the poor (1838), an orphanage for boys and girls (1836), a new cemetery (1827), a girls' school (1835), a teachers' training institute (1839) – these were some of the institutions that Berlin Jewry created or renewed. They had their counterparts throughout the other German cities and states.[171] The *Lehranstalt* founded under the will of Veitel Heine Ephraim in 1774, originally in the form of a *yeshivah*, became the precursor of the rabbinical seminary, when it was remodelled in 1856.[172]

Of course, the Torah lost even more of its sway. But it showed itself able to meet the new conditions of the nineteenth century. The sun set on the old *kehillah*, and rose on the new.

[171] D. Sorkin, *The Transformation of German Jewry, 1780–1840*, Oxford, 1987, pp. 115ff.
[172] Michaelis, 'The Ephraim family', p. 215.

3

A Tale of Two Cities: London, 1650–1880

Preamble

The modern Jewish community in London came into existence only a decade or so before the Berlin community. But this coincidence in time, and the common economic motive that invited Jews to both capitals, conceals a far more important difference: in Berlin, as I have shown, the community was from the outset subject to the growing supervision and control of the state whose support it also 'enjoyed'; in London, the state barely took cognisance of the existence of the Jews. This does not necessarily mean that the Jews of London, as compared with those of Berlin, enjoyed a greater liberty to order their affairs unimpeded by any outside source. In certain respects the very contrary prevailed; a bequest in favour of a *yeshivah* in Berlin was fulfilled with no hindrance[1] but in London the courts disallowed an identical bequest on the grounds that it was 'in contradiction of the Christian religion, which is a part of the law of the land'.[2]

But such impediments were rare and operated with arbitrary and inconsistent effect, and for the most part London Jewry was indeed free to order its affairs as seemed to its leaders, in their particular circumstances, best calculated to advance the aims and claims of the Torah. This was not of course their only motive, but it does help to explain why similar institutions should emerge in London and Berlin and thus answers to many of the questions relevant to Berlin will be sought also in the following pages: how synagogues were organized, the poor cared for, self-government administered, the relationship of lay and rabbinical leadership determined, liaison with government handled and the prerogatives of the Torah defended against the encroachment of the state.

If, however, the questions are the same, the answers must necessarily vary in accordance with the difference that divides a mercantile and absolutist Brandenburg from a constitutional and liberal Britain, to which

[1] See above p. 58.
[2] See below p. 83.

entry was virtually unrestricted. This must, for example, aggravate the problem posed by the immigrant poor and require an entirely different answer from a Brandenburg whence the Jewish poor were virtually excluded. Moreover, Britain's status as a great imperial power made it possible for Anglo-Jewry to concern itself with the religious and physical welfare of overseas Jewish communities. At another level, the gradual admission of Jews to the full enjoyment of British citizenship created acute tension in relation to the concern of the Torah for its own jurisdiction. But if the answers must necessarily differ, they will not for that reason depart from the same framework of concern.

A Community Foregathers

In 1290 Edward I expelled the Jews from England, but in the sixteenth and seventeenth centuries a handful of Portuguese Jews reappeared in London and Bristol in the guise of *marranos*.[3] They were accompanied later in the seventeenth century by an equally tiny handful of Sephardi Jews – Simon de Caceres, Antonio Fernandez Carvajal, Manuel Martinez Dormido and some few others. They also lived outwardly as Catholics and served Cromwell as army contractors and 'intelligencers'.[4] At the end of 1654 Dormido petitioned Cromwell for the regularization of his position, for aid in the recovery of his property from England's Portuguese allies and for the free entry of 'my nation'.[5]

In 1655 the 'movement' for re-admission took a more public turn when R. Menasseh b. Israel of Amsterdam, a Dutch Sephardi rabbi, millenarian, printer and pamphleteer, petitioned Cromwell in this sense. Behind this initiative stood the Navigation Acts of 1651, which sought to ensure that foreign goods imported into Britain from the colonies be carried in British ships or in ships belonging to the country where the goods originated. This would have eliminated Amsterdam Jewish commerce from trade with the British West Indies, whence raw sugar was imported for refining in Hol-

[3] C. J. Sisson, 'A colony of Jews in Shakespeare's London', *Essays and Studies by Members of the English Association*, xxiii (1938), pp. 38–51.

[4] L. Wolf, 'Cromwell's Jewish intelligencers', in Cecil Roth (ed.), *Essays in Jewish History*, JHSE, 1934, pp. 93–114; L. Wolf, 'Crypto-Jews under the Commonwealth', *TJHSE* I, (1895), pp. 55–88. For a description of Cromwell's relations with Dormido, see D. Katz, *Philo-Semitism and the Readmission of the Jews to England*, Oxford, 1982, pp. 193ff.

[5] See the documents in J. Kaplan (ed.), *Shivat ha-Yehudim le-Angliya*, Jerusalem, 1972, pp. 76ff.

land.[6] Such interests had therefore a powerful incentive to establish themselves in England.

Menasseh ben Israel served as their spokesman. But his hopes encompassed considerably more than the economic interests of the Amsterdam merchants. His purpose was also to further the messianic restoration of the Jews to their land. His pamphlet of 1650, *The Hope of Israel*, is devoted entirely to this cause. Its success, Menasseh argued, depended on the world-wide dispersion of the Jews, in fulfilment of Daniel 12:7 'and when the scattering of the holy people shall have an end, all those things shall be fulfilled'.[7] This exegesis was by no means novel.[8] In 1655, in his *Humble Address*, Menasseh gave it a contemporary application:

> Now we know, how our nation at the present is spread all about, and has its seat and dwelling in the most flourishing parts of all the kingdoms, and countries of the world, as well in America, as in the other three parts thereof; except only in this considerable and mighty island. And therefore this remains only in my judgement, before the Messiah come and restore our nation, that first we must have our seat here likewise.[9]

Menasseh's *Humble Address* to Cromwell and subsequent petition to the Council of State thus sought permission for the Jews to establish public synagogues, exercise their religion freely subject to their own laws (with the right of appeal to English civil law) and acquire a cemetery.[10]   But the overwhelming bulk of the *Humble Address* is devoted, not to furthering a messianic consummation, but to showing 'how profitable the nation of the Jews are'; merchandizing, Menasseh writes, is their 'proper profession'.[11]

---

[6] M. Arkin, 'Aspects of Jewish economic history', *JPSA*, 1975, pp. 103–11; H. Bloom, *Economic Activities of the Jews of Amsterdam*, repr., New York, 1969, p. 210.

[7] Kaplan, *Shivat ha-Yehudim* ('The Hope of Israel'), p. 56. The relevant part of the verse from Daniel is normally translated: 'and when they have made an end of breaking in pieces the power of the holy people, all these things shall be finished'.

[8] See the references in Shalom Rosenberg. 'Exile and redemption in Jewish thought in the sixteenth century', in B. Cooperman (ed.), *Jewish Thought in the Sixteenth Century*, Harvard, 1983, p. 428, n. 51.

[9] Kaplan, *Shivat ha-Yehudim* ('Humble Address'), pp. 84ff.; see also A. J. Saraiva, 'Antonio Vieira, Menasseh b. Israel et le cinquième empire', *Studia Rosenthaliana*, VI (1972), pp. 25–57.

[10] Katz, *Philo-Semitism*, p. 202

[11] Ibid., p. 88ff.; for the transition in Menasseh's thinking, see I. Schorsch, 'From messianism to realpolitik: Menasseh b. Israel and the readmission of the Jews to England', *PAAJR*, xlv (1978), pp. 187–208. The bulk of Menasseh's economic arguments are taken from Simone Luzzatto's famous *Essay on the Jews of Venice*

He enumerates five principal benefits from trade: the increase in tolls and customs receipts; the making available of goods from remote countries; 'the affoding of materials in great plenty for all Mechaniqs; as wooll, leather, wines; jewels, as diamants, pearles and such like merchandize'; the sale and export of manufactures; lastly, 'the commerce and reciprocall negotiation at sea, which is the ground of peace between neighbour nations, and of great profit to their own fellow-citizens'.[12] This emphasis was no doubt calculated to appeal to Cromwell's mercantilist policies.[13] It also accorded with Christian confidence in the purported trading abilities of the Jews. This view enjoyed wide currency in the contemporary world.[14] It chimed in too with a certain philosemitism that had accumulated in England since about the turn of the century.[15]

But talk of Jewish mercantile prowess cut both ways. Cromwell, in response to Menasseh's plea and internal pressure, summoned the Whitehall conference of politicians, lawyers, churchmen and merchants in December 1655. Whereas it was agreed that no legal obstacles obstructed Jewish settlement in England, no agreement concerning the conditions of settlement was attainable – largely, it seems, because of opposition from the London merchants.[16] As in the case of Brandenburg, rulers might welcome Jews for their supposed mercantile qualities, but those who fancied they might be exposed to Jewish competition did not. Menasseh set out for Amsterdam in disappointment but died at Middelburg en route. He had, at the lowest, succeeded in establishing the absence of obstacles to resettlement. This basis, however uncertain, invited the formation of a Sephardi community that did take slow shape in the later seventeenth century.[17]

The Lord Mayor and Corporation of the City of London initially attempted to halt this process and called for the expulsion of the Jews. In

---

(1638); see B. Ravid, "How profitable the Nation of the Jews are": the Humble Addresses of Menasseh b. Israel and the *Discorso* of Simone Luzzatto', in J. Reinharz and D. Swetchinski (eds), *Essays in Jewish Intellectual History in honor of Alexander Altmann*, Durham, N. Carolina, 1982, pp. 159–180.

[12] Kaplan, *Shivat ha-Yehudim*, p. 90.

[13] See D. Patinkin, 'Mercantilism and the readmission of the Jews to England', *JSS*, viii (1946), pp. 161–78.

[14] See above, p. 41.

[15] Katz, *Philo-Semitism*, passim; see also T. K. Rabb, 'The stirrings of the 1590s and the return of the Jews to England', *TJHSE*, XXVI (1974–8), pp. 26–33; and G. Lloyd Jones, *The Discovery of Hebrew in Tudor England*, Manchester, 1983.

[16] H. Pollins, *The Economic History of the Jews in England*, London/Toronto, 1982, pp. 33ff.; Katz, *Philo-Semitism*, p. 212. Katz's book also contains the fullest account available of the Whitehall conference (ch. 6).

[17] A. S. Diamond, 'The community of the resettlement, 1656–1684: a social survey', *TJHSE*, xxiv (1974), pp. 134–50.

1664, 1673–4 and 1685, it was suggested that either Jewish worship was illegal or that Jews were illegally failing to attend church worship. The community sought and obtained protection from both Charles II and James II.[18] Charles undertook to be 'their advocate and assist them with all his power'. R. Jacob Sasportas, *haham* (rabbi) of the Sephardi congregation, hailed this as 'a time in which God has seen fit greatly to ameliorate the condition of His people, bringing them forth from the general condition of serfdom into freedom ... in that we are free to practise our own true religion'.[19]

The records of the Spanish and Portuguese synagogue show that reliance was not exclusively heavenwards. In 1670–1 the congregation dispensed the sum of £22.8.10 'for various expenses on solicitors and goings and coming to the Parliament and bottles of wine that were presented'; and that of £10.17.6 in 1674–5 'by outlay in the house of Ishack Alvarez with the Duchess of Bokingam [sic].'[20] It was also customary for the congregation during at least the first century of its existence to make an annual gift to the Lord Mayor of London – a pipe of wine value £48, or a purse containing 50 guineas, or a silver salver holding sweetmeats or chocolate.[21]

The community took shape in complete disregard of Menasseh's messianic hopes, showing no wish to play its allotted part in the cosmic drama of redemption. In 1666, barely a decade after his departure, even the pseudo-messianic Sabbatean movement aroused virtually no echo in emerging Anglo-Jewry. Christians, rather than Jews, were stirred by the alleged messiah.[22]

Prudently, under the restoration, the Sephardic authorities did their

[18] Pollins, *Economic History*, pp. 38–9; H. S. Q. Henriques, *The Jews and the English Law*, Oxford, 1908, pp. 2–3, 152ff.; M. Wilensky, 'The royalist position concerning the re-admission of Jews to England', *JQR*, XLI (1950–1), pp. 397–409.

[19] A. Fraser, *King Charles II*, London, 1979, p. 218; see also L. Wolf, 'Status of the Jews in England after the re-settlement', *TJHSE*, IV (1899–1901), pp. 188–92: for the general hostility of the London merchants to the Jews, see T. Endelman, *The Jews of Georgian England, 1714–1830*, JPSA, 1979, pp. 20ff.; N. Osterman, 'The controversy over the proposed readmission of the Jews to England (1655)', *JSS*, III (1941), p. 323; L. Barnett (ed.), *Bevis Marks Records I*, Oxford, 1940, p. 9, 1664, p. 15, 1685.

[20] L. D. Barnett (trans.), *El Libro de los Acuerdos*, Oxford, 1931, pp. 53, 90. Alvarez Nunez (Ishack Israel) was a court jeweller and elder of the Sephardi congregation. The Duke of Buckingham introduced the 'Bill of Indulgence to all Protestant dissenters' in 1675; see also R. Barnett, 'Mr Pepys' contacts with the Jews of London', *TJHSE*, XXIX (1982–6), pp. 27–33.

[21] C. Roth, *Essays and Portraits in Anglo-Jewish History*, Philadelphia, 1962, pp. 108–12.

[22] M. McKeon, 'Sabbatai Svi in England', *AJSR*, II (1977), pp. 131–69.

utmost to obscure their Commonwealth origins. They deprecated strongly, for example, the proposed republication of the works of Menasseh b. Israel.[23] London in particular, and England in general, attracted many of the westward migrants characteristic of European Jewry in the seventeenth and eighteenth centuries.[24] In 1660 there were thirty-five Sephardi heads of families in London; by 1685 this had increased to ninety-two, and by 1695 to some 800 individuals including some 250 Ashkenazim. By 1720 the number of Sephardim alone is estimated to have reached a total of 1,050 altogether.[25] They came mainly from Portugal, Spain and their possessions (in flight from the Inquisition), or from Sephardi settlements in Hamburg, Amsterdam and Leghorn. Most were poor and dependent on the support of the wealthy. The latter were engaged in overseas trade, particularly as members of the East and West India companies, and as military suppliers and contractors. The Duke of Marlborough rewarded Solomon de Medina with a knighthood for his services in this role.[26]

During the eighteenth century the socio-economic profile of Anglo-Jewry changed radically through the influx of large numbers of poor Ashkenazi and Sephardi immigrants. In 1795, of the approximately 2,000 Sephardim in England slightly more than half were rated as poor by the secretary of the congregation.[27] Most had come in the second half of the century from Holland, Italy, North Africa, Portugal, Spain and Brazil.[28] The Ashkenazi community changed even more drastically, with some 6,000 immigrants in 1700–50 and another 8,000 to 10,000 by 1815, making a total of 25,000.[29] Most came from the small towns and villages of the German states and a smaller number from Poland. This continuing influx ensured that poverty would remain the besetting problem of Anglo-Jewry. The newcomers were destitute and unskilled and thronged the London streets as hawkers, pedlars and traders, offering a wide variety of cheap goods. In 1800 no less than one-tenth of the London Jewish population of 15,000 are estimated to have

---

[23] R. Barnett, 'The correspondence of the Mahamad of the Spanish and Portuguese congregation of London during the seventeenth and eighteenth centuries', *TJHSE*, XX (1964), p. 3.

[24] For a general picture, see Shulvass, *From East to West*, passim.

[25] A. S. Diamond, 'Problems of the London Sephardi community', *TJHSE*, XXI (1968), pp. 39–63.

[26] See O. Rabinowicz, 'Sir Solomon de Medina', *JHSE* (1974). Medina also had a textile warehouse which supplied the wealthy with luxury goods (Diana de Marly, 'Sir Solomon de Medina's textile warehouse', *TJHSE*, XXVII (1982), pp. 155).

[27] Endelman, *The Jews of Georgian England*, p. 32.

[28] Ibid., p. 170.

[29] Ibid., p. 173.

dealt in old clothes.[30] In the later nineteenth century and up to 1880 immigration continued at a lesser rate but this, together with natural increase, still brought the total Anglo-Jewish population to approximately 60,000. The entry of Jews from Eastern Europe marked the later 1850s and after.[31] By now the Anglo-Jewish profile had again changed; not only was a larger proportion than ever native born: also, for the first time since the earliest days of the community, the proportion of the poor had diminished. No doubt the two facts were connected. Be the explanation what it may, the careful calculations of Joseph Jacobs (1882) show that paupers and the recipients of communal charity still constituted about a quarter of the 46,000 Jews of London. The lower class (petty traders, servants and assistants) accounted for 19.6 per cent; a middle class (shopkeepers, low-income professionals and merchants) for 42.2 per cent, and the upper class (high-income professionals and merchants) for 14.6 per cent. The members of each class had an estimated average annual income respectively of £12, £26, £54 and £367.[32] Overwhelmingly, London Jewry had become *embourgeoisé*, and this was no doubt also true of the 15,000 Jews in the provinces.

From their first establishment the Jews in England were free of the charters, privileges, licences and statutes that trammelled and bedevilled Jewish existence elsewhere. And this endured (by contrast with Berlin). In 1773 Meyer Michael-David of Hanover compared Amsterdam and London with the German states in terms of heaven and hell.[33] The Jews in London could not participate in political and public life, but this exclusion (shared with Catholic and Protestant non-conformists) was only an incidental function of the inability to take the sacraments in accordance with Anglican rites. There was no ghetto or designated residential area; no taxes applicable solely to Jews or other *general* economic restrictions. A *specific* exception was the limitation to twelve Jews only of the 124 brokers permitted to operate on the Royal Exchange (1697) and the exclusion of Jewish retailers from the City. (From 1785 this was extended to baptised Jews.) City merchants also succeeded in excluding Jews from the Russia and the Levant companies. But these were trifling restraints, and the inability to participate in political life fully accorded with Anglo-Jewry's own desire to remain incon-

---

[30] V. D. Lipman, 'Trends in Anglo-Jewish occupations', *JJS*, II (1960), p. 205.

[31] V. D. Lipman 'The age of emancipation, 1815–1880', in V. D. Lipman (ed.), *Three Centuries of Anglo-Jewish History*, JHSE, 1961, p. 70.

[32] Joseph Jacobs, *Studies in Jewish Statistics, Social, Vital and Anthropometric*, London, 1891, pp. 14ff. The figures are discussed in Pollins, *Economic History*, pp. 90, 105ff., 114.

[33] Quoted G. Yogev, *Diamonds and Coral*, Leicester, 1978, p. 19.

spicuous.[34] On the other hand, religious tests of one sort and another had the effect of excluding Jews from entering any of the professions, so that trade, whether in money or in old clothes, was the primary occupation.[35] Only towards the end of the eighteenth and beginning of the nineteenth centuries do Jews appear as craftsmen – most frequently as watchmakers, goldsmiths, silversmiths and opticians, many of whom enjoyed royal patronage.[36]

A Legal Limbo

In all significant respects the individual Jew stood on the same legal footing as a Christian. In 1667 Jewish witnesses were permitted to take the oath on the Hebrew Bible ('Old Testament') and to cover their heads when so doing; and in 1697 it was held 'a Jew may sue at this day; but heretofore he could not, for then they were looked upon as enemies. But now commerce has taught the world more humanity.'[37] In 1744 it was determined in principle by Lord Hardwicke, the Lord Chancellor, 'that all persons who believe in a supreme being, who will punish them if they swear falsely, are competent witnesses, and should take the oath in the form binding upon them according to the tenets of their religion'.[38] Hardwicke's Act of 1753, intended to suppress clandestine marriages (26 Geo. II, cap. 33), explicitly excluded from its provisions (clause 18) any marriage between two persons both of whom professed the Jewish religion.[39]

Not only did the state make room for a second jurisdiction but it also gave its support to that jurisdiction. In 1733, in the consistory court of the Bishop of London, Mrs Andreas of the Spanish and Portuguese congregation sued her husband for restitution of conjugal rights. The defendant argued that the court had no jurisdiction because the marriage had been celebrated according to Jewish rites and not those of the Church of England. But the court accepted the validity of the Jewish ceremony and the case

---

[34] See below pp. 97–9.

[35] N. Perry, 'Anglo-Jewry, the law, religious conviction and self-interest (1655–1753)', *Journal of European Studies*, XIV (1984), p. 7.

[36] A. Rubens, 'Portrait of Anglo-Jewry, 1656–1836', *TJHSE*, XIX (1960), pp. 19–20.

[37] Quoted Henriques, *Jews and the English Law*, p. 189.

[38] Ibid., pp. 179ff.

[39] James Picciotto, *Sketches of Anglo-Jewish History*, rev. and ed. I. Finestein, London, 1956, p. 100; Henriques, *Jews and the English Law*, pp. 170–1; for the privileged position of Jews (and Quakers) in respect of Hardwicke's Act, see E. J. Cohn, 'Eheschliessung in englischen nicht-orthodoxen Synagogen', in *Festschrift zum 60ten Geburtstag von Rabbiner Dr Lothar Rothschild*, Bern, 1970, pp. 62–3.

was decided in favour of the plaintiff. At the end of the century two further cases in the Consistory court (Lindo *v.* Belisario, 1795, and Goldsmid *v.* Bromer, 1798) were noteworthy for the acceptance of expert evidence given by the members of the Portuguese and German rabbinical courts (*Batei Din*) in London. In these cases the guardian of one young girl and the wealthy father of another wished to secure the annulment of the girls' clandestine marriages. The forms of the ceremony were defective and contrary to Jewish law, it was argued. The ecclesiastical court sought the advice of the Jewish rabbinical authorities and their decision voiding the alleged marriages was accepted by the gentile court. The *Batei Din* were described as 'courts of great authority . . . and on matters of Jewish law entitled to the greatest respect'.[40]

But of course even England remained part of the diaspora, and to that extent 'the law of the land was the law'; and to that extent also Jewish autonomy, mediated through the Torah, was circumscribed. To what extent, precisely? It is extremely difficult to judge. The fact is that until 1845 and 1846, when the Jewish religion was admitted to the benefit of the Toleration Act of 1688 and a second Act relieved 'Her Majesty's subjects from certain penalties and disabilities in regard to religious opinions', uncertainty prevailed and the Jews lived in a 'legal limbo'.[41] Earlier, for example in the 1744 case of Da Costa *v.* De Paz, Lord Hardwicke held that a bequest in favour of the maintenance of a *yeshivah* was 'not a good legacy'. He added that 'this is a bequest for the propagation of the Jewish religion; and though it is said that this is a part of our religion, yet the intent of this bequest must be taken to be in contradiction of the Christian religion, which is a part of the law of the land'. The Toleration Act (1688) Hardwicke confirmed, had rendered legal the religion of the Dissenters, 'which is not the case of the Jewish religion, that is not taken notice of by any law, but is barely connived at by the Legislature'.[42] Similarly, in the case of Isaac *v.* Gompertz (1783–6), annuities in favour of Jewish education and charitable welfare were allowed, but not those for the support and maintenance of a

---

[40] J. Haggard (ed.), *Reports of cases in the Consistory Court of London*, *I*, London, 1822, pp. 216–61, 324–36, p. 4.

[41] I have borrowed the phrase from I. Finestein, *Post-Emancipation Jewry: The Anglo-Jewish experience* (seventh Sacks lecture), Oxford, 1980, p. 3; Henriques, *Jews and the English Law*, pp. 171ff.

[42] Henriques, *Jews and the English Law*, pp. 19–21; see also G. H. Gordon, 'Blasphemy in English criminal law', *JLA*, V (1985), p. 94. This argument was also used to exclude Jewish children from the benefits of local educational charities; see the Bedford charity case cited in N. Bentwich, 'More Anglo-Jewish leading cases', *TJHSE*, XVI (1945–51), pp. 152–4.

synagogue.[43] In these uncertain and inconsistent circumstances, Anglo-Jewry created *faits accomplis*, consciously or otherwise, which the law of the land had eventually to take account of.

The Synagogues and the Hierarchy

'In England . . . Jewish self-government did not exist.'[44] This is true in the sense that there existed no corporate entity, recognized by the state, with a more or less defined sphere of influence and obligations (as in Berlin), or any Jewish authority with effective coercive power. The absence of any such entity or authority was co-terminous with the 'legal limbo' in which Anglo-Jewry found itself. But it is not true that Anglo-Jewry created no range of institutions wherewith to meet the demands of the Torah – synagogues, schools, charitable bodies, slaughterhouses, etc. These institutions owed their being to purely voluntary initiatives; but their very existence created an involuntary community. The response to the obligations created by the Torah simultaneously brought into being a body of people distinguished in one way or another from their Christian neighbours.

Of all these institutions the synagogues were unchallengeably of primordial importance. Anglo-Jewry was certainly not assiduous in its worship – none the less the synagogues, either separately or as a group, constituted a source of power that generated virtually all the major benevolent, educational and political institutions of the community.[45] A multitude of minor philanthropic bodies, no less than major institutions such as the Jews' Free School, the Shechita Board, the Board of Deputies and the Board of Guardians, all arose as the response of synagogal leadership to changing needs and circumstances.[46] This could be so because the synagogues enjoyed an existence through time, a more or less constant membership of the wealthy, a consistent income and, of course, prestige. (This, obviously, does not mean that certain synagogues did not decline and others thrive.)

The first synagogue of the resettlement was founded in 1656. It was

---

[43] Henriques, *Jews and the English Law*, p. 22; these, and other inconsistencies and uncertainties, are discussed in R. Routledge, 'The legal status of the Jews in England, 1190–1790', *Journal of Legal History*, V (1982), no. 2, pp. 91–124.

[44] Endelman, *The Jews of Georgian England*, p. 142.

[45] This applied as much in the provinces as in London. J. Rumney writes: 'the synagogue, once it was founded, became the centre of all activities, and round it clustered all the manifold activities of an organised and settled community. Charities, schools, burial grounds all came under its aegis' ('The economic and social development of the Jews in England, 1730–1860, Ph.D diss., London, 1933, p. 27).

[46] For more detailed description of these institutions, see pp. 97–120 below.

located in a house in Cree Church Lane in the City, and the following year a plot of land in Mile End, east London, was acquired for use as a burial ground.[47] When John Greenhalgh visited the synagogue in 1662 he found more than 'one hundred men apparently of affluence and the ladies very richly attired'.[48] These were the Sephardi pioneers of Anglo-Jewry and hailed from Holland, Portugal and Italy. They were engaged in overseas trade, importing and exporting a wide variety of merchandise – wine, cloth, sugar, fish, and diamonds (from India).[49] By 1701, the community had prospered sufficiently to establish a permanent synagogue, modelled in some respects on the Amsterdam synagogue of 1675, at Plough Yard in Bevis Marks, in the City of London.

In the meantime, in 1690, the Ashkenazim established their own synagogue. They were virtually excluded from the Sephardi. The division went so deep that in 1744 a prosperous West India merchant, Jacob Israel Bernal, who wished to marry an Ashkenazi lady, had first to secure permission from his fellow-elders.[50] The Ashkenazi synagogue stood in Duke's Place, in the City of London. It was known later as the Great Synagogue and stood at the heart of the London 'ghetto'. At the price of considerable friction and tension two further Ashkenazi synagogues were formed in the eighteenth century, by process of fission from the Great – in 1706 the Hambro' (in Fenchurch Street) and in 1762 the New (in Leadenhall Street).

A few years later, the Westminster (later Western) Synagogue was also founded, in the vicinity of the Strand. Its progenitor was Wolf Liepman, grandson of the Berlin court Jew.[51] At the end of the century, some conventicles or *ḥevrot*-type synagogues already existed in east London, and by 1870 there were about another twenty *ḥevrot*, some with an associated friendly society.[52] The establishment of the Hambro' synagogue – so named because its founders, mainly Ashkenazim from Hamburg, followed the

[47] W. Samuel, 'The first London synagogue of the re-settlement', *TJHSE*, X (1921–3); A. S. Diamond, 'The cemetery of the re-settlement', *TJHSE*, XIX (1955–9).

[48] Greenhalgh's letters are extracted in appendix I to Samuel's article in preceding note, pp. 49–57.

[49] Pollins, *Economic History*, pp. 44–5; see also Yogev, *Diamonds and Coral*, passim, and the review by H. E. S. Fisher in *TJHSE*, XXVII (1978–80), pp. 156–65.

[50] Picciotto, *Sketches*, p. 149. By the nineteenth century such marriages had become much more frequent (cf. *Bevis Marks Records*, III, London, 1973, p. 5).

[51] A. Barnett, *The Western Synagogue through Two Centuries, 1761–1961*, London, 1961, pp. 22, 28. See also p. 000 above.

[52] Endelman, *The Jews of Georgian England*, pp. 136ff.; C. Roth, 'The lesser London synagogues of the 18th century', *MJHSE*, III (1937), pp. 1–7; V. D. Lipman, 'Jewish settlement in the East End of London, 1840–1940', in A. Newman (ed.), *The Jewish East End, 1840–1939*, JHSE, 1981, p. 29.

Hamburg rite – provoked the most vehement opposition of the Great. The authorities there obtained from the aldermanic court in the City an injunction prohibiting its establishment. This was successfully defied and the new foundation, amidst much scandal and acrimony, eventually came into existence.[53] The whole struggle illustrated the inherent thrust, evident amongst Sephardim as much as Ashkenazim, towards a centralized structure of government. Symptomatic of this thrust was the attempt of the three new foundations, as soon as they themselves were securely established, to suppress the foundation of any further bodies.[54]

In its heyday the synagogue leadership assumed a comprehensive authority over the activities of its members and deployed a wide range of services. The ordinances (*Ascamot*) of the Sephardi congregation of Bevis Marks of the late seventeenth century, which consciously follow the model of Amsterdam and Venice, provide *inter alia* for a regular subscription and a form of turnover tax on income; they prohibit the establishment of 'any other congregation in this city in London, its districts and environs'; they gave the governing body, the *Mahamad*, 'authority and supremacy over everything, and no person shall rise in the Synagogue to reprobate the decisions which they may take', under pain of excommunication; they require the donation of charity (only to be dispensed under the authority of the *Mahamad*); they regulate the conduct of synagogue services; they require business and brokerage disputes to be arbitrated before the *Mahamad*; they forbid the consumption of all meat save that from animals examined and slaughtered by the congregation's designated officials; they disallow the printing of any books by any member without the express permission of the *Mahamad*; they likewise prohibit 'dispute or argument on matters of religion with Guim' (gentiles) who must also not be urged 'to follow our holy Law'; they also forbid any member to speak 'in these realms in the name of the Nation or general affairs thereof' – this right the *Mahamad* reserved to itself.[55]

Similar regulations governed the Ashkenazi communities.[56] They manifest the same impulse to impose strict communal discipline, both within

---

[53] Diamond, 'Problems' pp. 57ff. gives a graphic account of the whole unsavoury episode.

[54] C. Roth, *The Great Synagogue, London, 1690–1940*, London, 1950, pp. 277–8.

[55] *El Libro de los Acuerdos*, pp. 1ff. R. Jacob Sasportas was one of the signatories to the *Ascamot*.

[56] See, e.g., Roth, *Great Synagogue*, pp. 67ff; Barnett, *Western Synagogue*, pp. 26–7. These regulations no doubt account for the fact that R. Tevele Schiff of the Great Synagogue refused to convert Lord George Gordon to Judaism. He had to go to Birmingham for this purpose; cf. Israel Solomons, 'Lord George Gordon's conversion to Judaism', *TJHSE*, VII (1911–14), pp. 222–71.

and without the synagogue.[57] A sentiment of insecurity in the initial period of settlement undoubtedly contributed to this imperative.[58] But the same concern persisted into the second half of the eighteenth century, and also in the provinces. The ordinances of the important Portsmouth congregation of 1766, for example, demanded of its members that 'they live in strict accordance with Jewish law'; and, should a dispute arise amongst them, 'they must not dare to go to the non-Jewish tribunal, but it is to be settled by our congregation. If it should be a hard matter however, then they should bring it before R. Tevele (Schiff) HaCohen, Chief Rabbi of the Great Synagogue in London.' The penalty for infringement of the law was a fine, which, it appears, had frequently to be imposed.[59]

Save for the *hevrot*, the synagogues, both Sephardi and Ashkenazi, were organized in a centralized, hierarchic and oligarchic spirit.[60] Not only did the principal Sephardi and Ashkenazi synagogues – Bevis Marks and the Great – distinguish at the outset between full, privileged members and those who rented seats, but their subscription and other fees and dues were such as to exclude the poor even from renting a seat.[61] If the poor wished to attend the Great Synagogue, then those who were domestic servants were not to wear their masters' livery lest, according to Roth, they introduce a 'servile atmosphere'.[62] Moreover, the poor were confined to a less favoured area of the synagogue, near the entrance.[63] Only privileged members had the right to vote for, and be elected to, honorary office in the synagogue, whether Sephardi or Ashkenazi. There were normally five such officers (two or three wardens, a treasurer and/or a charity overseer, the latter having the authority to dispense specified weekly sums to the poor). The honorary officers were flanked by a group of seven which functioned in an

[57] Picciotto, *Sketches*, p. 131; Roth, *Great Synagogue*, p. 36; A. Hyamson, *The Sephardim of England*, London, 1951, p. 69.

[58] See, for example, the remarks of the Rev. the Haham Moses Gaster in his *History of the Ancient Synagogue of the Spanish and Portuguese Jews*, London, 1901, p. 16.

[59] Quoted by the Rev. I. S. Meisels in his 'The Jewish Congregation of Portsmouth (1766–1842)', *TJHSE*, VI (1907); cf. also Dr A. Weinberg, *Portsmouth Jewry, 1730s–1980s*, London, n.d., pp. 23ff.

[60] For the following I am largely indebted to V. D. Lipman, 'Synagogal organiz-ation in Anglo-Jewry, *JJS*, Vols. I–II (1959–60), pp. 80–93.

[61] See also Roth, *Great Synagogue*, pp. 54ff. Certain Ashkenazi synagogues also had a category of members known as 'guests' and 'the poor of the congregation'. They are described as 'the pauper and semi-pauper proletariat of unattached persons', ibid.

[62] Ibid., p. 70. This also applied to the Western Synagogue (A. Barnett, *Western Synagogue*, p. 61).

[63] Roth, *Great Synagogue*, p. 169.

advisory capacity and was generally composed of former honorary officers.

A further extension of authority grouped all former honorary officers in a self-perpetuating oligarchy which constituted the governing body of the congregation. This body – the *Mahamad* in the Sephardi synagogue and the Vestry in the Ashkenazi synagogues – enjoyed supreme power within its own congregation: 'a relatively small group of ex-honorary officers, perhaps twenty or thirty in number ... elected the new honorary officers from a list prepared by the serving honorary officers and sometimes the committee; and the list could comprise only the privileged members who had to buy their privileged membership and be admitted by vote of the governing body.'[64]   This is made abundantly clear in ordinance 58 of the Laws of the Great Synagogue: 'The Committee shall consist of the Honorary Officers and of seven others called "Sheva Tovei ha-ir" ["seven good men of the city" – that is, elders] to be elected by the Vestry, from amongst such members of their own body who have either served or paid fine for the office of Warden, Treasurer or Observer.'[65] Not until the middle of the nineteenth century were the first steps taken towards extending the basis of power; and by the end of the century the status of privileged membership was abolished and all seat-holders became entitled to vote for their respective governing bodies, in both the Ashkenazi and Sephardi congregations.[66] But although differential membership might give way to equality, the hereditary principle remained in force, even in new foundations.[67]

Rabbis and their Courts

The continuity in lay leadership necessarily entailed continuity in the exercise of power, to an extent that diminished rabbinical authority – which does not of course indicate that this exercise of power also necessarily departed from the dictates of the Torah. If there was a division of responsibility – as there undoubtedly was – both institutions, lay leadership and

[64] Lipman, 'Synagogal organization', p. 84. The same sort of division prevailed in provincial synagogues; see, e.g., the entries for Birmingham and Sheffield in A. Newman (ed.), *Provincial Jewry in Victorian Britain*, London, 1975.

[65] Laws of the Great Synagogue revised, London, 5623–1863, no. 58, p. 14. The 'seven good men of the city' is an institution that goes back to the medieval Rhineland *kehillah* (see above pp. 35ff).

[66] Lipman, 'Synagogal organization', pp. 87–8; see also A. Newman, *The United Synagogue, 1870–1970*, London, 1976, pp. 11, 32–3.

[67] See, e.g., Rev. E. Levine, *The History of the New West End Synagogue, 1879–1929*, Aldershot, 1929, p. 41.

rabbinate, were subject to the same dictates. However, the Portsmouth ordinance that 'a hard matter' be brought before the rabbi of the Great must not suggest that the latter took a significant role in the self-government of London Jewry. On the contrary, the ordinances of the Great Synagogue (1722) enunciate the wide-ranging dominion of lay officers. They reserved to the latter the right to adjudicate disputes among members; only when the defendant had failed three times to answer a congregational summons was the plaintiff authorized to turn to the civil court, no mention being made of the rabbinical *Bet Din* in this context. The rabbi was not to officiate at a marriage or divorce or intervene in a private quarrel without the sanction of the wardens.[68] Moreover, he lacked a major disciplinary sanction: 'It shall not be lawful for the Chief Rabbi to pronounce *niddui* or *herem* [excommunication] against any member of the Congregation, nor (without the consent of the Committee) to deprive any member of his religious rights in the Synagogue.'[69] The distribution of power in the Sephardi congregation was not essentially different.[70] The ecclesiastical authorities were made 'entirely dependent' on the civil, comments Picciotto.[71]

The integration of the rabbi into the structure of power was sometimes facilitated in London, as in Berlin, by family connections; in the early eighteenth century, for example, Moses Hart, one of the twelve licensed 'Jew-brokers' and lay head of the Great Synagogue, secured the appointment of his brother Aaron as rabbi of the synagogue.[72] In the Sephardi world, the marriage of the Haham Benjamin Artom in 1873 to a sister of Mrs Reuben Sassoon, whose husband was a member of the *Mahamad*, furnishes a parallel.[73]

But matters went further than mere integration. At the end of the eighteenth and in the early nineteenth centuries, this question arose: were chief rabbis necessary? In 1801, by a 20–13 vote the privileged members of the Hambro' synagogue rejected this necessity.[74] There was an interregnum of ten years between Schiff's death and the appointment in 1802 of his successor at the Great, R. Solomon Hirschell; and an interregnum of twenty years (1784–1804) before R. Raphael Meldola was appointed haham at Bevis Marks. In the former case R. Moses Myers of the New doubled as chief rabbi at the Great, though precedence remained with the head of

---

[68] Roth, *Great Synagogue*, pp. 68, 80, 108, 266.
[69] Laws of the Great Synagogue, no. 159, p. 38. (*Niddui* is a less extreme form of excommunication than *herem*.)
[70] See, e.g., the scope of the *Mahamad's* decision-making powers above p. 86.
[71] Picciotto, *Sketches*, p. 154, n. 39.
[72] Roth, *Great Synagogue*, pp. 34–5; for Berlin, see above p. 61.
[73] Hyamson, *The Sephardim of England*, p. 343.
[74] Endelman, *The Jews of Georgian England*, p. 143.

the rabbinical court, R. Zalman Ansell.[75] In the Sephardi instance, the interval has been ascribed to the claim made by the lay leaders for 'powers also in areas that were not theirs'.[76]

It follows, therefore, that the areas of lay and rabbinical concern were differentiated. Very broadly speaking, they followed the same pattern as in Berlin, the laymen concerning themselves with 'political' matters and the rabbis with 'religious'. But this is a very fluid distinction – for example, was the donation in 1793 of £20 to build a synagogue in Charleston political or religious? In the eighteenth century the correspondence of the *Mahamad* of Bevis Marks reveals the Sephardi community's concern with the relief of Jews in Jamaica following on earthquakes in 1691 and, in the 1730s, disproportionate taxation imposed on the Jews there; discrimination against Jews in Barbados seeking British naturalization, and relief following a hurricane in 1781; assistance in finding a cantor for the congregation Shearith Israel of New York; and donations towards building a synagogue in Newport, Rhode Island. The congregation maintained separate funds for the ransoming of prisoners (from the Knights of Malta, Algerian pirates and the Turks) and for the support of the holy cities of Jerusalem, Hebron and Tiberias. Bevis Marks also co-operated with the London Ashkenazim in alleviating distress in Poland in 1710 and in trying to avert the expulsion in 1745 of the Jews from Bohemia (for whom a sum of nearly £900 was raised).[77]

The range of rabbinical activity was comparatively limited. The principal reason for this, amongst both Sephardim and Ashkenazim, was their resort to 'gentile courts'. The *parnassim* of Bevis Marks employed a solicitor, Philip Carteret Webb, to act for the congregation and sometimes also on behalf of individuals. Subject to his advice, sometimes after taking counsel's opinion, a variety of civil cases was dealt with. They frequently involved disputes arising out of wills, guardianships, bankruptcies and the disposition of property and estates.[78] This state of affairs applied in the 1720s and 1730s. A later case from London stands out by reason of its future ramifications. It is undated but presumably emanates from R. Tevele Schiff's court at the Great Synagogue – certainly some time before 1793 – and may well be the first of its type. It concerned the case of a London Jew who died of gallstones after an operation: was it then permissible for the surgeons

[75] A. B. Levy, *The 200-year-old New Synagogue, 1760–1960*, London, 1960, pp. 12–13; H. Simons, *Forty Years a Chief Rabbi*, London, 1980, p. 13.

[76] M. Beneyahu, 'Vikuhim ba-kehilah ha-sephardit ve-ha-portugesit be-London', *Michael*, X (1986), p. 31 (Heb. Sec.).

[77] All the above is based on Barnett, 'Correspondence of the Mahamad', pp. 1–50.

[78] See the material cited in Diamond, 'Problems', pp. 41ff.

to dissect the corpse in the interests of medical knowledge or did this amount to desecration of the corpse and thus conflict with the law? The dispute was first submitted to R. Leib Fischeles, who passed it on to his relation R. Ezekiel Landau, chief rabbi of Prague. Landau summed up the issues pro and contra and concluded with a heavily qualified endorsement of the practice of dissection.[79] In the first four decades of the nineteenth century, it is clear that R. Solomon Hirschell, chief rabbi at the Great from 1802 or 1803 to 1842, had very few civil cases to deal with. 'Every dispute, even between brother and brother, comes before the Magistrate and Law courts', declared Solomon Bennett, Hirschell's critic.[80]

Most of the cases that came before Hirschell's court concerned questions of conversion and personal status.[81] He had to deal with some fifteen divorce cases annually.[82] These often involved Jewish convicts or Jews sentenced to transportation to Australia.[83] Their spouses were granted 'conditional divorces', whereby the divorce took immediate effect, provided the 'divorced wife' simultaneously undertook not to remarry during the term of her 'husband's' sentence. The couple could then be re-united or the 'wife' become free to remarry should the divorced 'husband' not return.[84] Hirschell also sought to safeguard the position of married women whose husbands were serving overseas against Napoleon.[85] He administered an oath to a widow in substantiation of her claim against the Phoenix Assurance Company.[86] He arranged for the burial of a child, born to a Jewish father and his non-Jewish 'common-law wife', in a Jewish cemetery.[87] He also permitted the circumcision of a male child, born to a non-Jewish woman, who had been converted during her pregnancy, to be performed on the Sabbath, thus over-riding the Sabbath.[88] The court exercised its disciplinary powers when it imposed penalties on a Jew who sold non-kosher cheese to fellow Jews; and on traders at Sheerness who boarded a ship on the Sabbath

[79] *Noda Biyehuda*, no. 210.

[80] Quoted Duschinsky, *The Rabbinate of the Great Synagogue*, p. 148.

[81] R. Jacob Zimmels, 'Psakim u-Tshuvot mi-bet dino shel R. Shlomo bar Zvi [Rabbi Solomon Hirschell]', in *Essays presented to Chief Rabbi Israel Brodie*, London, 1967 (Heb. Sec.), pp. 219ff.

[82] Simons, *Forty Years*, p. 45.

[83] About 400 Jewish convicts were transported overseas during Hirschell's rabbinate (Simons, *Forty years*, p. 77).

[84] E.g. Zimmels, 'Psakim u-Tshuvot', no. 2, p. 223, and no. 13, p. 232.

[85] Simons, *Forty Years*, p. 34. (In the absence of further information I presume this also means the granting of conditional divorces, as in the case of spouses of convicts transported overseas: see preceding fn.).

[86] Zimmels, 'Psakim u-Tshuvot', no. 6, p. 226.

[87] Ibid., no. 16, p. 234.

[88] Ibid., no. 9, pp. 228–9.

for the purpose of collecting their debts from the sailors.[89] Hirschell conducted a very exhaustive correspondence on behalf of ritual slaughterers and cantors, and about ritual matters, with communities in North America (Philadelphia, Charleston, New York), Australia and Tasmania as well as Eastern Europe. Because of the expense this correspondence entailed, Hirschell secured certain postal concessions from Francis Freely of the Post Office Board.[90]

It is clear that Hirschell could in fact only exercise authority over the poorer members of Anglo-Jewry. And his critic Bennett did not fail to point this out:

> seeing that the Royal Exchange, the Stock Exchange, and the coffee-houses adjoining are all filled with Jew-merchants transacting business on the *Sabbath* and *holy days quite public.* The Rabbi is also aware that the most part of the Jew merchants transact business in their *counting and ware-houses on the Sabbath* days without exception; that Jewish shop-keepers many of them keep their shops open on the Sabbath day. I have often seen myself Jewish picture dealers of pretended piety, furniture and clothes-sellers, attend public sales on the Sabbath day, all without blushing before the Christian community . . . and yet our pious grand Rabbi never rebukes the generality or any individuals for doing so. And why? We have sufficient reason to conjecture, because it would not answer so well his purpose, or because his followers would look upon him with a frown.[91]

[89] Ibid., nos 14 and 5, pp. 233 and 225–6. (Outside London, of the eleven earliest Jewish communities, eight were established in seaports, including the three main naval towns of Portsmouth, Plymouth and Chatham: see G. Green, 'Anglo-Jewish trading connections with officers and seamen of the Royal Navy, 1740–1820', *TJHSE*, XXIX [1982–6].

[90] Simons, *Forty Years*, pp. 55, 66, 75, 89.

[91] Solomon Bennett, 'The present reign of the synagogue of Duke's Place displayed, London, 1818', quoted A. Barnett, 'Solomon Bennett: artist, Hebraist, controversialist (1761–1838)', *TJHSE* XVII (1951–2), pp. 91–111; see also Duschinsky, *The Rabbinate of the Great Synagogue*, p. 149. Hirschell left a personal fortune of £14,000, though his salary was £250 p.a. His biographer writes: 'he was known to have been a fine mathematician, and it must therefore be assumed that he applied his financial acumen successfully to speculate on the Stock Exchange. His close friendship with such City giants as the Keysers, Goldsmids, and Rothschilds would have proved advantageous to him in the City of London money markets. The mention in his Will of his holdings in English and foreign bonds bears out this supposition as being the source of his wealth' (Simons, *Forty Years*, p. 102). One

Later in the century, Nathan Marcus Adler, successor to Hirschell, dealt mainly with cases of divorce, missing husbands and remarriage – at least during his early years in London. These cases involved immigrants to England from Eastern Europe.[92]

The Cousinhood and the Nineteenth Century

By the end of the eighteenth and beginning of the nineteenth centuries, the original two synagogues of the resettlement – Bevis Marks and the Great – had grown only to five. None the less this base proved strong enough to create and support a network of philanthropic and political institutions, which in many respects prefigured the future shape of Anglo-Jewry as a whole. As earlier, the Ashkenazi and Sephardi synagogues sought to make their respective congregations co-terminous with the actual community and to control their members' intercourse with the Christian world. But the threat and even the reality of the *herem* – excommunication – had less and less force.[93] The synagogues of course remained purely voluntary – as did adherence to the community in general – and the Ashkenazim could no more silence a dissident critic of R. Hirschell such as Solomon Bennett than the Sephardim could prevent the defection of a Samson Gideon or, later, an Isaac Disraeli or the economist David Ricardo.

Thus the structure of the eighteenth-century community continued into the nineteenth. But it was modified in three ways: first, by the consolidation of what Finestein has designated 'the Anglo-Jewish pluto-aristocracy' and Bermant, with equal felicity, 'the cousinhood'.[94] The two designations complement each other admirably in that consanguinity and wealth went hand in hand. This alliance was fortified by another feature characteristic of the nineteenth century. Hitherto, writes one keen observer of the Anglo-Jewish scene, 'many Jews realised large fortunes; few retained them beyond one or two generations.'[95] In the new century wealth enjoyed greater longevity. This happy circumstance enabled the 'cousinhood' to monopolize all major communal positions. An example from 1870: in that year Sir

---

of Hirschell's sons, R. David Berliner, became a banker in Jerusalem – cf. A. Blumberg, 'The British and Prussian consuls at Jerusalem and the strange last will of Rabbi Hirschell', in *Zionism*, I (Spring 1980), pp. 1–8.

[92] S. Singer, 'Orthodox Judaism in early Victorian London, 1840–1858', Ph.D thesis, Yeshiva University, New York, 1981, p. 31.

[93] Endelman, *The Jews of Georgian England*, ch. 4 passim.

[94] Finestein, *Post-Emancipation Jewry*, p. 5; C. Bermant, *The Cousinhood – the Anglo-Jewish Gentry*, London, 1971.

[95] Picciotto, *Sketches*, p. 167.

Anthony de Rothschild became first president of the newly formed United Synagogue whilst Lionel Louis Cohen was president of the Board of Guardians – both men were descended from Levi Barent Cohen, the former being his grandson, the latter his great-grandson. The treasurer of the Board of Guardians was Baron Ferdinand de Rothschild, who was married to a niece of Sir Anthony. Sir Moses Montefiore, president of the Board of Deputies, was uncle to Sir Anthony, who had himself married a niece of Sir Moses.[96] As always the path to national communal advancement began in the synagogue: I take at random the seven Sephardi representatives on the Board of Deputies in 1854, of whom six had also belonged (or would belong) to the *Mahamad* (the supreme governing body of the Sephardi synagogue), namely Sir Moses Montefiore (1815), Judah Aloof (1842), Isaac Foligno (1844), Nathaneel Lindo (1845), Joseph Sebag (1853) and Solomon Sequerra (1856).

One estimate puts the number of inter-related ruling families at some 200, another at 20-odd.[97] But this apparent discrepancy is easily resolved: where did one family end and another begin? The families were not homogeneous in either their political or religious outlook – some were Tory, some Liberal; some Ashkenazi, some Sephardi; some traditionalist in religion, some reform. But their combined influence necessarily reinforced the centralized direction of communal life, all the more so as the bulk of the cousinhood derived its wealth from a limited range of finance-based occupations: private banking, insurance, bullion-broking, loan-contracting and stock-broking.

Wealth, of course, provided the leisure required for communal service. But it also had to be allied with a readiness to take up what Lionel Louis Cohen, lauded as 'the ablest communal administrator in Anglo-Jewish history', called 'our hard, dry and monotonous work'.[98] The ethos of *richesse oblige* was not in fact lacking. 'Service in the communal organisation was in my youth a privilege', wrote Radcliffe Salaman in 1954.[99]

The second factor to characterize institutional life in the nineteenth

---

[96] Adapted and simplified from Todd Endelman, 'Communal solidarity among the Jewish elite of Victorian London', *Victorian Studies* (Spring 1985), pp. 495–6; for other examples, see below p. 101. The Board of Guardians is discussed below, pp. 117ff.

[97] V. D. Lipman, 'The Anglo-Jewish community in Victorian society', in D. Noy and I. Ben-Ami (eds), *Studies in the Cultural Life of the Jews in England*, Jerusalem, 1975, p. 153; R. Salaman, 'Whither Lucien Wolf's Anglo-Jewish community?', *JHSE*, London, 1954, p. 19.

[98] Quoted I. Finestein, 'Anglo-Jewish Opinion during the struggle for emancipation', *TJHSE*, XX (1959–61), p. 133.

[99] Ibid., p. 20; see also Endelman, 'Communal solidarity', p. 506.

century was its modest conversion into an agency of the state – in other words, the state made certain demands of the institution to which the latter had to conform, forfeiting therefore a degree of freedom. But the relationship was reciprocal, so that, in its turn, the institution was guaranteed a degree of recognition. In the long run this was a consequence of the successful campaign waged for political emancipation in the 1830s–50s. It proved impossible to combine the prerogatives of full citizenship with the maintenance, in all respects, of a separate legal enclave. The operation of the Aliens Acts of 1793, 1798 and 1803 during the Napoleonic wars provided an early intimation of the changing relationship. The synagogues acted as intermediaries, registering the particulars of Jewish aliens (who would otherwise have been liable to imprisonment and transportation) and transmitting the information to the authorities.[100] But the Board of Deputies became the main agent of the state *vis-à-vis* Anglo-Jewry and also the latter's main agent *vis-à-vis* the state. Therefore, although its actual legal standing had a very narrow base, it is not fanciful to see the Board in the same light, *toutes proportions gardées*, as the legally recognized and constituted Jewish community in Prussia (under the law of 1847).[101] It also had some of the characteristics of the French Consistoire Central, in acting as a channel for government policy.

The third feature characteristic of the nineteenth century was the growth of combined Sephardi–Ashkenazi endeavour. No doubt the decline of the Sephardim helped to make this co-operation possible. In 1800 Bevis Marks had a membership of 242; in 1841, 193.[102] After the death of Raphael Meldola in 1828 no haham was appointed until 1866. The number of members subscribing and offering to the congregation declined from 222 in 1837 to 161 in 1848.[103]

The bearing of these new features of the Anglo-Jewish scene would be irrelevant had Anglo-Jewry succumbed to the messianism of the early nineteenth century. This took hold of certain Jewish communities in parts of Eastern Europe and the Ottoman Empire. It was fed from manifold sources: the upheaval of the revolutionary and Napoleonic wars, the intensified hardships of the Jews in Russia (such as the conscription of

---

[100] Picciotto, *Sketches*, p. 234; Roth, *Great Synagogue*, p. 203, fn. 1. V. D. Lipman in 'Migration and Settlement', *JHSE* (1971), pp. 47–58, gives a list of the 138 aliens registered at Bevis Marks, 1803.

[101] See W. Breslauer, 'Vergleichende Bemerkungen zur Gestaltung des jüdischen Organisationslebens in Deutschland und England', in H. Tramer (ed.), *In Zwei Welten*, Tel-Aviv, 1962, pp. 87–96.

[102] Simons, *Forty Years*, p. 27.

[103] See G. H. Whitehill, 'Introduction to Bevis Marks Records, III', *JHSE* (1973), pp. 3–4.

Jewish boys into the Russian army in 1827), Mehemet Ali's invasion of Palestine in 1832, etc., to say nothing of a messianic prediction in the mystical classic, the *Zohar*, that identified the calendrical equivalent of 1840 as the year of the messianic advent. R. Solomon Hirschell strongly disapproved of the movement: 'would that the men of our covenant who do not have the strength to be content with what they have in the Holy Land still lived outside the Land and did not "stir up love till it please" [Song of Songs, 2:7].'[104]

The movement was represented in England by Joseph Crool, who was born in Hungary, came to England at the turn of the eighteenth century, held posts at congregations in Manchester and Nottingham and eventually taught Hebrew at the University of Cambridge in the absence of the Regius Professor of Hebrew. He was not only a vigorous and articulate opponent of missionary work amongst Jews but also propounded a Jewish version of the theory of the Fifth Monarchy. Crool at first expected the restoration of the Jews to take place in 1830, but he later advanced the date to 1840. In two pamphlets of 1829 Crool contrasted the four empires of the world – 'empires of destruction, of misery, of slaughter, of cruelties' – with the coming fifth empire. This would be of 'a different kind . . . no Satan, no enemy, no sin, no war, no death, no sickness, no sorrows, no weeping, no crying – but joy and gladness shall reign in the world . . . In short the Fifth Empire will be heaven on earth.' Crool continues: 'by a particular calculation of my own, it appears to me that the following ten years will produce strange things in the world, and it further appears that all things will be accomplished by the year 5600 of the creation of the world [1840 by the Christian calendar]'.[105] In the second pamphlet Crool summoned the Christian world to repent of its treatment of the Jews: 'eleven years is only a short time; yet in that time great things may be done. Make haste, lest you repent when it will be rather too late, and particularly when you know not whether you are not one of the last generation.'[106]

In the 1830s no more than in the 1660s did Anglo-Jewry give any credence to messianic hopes and eschatological prophecies. On the contrary, Crool was not only reproved by the traditionalist R. Hirschell but also rebutted by the reformer Francis Henry Goldsmid: 'the Jewish religion', Goldsmid wrote, 'leaves the period when her predictions shall be

---

[104] For the whole picture, cf. A. Morgenstern, *Meshihiyut ve-yishuv Eretz-Yisrael*, Jerusalem, 1985, esp. ch. 2. Hirschell is quoted ibid., p. 107. This is one of the passages interpreted as an adjuration to Israel not to return prematurely en masse to the Promised Land – see R. Jose b. Hanina in TB Ket., 110b–111a, and below, p. 164.

[105] Joseph Crool, *The Fifth Empire*, London, 1829, pp. 72–3.

[106] Joseph Crool, *The Last Generation*, London, 1829, p. 23.

accomplished wholly indefinite – because the devout Jew has no greater reason for supposing that the re-establishment of his race in Palestine will take place during the next twenty, than that it be delayed to the end of the next one thousand years.'[107]

Crool had no following. He was at best a marginal individual. He was quite unable to halt the movement towards the restructuring of Anglo-Jewish life.

Organs of Self-government

A first token of the new community showed itself in 1804 when what came to be known as the London Board of Schehitah was formed. This body supervised the provision and distribution of ritually slaughtered (kosher) meat in England and authorized slaughterers to operate throughout the British empire. The Board is of note on two accounts: first, because it was of synagogal origin; second, because it brought together the Ashkenazi and Sephardi congregations in a common enterprise. Previously both congregations had separately organized the supply of kosher meat (although there had been attempts to co-operate in 1745 and in 1792).[108] But in 1804 a conference of five representatives from Bevis Marks and three from each of the three principal Ashkenazi synagogues (the Great was represented by Baron Lyon de Symons) resolved that the four congregations agree to work together in 'adopting and supporting a plan for the better regulating the *Shehita,* and more effectively securing kishrut [sic] in the meat to be eaten by Jews under the sole direction of the Bet Din and Haham'.[109] The profits of the Board's operations, derived from a levy on each animal slaughtered, were divided equally amongst the four constituent synagogues. Their trustees administered these funds. R. Hirschell's particular role was to authorize the slaughterers practising under the Board's aegis, and during the years 1822–42 he authorized some 150, hailing mainly from Poland, Russia and Germany. They functioned in London and virtually all the provincial and Scottish towns and cities with a Jewish population. Also overseas: in 1829 Aryeh b. Jacob Hazan was licensed to practise his craft in Jamaica.[110]

On the whole Anglo-Jewry eschewed direct and public entry into the national political realm. From 1688 and at least until 1819, those members

---

[107] F. H. Goldsmid, *Arguments Advanced against the Enfranchisement of the Jews,* London, 1831, pp. 10–11.

[108] A. M. Hyamson, *The London Board for Schechita, 1804–1954,* London, 1954, pp. 7ff.

[109] Ibid., p. 11.

[110] Duschinsky, *The Rabbinate of the Great Synagogue,* p. 117 and pp. 264–73.

of the Sephardi congregation who took part in political matters or voted in any political contest exposed themselves to the threat of excommunication.[111] Similarly, in 1664, 1785 and 1831 the Ascamot of Bevis Marks repeatedly prohibited the printing of books without the express permission of the *Mahamad*, 'it being one of the principal points on which depend our union and preservation, that there should be no dispute on matters of religion, between us and the people of this country, and that we should not enter into controversy on reasons of state, from which, beside the offense which they generally occasion, more disastrous consequences may result'.[112]

But this was perfectly compatible with action when particular Jewish interests were at stake – as they undoubtedly were in the 1740s and 1750s. In 1738 publicity was given to a decree of 1271 prohibiting the acquisition of land by Jews; in 1744 (in Da Costa *v.* De Paz) a bequest in favour of a *yeshivah* was ruled invalid, the Christian religion being 'part of the law of the land' (see above p. 83); in 1746 a bill that would have facilitated the naturalization of Jews failed, by only two votes, in the Irish House of Lords.[113] And as a constant aggravation, there was the limitation of the number of 'Jew-brokers' to twelve and the inability to conduct retail business in the City of London.

In 1746, therefore, the *Mahamad* secured the adoption by the Sephardi elders of a resolution to appoint a committee 'to make use of any opportunity that there may be for the benefit of our Nation, and recommend them to take, in case of necessity, in time the advice of the best legal authorities of the realm, and power is given to them to call to their assistance any person of our Nation'. Although the 'Senhores Deputados' were required to keep a minute book, they were also assured that they would never be called on to produce it. They were to act on majority rule.[114] A 'committee of diligence' of five leading City merchants and Sephardi notables was then appointed. Benjamin Mendes da Costa took the presidency.[115]

The first test of the committee came in 1753 in relation to the 'Jew-Bill'. This would have made it easier for foreign-born merchants to become naturalized British subjects and also had favourable implications for the status of native-born Jews and their right to own landed property.[116] The

[111] Gaster, *History of the Ancient Synagogue*, p. 88.

[112] N. Laski, *The Laws and Charities of the Spanish and Portuguese Jews Congregation of London*, London, 1952, pp. 102–3.

[113] L. Hyman, *The Jews of Ireland*, London/Jerusalem, 1972, pp. 46–7.

[114] Quoted and translated Hyamson, *Sephardim*, p. 125.

[115] For an interesting account of the rise and decline of this family, see N. Perry, 'La chute d'une famille sefardie', *Dix-Huitième Siècle*, XIII (1981), pp. 11–25.

[116] Liberles, 'The Jews and their bill', pp. 29–35; C. Roth, *A History of the Jews in England*, 3rd edn, Oxford, 1978, p. 214.

'committee of diligence' actively employed the services of Philip Carteret Webb, attorney, antiquary and Whig politician. Through him payments were channelled to House of Commons clerks 'and others in official positions'.[117] Joseph Salvador, of the Jessurun Rodrigues family, first Jewish director of the East India Company and later loan underwriter to the government in the Seven Years War, was also active in the cut and thrust of pamphlet and polemic. To no avail – swift defeat in 1754 followed success in 1753.[118]

Not until 1760 did a more or less formal body composed of both Ashkenazim and Sephardim come into existence. The precise occasion was the latter's presentation of a dutiful address to George III on his accession. The Ashkenazim objected to this independent action, proposing that 'each Nation should communicate to the other what they were doing in public affairs.' By way of sequel the Sephardim resolved in January 1761 that 'Whenever any publick affair should offer that may Interest the Two Nations We will on our part Communicate to the Committee of the Dutch Jews Synagogues what we think proper should be Done. And that we desire the said Gentlemen may do the same.'[119] 'Public affair' must be construed in a limited sense, as applying only to such matters as affected the interests of Jews. Any intervention in national 'public affairs' would have been utterly at odds with the Sephardi tradition and doctrine of political passivity.[120] The line here was drawn as early as 1763: during George III's negotiations in Paris with the American colonies, the six Sephardi deputies, headed by Joseph Salvador, held back from sending an address of congratulation to George III on the conclusion of peace: 'peace or war being political concerns, addressing would be taking a part in matters we ought to avoid', it was held. Only 'when the subject relates to the King's person or family' would an address be fitting.[121]

On the other hand, 'public affairs' as applying to Jews were construed in a very broad sense. This became all the more true when, in 1805, deputies from the three Ashkenazi congregations were invited to join their *confrères* from Bevis Marks 'for the purpose of watching all acts of Parliament, Acts of government, Laws, Libels, Addresses or whatever else may

[117] Hyamson, *Sephardim*, p. 128, n.1.

[118] For a full account of this episode see T. W. Perry, *Public Opinion, Propaganda and Politics in 18th Century England*, Cambridge, Mass., 1962; for Salvador, see M. Woolf, 'Joseph Salvador, 1716–1786', *TJHSE*, xxi (1968), pp. 104–37.

[119] C. Roth (ed.), *Anglo-Jewish Letters, 1158–1917*, London, 1938, no. LXVII, p. 148.

[120] See above p. 86.

[121] Minute Book 1, November, 1760–April, 1828, p. 18b.

affect the body of Jews'.[122] But this broad concern is already apparent from the record of the late eighteenth and early nineteenth centuries, when deputies met very infrequently – on an average about once every decade. Their activities merged imperceptibly with those that the Sephardim on their own initiative had already been engaged in. Thus in 1766, deputies addressed a petition to the Duke of Richmond, 'one of his Majesty's Principal Secretaries of State', to secure for the Jews of Port Mahon (Minorca) permission to re-establish a place of worship such as they had enjoyed before the island's capture by France; in the invasion scare of 1779 congregants were advised to join 'such loyal associations as may be formed'; in 1805, deputies demanded from the editor of the *St James Chronicle* an apology and retraction of an anti-Jewish libel, on threat of prosecution (which was not in fact proceeded with); and the following year they took up the case of the conversion of Mrs Moss and her five children by the London Missionary Society.[123] In 1829 a petition was prepared for presentation to the House of Lords, seeking relief from the political and civil disabilities under which Jews laboured. In this connection the land question reappeared when the deputies invited Nathan Meyer Rothschild and Isaac Lyon Goldsmid to their session on 16 April 1829. The former told the eleven deputies present that the petition should also ask for 'the full protection in holding and conveying of Landed Property and etc. He also strenuously advised that for the present not a single observation should be published in the daily Papers on the Subject, being convinced that any Controversy would prove fatal to the object in view.'[124]

The Board originated in the synagogue and by virtue of this fact reproduced the same socio-economic structure. Moses Montefiore, for example,

[122] Ibid., p. 28b.

[123] The above is based on C. Emanuel, *A Century and a Half of Jewish History*, London, 1910, pp. 5–16; see also Minute Book 2, March 1829–January 1838, pp. 11b, 27b, 29b.

[124] Minute Book 2, March 1829–January 1838, pp. 8–9; Emanuel, *A Century and a Half*, pp. 15ff. The prime minister, the Duke of Wellington, with whom Rothschild had been in contact, proved unsympathetic to the petition, explaining through an intermediary that he had no wish to create further hostility to the government following on the controversy already generated by the Catholic Emancipation Act of 1829 (Emanuel, *A Century and a Half*, pp. 24 ff.). Jews in fact *did* own land and evidently with good title. Chief Justice Lord Ellenborough would hardly have bought Abraham Goldsmid's estate at Roehampton otherwise. But Benjamin Goldsmid, brother to Abraham, chose to register his property in the name of an employee; and in 1830 when Moses Montefiore wanted to purchase an estate at Ramsgate he was unable to and had to rent the property for three years (Perry, *Public Opinion*, pp. 7, 11; A. Gilam, *The Emancipation of the Jews in England, 1830–1860*, New York/London, 1982, pp. 10–11; Liberles, 'The Jews and their bill', p. 34).

graduated, as it were, from his position as president of the Sephardi congregation (1818) to his election as president of the deputies (1835). His immediate predecessor was his maternal uncle, Moses Mocatta, who had earlier sponsored Montefiore's membership of the stock exchange; and when Montefiore finally retired in 1874 at the age of ninety, he was succeeded by three nephews in turn: Joseph Mayer Montefiore (1874), Arthur Cohen (1880) and Joseph Sebag-Montefiore (1895). Moreover, there was a tendency for the cousinhood to extend its influence to provincial synagogues, when these came to elect deputies. As late as about 1900 Redcliffe Salaman, an outlying member of the cousinhood, received 'a charming letter' from Leopold de Rothschild. The letter suggested that 'I should take an active part in communal affairs and should join the Board of Deputies, to which end he would arrange that I should sit as a representative of a small provincial town, which he named.'[125]

The Board meanwhile slightly regularized its procedure in 1817 by authorizing any five deputies to summon a meeting independently of the president's right.[126] In 1835 it acquired its first constitution, 'convinced that it would be of essential advantage to the interests of the Jews of Britain, that in all matters touching their political welfare they should be represented by one Body, and inasmuch as the general Body of Deputies have long been recognised as their representatives, it is highly desirable for the general good that all the British Jews should so acknowledge them'. The constitution provided for the elections of deputies every five years from the main London synagogues and those other 'Congregations as were of sufficient size to merit them'. The constitution authorized deputies 'to adopt such measures as they may deem proper' to achieve their objects, defined a quorum, apportioned its expenses amongst the synagogues and determined voting procedure.[127] At this time the Board had twenty-two deputies. Later the number of deputies varied considerably. In 1853 there were fifty-eight of whom twenty-six were elected by six London synagogues and thirty-two by twenty-eight provincial synagogues; in 1859 the fifty-eight were more than halved to twenty-five; in 1883, twenty-seven deputies represented fourteen London synagogues and eighteen represented eighteen provincial synagogues.[128]

[125] Salaman, 'Whither Lucien Wolf's', p. 20.

[126] Minute Book 1, pp. 13, 15.

[127] Ibid., 2, pp. 94ff. (11 May 1835).

[128] A. Newman, *The Board of Deputies of British Jews, 1760–1985*, London, 1987, pp. 15ff. For a time in mid-century the Board tolerated a system of 'rotten boroughs' whereby provincial synagogues 'sold' their representation to wealthy Londoners, who paid the provincial synagogue's affiliation fees and became its elected deputies (Stuart Cohen, 'Sir Moses Montefiore and Anglo-Jewry', Proceedings of the 9th

In 1837 the Board acquired a salaried secretary;[129] and in 1838 the Board recommended to its synagogues that all seat-holders (not only the privileged) be entitled to vote for deputies.[130] Not until 1853 were the proceedings of the Board made accessible to the press, although this had been urged since 1844.[131]

In May 1836 the deputies resolved to inform the chancellor of the exchequer that they were 'the only official channel of communication for the secular and political interests of the Jews'.[132] In December this resolution was communicated to the congregations, which were 'invited to entrust their political Interests to us as recognised representatives of the British Jews'.[133] In effect the government recognized this status without demur; in the same year, pursuant to the Marriage Act of 1835, it was enacted that the Registrar-General was to 'furnish marriage registers to every person whom the President for the time being of the London Committee of Deputies of the British Jews should certify in writing to be secretary of a synagogue in England of persons professing the Jewish religion'.[134]

The cousinhood dominated the deputies, and by virtue of this fact it might be supposed that their own class interests would be of primary concern. This was not so. Deputies understood 'the secular and political interests' of Anglo-Jewry in a wide sense, as embracing those of all classes of Jews, particularly their religious welfare. In 1841 the Board obliged the *Tablet* journal to retract a libellous accusation of murder against the Jews of Damascus; in 1842 it intervened with the Poor Law Commissioners on behalf of the Jewish poor 'whose religious scruples prevented them from entering the workhouse'; it could not secure the exemption of Jews from the operation of the Poor Law Act, only an assurance of goodwill from the Poor Law Commissioners. Also in 1842, following representations made by Moses Montefiore to Sir Robert Peel, synagogues were put 'in the same position with all other places of worship' in regard to a proposed income tax; in 1843 proposed educational clauses of the Factory Bill were abandoned following a meeting between the Board and Lord John Russell; in 1847

World Congress of Jewish Studies, Division B, Jerusalem, 1986, III, pp. 128–9). Thus, in 1854, of the total of thirty-two provincial deputies, eleven lived in London (N. Grizzard, 'The provinces and the Board, 1851–1901', in Newman, *Provincial Jewry in Victorian Britain).*

[129] Minute Book, 2, p. 114.

[130] Ibid., p. 135ff.

[131] I. Finestein, 'The uneasy Victorian: Montefiore as communal leader', in Sonia and V.D. Lipman (eds), *The Century of Moses Montefiore*, Oxford, 1985, pp. 51, 54.

[132] Minute Book 2, pp. 94, 105.

[133] Ibid., pp. 109–10.

[134] Emanuel, *A Century and a Half*, p. 26.

deputies, on behalf of Louis Nathan, president of the Jewish congregation of Hobart Town, Van Dieman's Land (later Tasmania), took up the case of a Jewish girl of fourteen forcibly converted to Christianity; and later in 1847 the Board unsuccessfully attempted to secure for the Jewish congregation of Sydney a share in the government's grant for ministers of religion. In 1872 the Board formed a committee to consider the religious welfare of Jewish children at industrial schools or reformatories where they might be forced to conform to 'religious discipline imposed upon inmates belonging to this denomination'; also in 1872 it was resolved to speak to the Home Secretary to secure exemption from Sabbath and festival labour for Jewish prisoners in Wandsworth Gaol (as was the case in all other prisons).[135]

The deputies, clearly, were anything but a revolutionary body. They worked strictly within the status quo and it might well be argued that here the activities of the cousinhood were irrelevant to the besetting problem of Anglo-Jewry – its poverty. But this argument would overlook the effort made by the deputies to secure governmental aid for education – the means to economic advancement[136] – and also the part taken in this respect by other agencies of the cousinhood, such as the Jews' Free School and the Board of Guardians.[137]

But if broader struggles were disregarded, this did not of course exclude their exploitation when those struggles succeeded. Take the example of political emancipation: Montefiore and, under his sway, the deputies held aloof from the struggle, on religious grounds, but once it succeeded and Jews, from 1858, took their seats as Members of Parliament, Montefiore perceived how this might be turned to the Board's advantage. In 1868 he toyed with the idea of admitting those Members of Parliament who were Jewish to *ex officio* membership of the deputies, 'as the best medium of expressing the sentiments of the Board in the House of Commons'.[138] This was never proceeded with. Its nearest approximation was a conference in 1910 with Jewish Members of Parliament over the provisions of a bill regulating shop opening hours. This would, had it been left unaltered, have adversely affected the interests of Jewish traders.[139]

Abroad also, the deputies, by virtue of the strength that accrued to them as a British body, took steps to defend Jewish welfare; and again they enjoyed the good offices of the British government. In 1840, when Moses

---

[135] For all above, see Minute Books 5 (May, 1841–February, 1846), pp. 69, 117, 136, 197; 6 (March, 1846–December, 1850), pp. 35, 98; 11 (June, 1871–March, 1878), pp. 59ff., 167.

[136] See below, p. 112.

[137] See below, pp. 115ff.

[138] M. Montefiore, *Diaries*, ed. Louis Loewe, 2 vols, London, 1890, II, p. 223.

[139] Emanuel, *A Century and a Half*, p. 182.

Montefiore as president of the deputies travelled to Damascus to defend local Jews against the accusation of ritual murder, Palmerston, the Foreign Secretary, commended his mission to British envoys in Egypt and Constantinople. He thus secured Montefiore's entrée to the sultan of Turkey and Mehemet Ali.[140] On the voyage to Russia in 1846 (seeking to annul the forcible expulsion of Jews from western frontier zones) Lord Aberdeen, the Foreign Secretary, provided Sir Moses with letters to the British ministers at St Petersburg and Berlin;[141] and in 1877 the Foreign Office, at the instance of Sir Moses, used its influence to avert the forcible conversion of Jews in Persia.[142] On at least one occasion Montefiore travelled in a vessel put at his disposal by the Royal Navy – from Gibraltar to Morocco in 1863.[143]

It is noteworthy that although the deputies normally preferred to work through their influence with government or sympathetic parliamentarians, they also took international issues to public attention. In May 1840 they publicized the injustices committed at Damascus through advertisements in the leading daily and weekly papers of London, Liverpool, Birmingham, Manchester, Edinburgh, Dublin, Bristol, Exeter, Plymouth and Brighton; and when Montefiore, en route for Damascus, wrote to his fellow deputies in London, he reported the presence of representatives from *The Times* and the *Morning Chronicle*, 'for the transmission of any intelligence that may arrive'.[144] The Board also initiated a public meeting of protest at the Mansion House with spokesmen and a platform mainly of Christians.[145]

In all these ways, the deputies sought to make it possible for Jews to observe the Torah. Obviously, not all their activities belonged to this category. It would be difficult to argue that the Torah required N. M. Rothschild to be able to purchase landed estate. But the thrust is unmistakeable. This was all the more so by virtue of the intimate association that developed between Moses Montefiore and the rabbi of the Great Synagogue, Nathan Adler. Hirschell, Adler's predecessor, had deliberately held

---

[140] *Diaries*, I, p. 215.

[141] Ibid., p. 325; see also the documents reprinted in J. Frankel, 'The Russian-Jewish Question and the Board of Deputies' in *Transition and Change in Modern Jewish History* – Essays in Honor of S. Ettinger, Jerusalem, 1987, pp. liv ff.

[142] *Diaries*, II, p. 290.

[143] Ibid., p. 151.

[144] Minute Book 3, pp. 132ff., 279ff.; cf. also Frankel, 'The Russian-Jewish Question', p. xxxvii.

[145] J. Frankel, 'Crisis as a factor in modern Jewish politics', in J. Reinharz (ed.), *Living with Antisemitism*, Hanover/London, 1987, p. 53.

aloof from all public activity.[146] Not so Adler: when Montefiore, writes the editor of his diaries, 'as President of the Board of Deputies, or of any other institution, had to give his opinion on religious matters, he invariably referred to the Spiritual Head of the community for guidance; he regarded a word from him as decisive, and obeyed its injunctions at whatever cost to himself'.[147] Montefiore 'espoused the Rabbi's conduct in everything', writes another observer.[148] This was exemplified in 1851 when the Board was seeking to obtain for Jewish schools a share in parliamentary educational grants. The Privy Council agreed, enquiring, however, whether the schools would be open for inspection, though only in respect of secular subjects, such inspection to be carried out only by laymen. Were these conditions acceptable, Montefiore asked Adler? Only on receipt of Adler's assent were the negotiations proceeded with.[149] Montefiore and Adler dominated the Board from the mid-1840s till the 1870s.

Marriage, Divorce and 'the Law of the Land'

The overall harmony that developed between deputies and the government undoubtedly enhanced and enlarged the efficacy of the Torah. But in certain respects it also limited its power. This applied to the community's authority exercised by the rabbinical court (the *Beth Din*) in respect of marriage and divorce. This weakening was all the more pronounced by reason of its association with the simultaneous campaign waged by certain members of the community for political emancipation. The issue of marriage concerned not the state's recognition of the validity of the form of Jewish marriage but rather the capacity to marry – more particularly whether a Jewish marriage, the parties to which infringed the prohibited degrees enacted by the law of England, could lawfully be celebrated although it conformed to the rabbinical understanding of the prohibited degrees. A second issue concerned the exclusive power of the rabbinical court to dissolve a marriage contracted under Jewish auspices. In both cases, the Jewish community forfeited its authority and yielded to the law of the land.

---

[146] See his letters of 1833 and 1836 to Sir Isaac Lyon Goldsmid, quoted S. Stein, *The Beginnings of Hebrew Studies at University College*, London, 1952, pp. 6–7.

[147] *Diaries*, I, pp. 301–2.

[148] Rev. Moses Margoliouth, *The History of the Jews in Great Britain, III*, London, 1851, p. 100; cf. also M. Friedlander, 'The late chief rabbi Dr N.M. Adler', *JQR*, no. 2 (1889–90), pp. 376–8.

[149] Report of the Committee appointed on the subject of parliamentary grants for education to Jewish schools, London, 1852, esp. pp. 5–13.

The first issue did not arise, it seems, before the enactment of Lord Lyndhurst's Marriage Act of 1835. Section 2 declared as 'absolutely null and void' all marriages between persons 'within the prohibited degrees of consanguinity or affinity'. These degrees were not defined there but they would have excluded marriage with a deceased wife's sister or between uncle and niece, both permissible under rabbinic law.[150] It was not absolutely clear that Jewish matrimonial law was in fact included within the scope of Lyndhurst's Act. In any case, Moses Montefiore, newly elected president of the deputies in 1835, took the opinions of Rabbis Hirschell and Meldola, respective spokesmen for the Ashkenazi and Sephardi congregations. Thus fortified, Montefiore sought to ensure that the proposed bill had no adverse effect on the authority of the rabbinical courts. As Judge Finestein points out, it was in the face of this possibility that Montefiore wrote in his diary in 1837: 'I am most firmly resolved not to give up the smallest part of our religious forms and privileges to obtain civil rights.'[151]

But the deputies moved too slowly. A parliamentary bill promoted by Montefiore in 1837, intended to amend Lyndhurst's Act, failed. The Board had to take cognisance of the possible effect of the Act to the extent of advising congregations in 1844 that their officers 'should withhold their sanction' from marriages falling within the prohibited degrees as defined by the law of the land.[152] It also issued the severest warnings against 'clandestine proceedings in marriage'. These were marriages contracted in full accordance with Jewish law but which failed to comply with the law of the land in not being registered by the marriage secretary of a synagogue certified by the president of the deputies.[153] Such a marriage apparently took place in 1847 in London between Solomon Abrahams of Warsaw and Hannah Shuh of Hamburg.[154]

In 1866, chief rabbi Nathan Marcus Adler, much against his will, accepted 'the law of the land'. He informed the Royal Commission on the Laws of Marriage of that year that if a marriage was to be 'normal and valid according to Jewish laws' it must first be 'fully ascertained that the persons between whom the marriage is to be contracted do not stand within the prohibited degrees of consanguinity or affinity prohibited by the Jewish laws

---

[150] See I. Finestein, 'An aspect of the Jews and English Marriage Law during the emancipation: the prohibited degrees', *JJS*, VII (1965), no. 1, pp. 6–7. I wish to acknowledge the indebtedness of the present section to Judge Finestein's article.

[151] *Diaries*, I, p. 111, cf. also Minute Book 2, pp. 100ff., 113ff.

[152] Emanuel, *A Century and a Half*, p. 49; Finestein, 'An aspect of the Jews', p. 11.

[153] See above p. 102.

[154] Minute Book 6, p. 94.

or *the law of the land*.[155] Salomons, one of the prime protagonists of emancipation, wished to go further and altogether remove the deputies' control over Jewish marriages. But this further weakening of its authority the Board succeeded in thwarting.[156]

Salomons – this time accompanied by Lionel de Rothschild, later the first Jewish member of Parliament (1858) – had greater success with divorce than marriage. The civil divorce court, established in 1857 as part of the Matrimonial Causes Bill, initially lacked the power to dissolve a Jewish marriage. This remained with the Jewish court. But it would, under the bill, have become possible for a marriage contracted under Jewish law to be dissolved under English law. Thus the offspring of any subsequent remarriage would have had to be regarded as illegitimate unless the first marriage had been dissolved also by the rabbinical court. The objectionable clause in the bill read as follows: 'as soon as this act shall come into operation, all jurisdiction now vested in or exercised by any ecclesiastical court or person in England in respect of divorces *a mensa et thoro* . . . shall be vested in Her Majesty . . . [to be] exercised in the name of Her Majesty in a court of record.'

But to chief rabbi Adler, Montefiore and the majority of deputies, this provision was 'a great interference with our rights and privileges'. They also argued, pragmatically, that the divorce procedure at the rabbinical court would be less costly and offered wider grounds for divorce than those available under the bill. For all these reasons Adler successfully persuaded deputies to press Parliament to add to the bill a further clause: 'nothing herein contained shall give the Court hereby established jurisdiction in relation to any marriage of persons both professing the Jewish religion contracted or solemnized according to their own usages.'

The Lord Chancellor accepted this addition. But at the bill's third reading in the House of Lords it was omitted, following intervention by Salomons and Rothschild. Adler continued to fight and again persuaded the Board to petition Parliament to reinstate the clause on the bill's passage through the House of Commons. This time the government refused. After 1866, the Jewish court refused to grant a Jewish divorce until after the English civil courts had similarly ruled.[157]

The agitation had a political as much as a religious objective. Lionel Rothschild, though a deputy for the Ashkenazi Great Synagogue, promised to 'exert himself to the utmost' to nullify any special legal status for the

---

[155] Quoted Finestein, 'An aspect of the Jews', p. 14 (italics added).

[156] Emanuel, *A Century and a Half,* p. 88; A.M. Hyamson, *David Salomons,* London, 1939, pp. 47–8.

[157] M.D.A. Freeman, 'Jews and the law of divorce in England,' *JLA,* IV (1981), pp. 276–88.

English Jew. His stand cannot be divorced from the renewed campaign for political emancipation. Only a year after the civil divorce court was established Rothschild was able to take his seat in the House of Commons (1858). His supporters over the marriage and divorce bill made clear the connection between political advancement and the abrogation of rabbinical power. Salomons, for example, elected lord mayor of London less than two years previously, even demanded that 'the power of divorce by the Jewish ecclesiastical authorities be entirely abrogated'. This separate jurisdiction emphasized the separate national identity of the Jew. Salomons was supported inside the Board by Alderman Benjamin Phillips, who in 1865 followed Salomons as the second Jewish lord mayor of London. 'As Englishmen', declared Magnus, deputy for the Sheerness congregation, 'when they were seeking their rights as such from the country, they ought to submit to the general laws, like the professors of every other religion.'[158] With these words Magnus, like his sympathizers, revealed a new front in the perennial conflict over the limits of 'the law of the land'. From another standpoint, the debate disclosed the growing subordination of Anglo-Jewry to the democratic state. The price of political freedom was the diminution of legal freedom.

Rich, Poor and Self-help

The poor, I repeat, were the besetting problem of London Jewry. This was a consequence of continual immigration. England in general and London in particular attracted Jews from Western Europe (especially the Low Countries), the German lands, Eastern Europe, Italy, Gibraltar and North Africa. Over the whole of the eighteenth century alone, numbers increased at least fifteen-fold, from about 1,000 to 15–20,000. The growth was most marked in the second half of the century. Between 1690 and 1734 the average number of immigrants was c.250 a year; from 1750 to 1800 c.400. In the first half of the nineteenth century it dropped to c.300 and rose again between 1850 and 1880 to 300–400.[159] The influx attained such proportions that the resources deployed by local charities and such welfare services as existed failed to provide for the needs of the newcomers. And in this connection it must always be borne in mind that all response to this situation

[158] All the above is based on Emanuel, *A Century and a Half*, p. 71, and the reports of deputies' debates in the *Jewish Chronicle* of 26 June, 3 July and 10 July 1857; see also I. Finestein, 'Anglo-Jewry and the law of divorce', *Jewish Chronicle*, 19 April, 1957.

[159] For all the above, cf. V.D. Lipman, *The Social History of the Jews in England, 1850–1950*, London, 1954, pp. 6–8, 65–6.

could only be voluntary. The contrast between the established Jewish communities of the continent and the disestablished Anglo-Jewish community was made prominent in a publication of the Great Synagogue:

> although in France, Holland, Hamburgh, etc., the law of the land authorises the Jewish congregations to levy a rate on their brethren for their Synagogue establishment and the maintenance of their poor, the laws of England do not permit a compulsory tax to be raised by any separate community without a special act of Parliament; hence, the only resource and hope of this Congregation rest on the voluntary contributions of its members.[160]

With the immigrants came the problem of crime, for the newcomers were overwhelmingly poor and unskilled.

One Sephardi response to the influx was certainly discouragement. 'The heads of the Jews were constrained to remember that they were strangers in a foreign country, surrounded by a population which, if not openly hostile, at all events eyed them with distrust and jealousy, and where the slightest offence against the laws of the land might entail misery and expulsion to all of their race.'[161] As early as 1670, for example, the *Mahamad* decreed that all foreigners requiring assistance should quit England in five days, not be permitted to enter the synagogue and receive from its funds as much as it could spare.[162] In 1710 'Italianos and Berberiscos' (Italians and North Africans) were to be supplied with food for only three days and then given 10 shillings to leave the country.[163] Other measures taken by the *Mahamad* included a complaint to the lord mayor of the foreign paupers besieging the synagogue (1669) and a warning to the synagogue's agents in Holland (1692) and Leghorn that the congregation was already overwhelmed with indigent refugees from Portugal and elsewhere (1705, 1706).[164]

It was also open to the *Mahamad* to encourage the emigration of the poor, and this was a course followed in the 1730s. By means of travel subsidies and participation in the Crown's charter for the colonization of

[160] *Laws of the Great Synagogue*, preface, pp. vi–vii.

[161] Picciotto, *Sketches*, pp. 33–4.

[162] Ibid., p. 40.

[163] Gaster, *History of the Ancient Synagogue*, pp. 21–2, 149; cf. also E.R. Samuel, 'The first fifty years', in V.D. Lipman (ed.), *Three Centuries of Anglo-Jewish History*, Cambridge, 1961, p. 35.

[164] Barnett, 'Correspondence', p. 3; Diamond, 'Problems', p. 40; Endelman, *The Jews of Georgian England*, pp. 167–8; Pollins, *Economic History*, pp. 62ff.

Georgia in 1732, Sephardi families were sent to Barbados, Jamaica, Georgia and Carolina.[165] As late as 1842, the London *Voice of Jacob* recommended 'emigration to new colonies' as a solution to the problem created by 'the masses of our brethren reduced to a state of hopeless poverty';[166] and in 1871 the *Jewish Chronicle* warmly welcomed 'a very material increase (in 1870) of the number of poor Jews who have left this country to seek subsistence elsewhere'.[167]

Those who remained, in the eighteenth century, were dependent on the facilities provided by the three Ashkenazi synagogues and Bevis Marks. From their initial establishment each had an elected officer whose task it was to dispense relief in cash within predetermined limits. This duty encompassed not only the synagogue members fallen on hard times but also 'the foreign poor'. The synagogues functioned as welfare centres, providing free medical and burial facilities to the poor. From the end of the seventeenth century and into the eighteenth the Sephardim had also established a number of charities that provided appropriate services for the sick, the bereaved, mothers in childbirth, orphaned brides, the aged, intending emigrants etc.

By 1731 the number of families of the sick poor attached to Bevis Marks already amounted to 254, probably more than half the total Sephardi population.[168] This was the context to the establishment of a hospital in 1748, funded by synagogue members.[169] First situated in Leman Street, the hospital had a medical staff that included a dispenser, a matron, an apothecary, a nurse and two midwives. It is claimed to have been 'the first hospital in England designed from the outset to include care for maternity cases'.[170] The rate of infant mortality showed a rapid decline: in 1734–43 it was 32.9 per annum; in 1744–53, 20.5; and in 1754–63, 17.3.[171] The Sephardim also maintained an orphanage (1703) and a society that apprenticed boys to useful trades (1749).[172]

---

[165] Endelman, *The Jews of Georgian England*, pp. 168–9; Picciotto, *Sketches*, pp. 144–5; L. Hühner, 'The Jews of Georgia in colonial times' *AJHS*, X (1902), 65–95; R. Barnett, 'Dr Samuel Nunez Ribeiro and the settlement of Georgia', in *Migration and Settlement – Papers in Anglo–American Jewish History*, London, 1971, pp. 82ff.

[166] *Voice of Jacob*, 16 September 1842.

[167] *Jewish Chronicle* 10 March 1871.

[168] R. Barnett, 'Dr Jacob de Castro Sarmento and Sephardim in medical practice in 18th century London', *TJHSE*, XXVII (1978–80), p. 90.

[169] Ibid., p. 91.

[170] Ibid., p. 95.

[171] Diamond, 'Problems' *TJHSE*, XXI, p. 61, n. 18.

[172] A.P. Arared, *Apprentices of Great Britain, 1710–1773*, with an introduction by R. Barnett, *TJHSE*, XXII (1968–9), p. 146.

The London Ashkenazim were slower to create comparable facilities, though the need was certainly no less. In 1830 Moses Montefiore visited the Jewish poor, as member of a joint Sephardi–Ashkenazi committee of the deputies: 'we witnessed many very distressing scenes', he noted, 'parents surrounded by children, frequently six or seven, seldom less than two or three, with little or no fire or food, and scarcely a rag to cover them; without bed or blanket, but merely a sack or rug for the night . . . Few had more than one room, however large the family . . . Of those who had two rooms, the upper one was most miserable, scarcely an article of furniture.'[173]

Closely associated with poverty was crime amongst Jews. This was directed mainly against property, and took the form of pickpocketing, shoplifting, burglary and trafficking in stolen goods. In the 1760s and after, more and more Jews were sentenced at the Old Bailey to death or transportation.[174] One such case was that of Feibel Fibemann, the fifteen-year-old son of an immigrant from Oldenburg, now living in London. The father was about to take up a position as teacher-cantor-slaughterer at the Dover Jewish congregation when Feibel and another boy were arrested for stealing a handkerchief worth tenpence. In 1771 Feibel was sentenced to seven years' service as a 'transport' in British North America, where he would be sold into servitude for the period of his sentence. The distraught father wrote to a cousin, Meyer Josephson of Pennsylvania, imploring him to have the boy 'bought out' by Jews. This did sometimes happen but not apparently in this case.[175]

A particularly notorious crime was the 'Chelsea murder' of 1771, when a gang of Polish Jews murdered a servant whilst committing burglary. The repercussions impelled Ashkenazi leaders to petition the government for the removal of the facilities for free immigration offered by Post Office package-boats. The lord mayor at the same time offered free passes to any poor Jew desirous of returning to his native land.[176]

The Jewish notables enthusiastically co-operated with the civil authorities in the suppression of crime, especially dealing in stolen goods. In 1766, the wardens of the Great Synagogue, Napthaly Franks and Napthaly Hart Myers, both American-born, wrote to the Bow Street magistrate, Sir John Fielding, that in so co-operating they were convinced 'we shall receive the applause of every Jew, who is not totally ignorant of the Law of God, the Duty of his own religion, the true regard of Public justice, and the obedience

[173] *Diaries*, I, p. 80.

[174] Endelman, *The Jews of Georgian England*, pp. 196ff.

[175] All the above is based on J.R. Marcus, 'Shed a tear for a transport', in Sh. Yeivin (ed.), *Studies in Jewish History presented to Raphael Mahler*, Merhavia, 1974 (Engl. Sec.), pp. 53–61.

[176] Roth, *History of the Jews*, p. 236.

due to the laws of this Kingdom.'[177] This co-operation was all the closer because Jewish criminality at this time provoked a variety of anti-Jewish manifestations, in London and the provinces.[178] When the Chelsea murderers were hanged at Tyburn, the community not only utterly dissociated itself from them but also warned all its members, through an announcement read in every synagogue, not to venture on to the streets.[179]

A cycle of deprivation had established itself through the inability of the Jewish poor to provide education and/or some form of vocational training for their children.[180] At the beginning of the nineteenth century Joshua Van Oven, honorary physician to the Great Synagogue, stated the problem very fairly when he argued that although there was 'no circumstance more distressing to the Jewish father than how to put his son forward in life in some industrious occupation', religious observance stood in that father's way. A Jewish apprentice could not share his Christian master's food, work all day Friday or at all on Saturday and would require leave for the Jewish holidays. The poor were 'totally deprived of the possibility of acquiring a trade, or of being employed at day-work more than four days and a half in the week, unless extra on Sundays', Van Oven concluded.[181] He therefore proposed the establishment of a 'House of Industry' to teach handicraft and trades, to be financed by appropriating part of the general rates for the Jewish poor or, when this was rejected as impracticable, by a form of Jewish self-taxation.[182] This was rejected, most vehemently so by the Sephardim; and in any case the proposal made virtually no progress in Parliament.[183]

But the poverty of the Jews was not due solely to the impediment created by religion; anti-Jewish prejudice also contributed. 'There have been many

---

[177] Roth, *Anglo-Jewish Letters*, pp. 156–7.

[178] Bill Williams, *The Making of Manchester Jewry, 1740–1875*, Manchester 1976, pp. 7ff.

[179] Roth, *History of the Jews*, p. 236; Williams, ibid.

[180] Endelman, *The Jews of Georgian England* pp. 186ff.

[181] *Letters on the Present State of the Jewish Poor in the Metropolis*, London, 1802, pp. 11–12. Sometimes economic considerations cut across religious. A man signing himself 'An involuntary Jewish pedlar' wrote as late as 1853: 'how can it be expected that Jews should either follow or excel in handicraft trades when Christians *cannot*, and Jewish workers *will* not, except in some few (very few) cases employ Jewish workmen? Christians *cannot* employ us on account of our Sabbaths and festivals, and Jews *will not* on the same account . . . I was brought up to a trade as a workman but years since was obliged to abandon it, and became a hawker and pedlar because I could not get employed by Jews, and I would not abandon my religious observances to be employed by Christians' (*Jewish Chronicle*, 13 May 1853). My attention was drawn to this letter by the kindness of Mr David Cesarani.

[182] Ibid., pp. 17–19, 34.

[183] Endelman, *The Jews of Georgian England*, pp. 231ff.

instances in this metropolis', wrote a contemporary observer, 'of all the journeymen in a shop threatening to strike if a Jew were admitted as a journeyman.' In 1813 the London Missionary Society reported: 'there are 4 or 5 boys fit to be put out as apprentices wherever proper masters can be provided for them, but the committee are sorry to find that there is still a disinclination amongst Christians to receive Jews into their families.'[184] We hear also of George Myers, a converted butcher, whose employment in the Leadenhall meat market in London came to naught: 'it was no sooner discovered that he was a Jew than every man in the employ of the carcase butchers refused to work with him.'[185]

This was the immediate background to a sustained educational programme: the establishment, largely at the hands of the Goldsmid family, of the Jews' Hospital Neveh Zedek (1807) and the Jews' Free School (1817). The former housed an asylum for the elderly and also incorporated a workshop in which the boys were taught to make shoes, chairs and furniture, and the girls instructed in domestic tasks. On leaving school, the boys were apprenticed to skilled artisans and the girls entered domestic service.[186] But the numbers of both sexes were limited and the training was poor, so that by 1844 only 223 children had been either apprenticed or placed in domestic service.[187] Moreover, the founders of the Hospital had no wish to encourage immigration and therefore made it a condition of entry to the school that the parents of boys admitted had to have lived in the United Kingdom for at least ten years, two years of it in London; for orphans the period of residence was limited to nine years with two in London.[188]

The Jews' Free School was an altogether more ambitious undertaking. This developed again from a mixture of motives – not only *richesse oblige* and the desire to protect the good name of the community from the stigma of poverty and crime, but also as a means to thwart the efforts of the free schools established by the London Society for the Promotion of Christianity amongst the Jews and by the London Missionary Society. Here was an issue on which Jews co-operated, whatever their other differences. Joseph Crool, the 'fifth monarchy man', took an active part in pamphleteering against the missionaries;[189] so did his opponent, R. Hirschell, who sent a

---

[184] Rumney, 'Economic and social development', pp. 179–80.

[185] Ibid., p. 175.

[186] Endelman, *The Jews of Georgian England*, pp. 236ff.; cf. also L. Wolf, 'The origin of the Neve Zedek', in C. Roth (ed.), *Essays in Jewish History*, JHSE, 1934, pp. 193–9.

[187] Endelman, *The Jews of Georgian England*, p. 241.

[188] E.S. Conway, 'The origins of the Jewish Orphanage', *TJHSE*, XXII (1970), p. 55.

[189] H. Meirovich, 'Ashkenazic reactions to the conversionists, 1800–1850', *TJHSE*, XXVI (1979), pp. 16ff.

deputation of authorities from the Great Synagogue to protest to the treasurer of the London Society;[190] and in a sermon that was also distributed in the Jewish quarter of London, Hirschell sternly condemned the schools as 'a decoying experiment . . . to entice innocent Jewish children . . . from the observance of the Law of Moses'. He warned that all parents who sent their children to such schools 'will be considered as if they themselves had forsaken their religion, and been baptised; and shall lose all title to the name of Jews, and forfeit all claims on the Congregation both in life and death'.[191] Hirschell clearly had much success, at least in the short term.[192]

But the missionary schools undeniably met a need, admitting, for example, 219 pupils between 1809 and 1814.[193] This total of course compared very favourably with the ten boys and eight girls admitted to the Jews' Hospital school in 1807, and testifies to the eagerness with which parents sought education for their children, even from a Christian source.

The Jews' Free School, financed from a wide body of subscribers, was grafted on to the existing *Talmud Torah* of the Great Synagogue. The synagogal origin was again crucial to a major Anglo-Jewish institution, although it also enjoyed the patronage of the Rothschild family.[194] Its guiding force was Joshua Van Oven, the physician. The school was eventually opened in 1817 and enjoyed a growing intake – from 102 (1817) to 550 (1824) and to more than 1,000 by mid-century.[195] Its importance, economically, derived from the vocational training it provided and the apprenticeship system it operated. The hospital or the school paid the indenture fee when the intending apprentice reached the age of thirteen. Very little is known concerning the number of boys trained in this way or the trades to which they were apprenticed. Data from 1823–39 of fifty-three Sephardi boys, apprenticed through a Sephardi charity, suggest that tailoring (twelve boys) and shoe-making (ten) were amongst the more popular, but smaller numbers entered virtually every London trade.[196] In

---

[190] Ibid., pp. 12–13; *Thirteenth Report of the Missionary Society*, London, 1807, pp. 266–7.

[191] The 'caution' in summary form is reproduced in S.S. Levin, 'The origins of the Jews' Free School' *TJHSE*, XIX (1955–9), p. 106; Beneyahu, 'Vikuhim ba-kehillah', p. 32.

[192] Meirovich, 'Askenazic reactions', p. 12.

[193] Ibid., p. 9; see also M. Scult, 'English missions to the Jews', *JSS*, XXXV (1973), no. 1, pp. 3–17.

[194] Levin, 'Origins of the Jews' Free School', passim.

[195] Endelman, *The Jews of Georgian England*, p. 243. The Jews' Infant Schools and the Stepney Jewish School showed the same measure of growth (E. Black, *The Social Politics of Anglo-Jewry, 1880–1920*, Oxford, 1988, pp. 111ff.).

[196] Pollins, *Economic History*, pp. 120ff.

this particular way, on however limited a scale, Anglo-Jewry fulfilled the Talmudic demand: 'whoever does not teach his son a trade is as though he brings him up to be a robber.'[197] In the English context this was part of a policy that sought to create a class of respectable, self-supporting English Jews, not hereditary proletarians. It is true that when chief rabbi Adler proposed an expansion of the school curriculum, the managers replied that the school existed in order to give pupils 'an elementary education consistent with their station'.[198] But this station was never considered immutable.

Later, the aspiration to upward social mobility was extended to embrace anglicization. The two were in fact interdependent and inseparable. In 1881, when faced with the first wave of mass immigrants from Eastern Europe, the *Jewish Chronicle* correctly identified the issue at stake. What the young foreign Jews required was 'a thoroughly English education . . . to transform them into Englishmen . . . We can place a young Pole in the Jews' Free School with the assurance that at the end of his training he will be turned out a young Englishman.'[199] A few years later, when the *Chronicle* discussed the activities of the Working Men's Club, the Jews' Free School, the Board of Guardians and the Jewish Buildings, it concluded by bringing them all under the same umbrella and defined the central issue of Anglo-Jewish philanthropy as 'how to anglicise the foreign poor'.[200]

I now turn to some of these institutions in a little more detail.

The Jews' Free School was the first example of an instrument of embourgeoisement and denoted a conscious attempt at social engineering. It set a precedent for later bodies that also sought to combine instruction – in the broadest sense – with anglicization, all in the interests of bringing the Jewish poor and working class closer to the cousinhood. The introduction of socialism, the growth of immigration, which was itself frequently the bearer of radical ideas, and the antisemitism that marked the mid-1870s, stimulated by Disraeli's pro-Turkish and anti-Russian foreign policy in the middle-

---

[197] TB Kidd. 29a.
[198] Quoted L.P. Gartner, 'East European Jewish immigrants in England', *TJHSE*, XXIX (1982–6), p. 308, n. 13.
[199] *Jewish Chronicle*, 12 August 1881.
[200] 15 May 1885. The same issue also mentions the 'great danger that . . . a little Poland [will be created] in the East End of London'. The 'Jewish Buildings' are a reference to the Rothschild dwellings planned in 1885, following a United Synagogue report into housing conditions, and opened in 1887 – see J. White, *Rothschild Buildings*, London, 1980. Stanley Kaplan, 'The Anglicization of the East European Jewish immigrant as seen by the London *Jewish Chronicle*, 1870–1897' *Yivo Annual of Jewish Social Science*, x (1955), pp. 267–78, deals extensively with this recurrent theme.

eastern crisis, gave added impetus to the cousinhood's policy. The solidarity enjoined by the Torah also required to be activated or at least reinforced by motives of self-preservation.[201] An early reaction to at least the former factors was the establishment of Sussex Hall (so named after the philosemitic Duke of Sussex). It was founded in 1845 as a sort of Jewish 'Mechanics' Institute'. Lectures on contemporary issues, a library and a reading room educated the Jewish poor in the mores and standards of English life, and it was thus hailed by the *Hebrew Observer* (20 October 1854): 'there cannot be a more efficient antidote to the poisonous doctrines of socialism, communism, chartism and other utopian solutions lauded by designing demagogues or short-sighted philanthropists than this frequent intercourse between the higher and lower classes on the common ground afforded by the platform of the . . . Institution;'[202] and when the Jewish Working Men's Club and Institute was founded in 1874, the *Jewish Chronicle* commented on the first annual report that it would help to broaden the occupational composition of the Jewish working class and also to anglicize new immigrants: 'it is clearly the interest of the Jewish community to rid them as soon as possible of all those externals not rarely repugnant to English feeling and to imbue them with English sentiments and notions.'[203]

These ventures in social engineering extended also into the use of religion as a means of social control. The formation of the Hebrew Socialist Union by Aaron Lieberman in 1876 had already alarmed communal leaders. In 1885 the publication of the *Arbeter Fraint* (Worker's Friend), with an explicitly socialist message directed at the immigrant poor, confirmed these fears. Part of the answer came in the form of the Federation of Synagogues, initiated by Samuel Montagu (later Lord Swaythling), but at this time Liberal Member of Parliament for Whitechapel in East London, where many of the immigrants had settled. Under the aegis of Montagu and his sympathizers, the Federation, founded in 1887, grouped together the old and new *hevrot* of East London in an effort to counteract the socialist appeal,

---

[201] Ber Borochov, the great analyst of the particular Jewish socio-economic structure and ideologist of socialist Zionism, described the philanthropic activities of 'the plutocracy and communal leaders' as having one aim '*to obtain the recognition of the neighbouring peoples and to achieve personal integration in the Galut* [diaspora]', *Nationalism and the Class Struggle*, Engl. trans., Westport, 1973, p. 105 (italics in original). But this is surely too narrow.

[202] Quoted Finestein, 'Anglo-Jewish opinion', pp. 128–9; for the history of the institution, see A. Barnett, 'Sussex Hall – the first Anglo-Jewish venture in popular education', *TJHSE*, XIX (1955–9), pp. 65–79.

[203] 31 March 1876; H. Pollins, *A History of the Jewish Working Men's Club and Institute, 1874–1912*, Oxford, 1981, gives a comprehensive account of the genesis and activities of the Institute.

provide improved satisfaction for the religious needs of the immigrants and blunt the thrust of agitation directed against immigration altogether.[204]

In terms of social engineering, pure and simple, as a means to enhance the living standards of the poor the most ambitious and comprehensive venture was the foundation of the Board of Guardians in 1859. This had its origin in discontent with the system of casual relief operated by the synagogues, which revealed itself to be less and less efficient. It was arbitrary and pauperizing, degraded the poor, generated recurrent wrangling amongst the synagogues and duplicated resources in that it overlapped with the work of the voluntary charities. Some co-ordination was introduced in 1834 through an inter-synagogal agreement initiated by Nathan Mayer Rothschild, on behalf of the Great Synagogue.[205] But not until 1858–9 did the three Ashkenazi synagogues jointly agree to establish a Board of Guardians financed from their individual resources. Legacies, endowments, annual contributions and gifts in kind also augmented its funds and by 1879 accounted for more than nine-tenths of the Board's income.[206]

In this fashion the synagogues of Anglo-Jewry once again gave rise to a major communal institution. The moving spirits came from the Great Synagogue – Ephraim Alex, a successful dentist, the first president, and Lionel Louis Cohen, a stockbroker and kinsman of the Rothschilds, the first secretary. Opposition came from some of the Reform synagogue (Sir Francis Goldsmid, Simon Waley and Professor David Marks) who feared lest an extension of relief to the foreign born encourage a further influx of immigrants.[207] As a concession to this argument those immigrants with less than six months' residence in the United Kingdom were refused relief. But arguments for delay could not withstand the alarming evidence of distress in 1858–9 due to the severe winter and the trade depression.[208]

The new organization rapidly developed facilities that took it far beyond immigrant welfare, despite the latter's unquestioned and enduring importance. Obviously, if the poor could be prevented from coming to England altogether or, if they did arrive, at least encouraged to emigrate, that was the best solution. That is why the Board's Thirteenth Annual Report (January–December 1871) referred with approval to emigration having been 'fairly active during the year';[209] and also to the deterrent effect on intending

[204] G. Alderman, *The Federation of Synagogues, 1887–1987*, London, 1987, pp. 13ff.

[205] Lipman, *Social History*, pp. 54ff.

[206] V.D. Lipman, *A Century of Social Service, 1859–1959*, London, 1959, p. 39.

[207] Ibid., p. 26.

[208] Ibid., pp. 24–5.

[209] London, 5632–1872, p. 12; see also 21st Annual Report (5640–1880), pp. 9–10.

immigrants 'of the futility of an application [for assistance] following immediately on arrival'.[210]

However, if such measures failed – as they did, given the deteriorating conditions for Jews in Eastern Europe – then the Board committed itself to a wide-ranging exercise in philanthropy. Operating through a system of committees, the Board took within its purview medical relief, aid to emigrants, sanitary inspection, the distribution of fixed allowances to the aged and indigent of food and clothing, the investigation of applicants' circumstances on behalf of other charities and the provision of funerals, and it expanded the work of the apprenticeship system for boys originally introduced by the Jews' Free School. Girls were trained in dressmaking, shirt- and collar-making and embroidery. It is impossible to assess the impact of these measures, but by 1879 there were eighty-five apprentices, distributed amongst such trades as furniture (thirty-seven), boots and shoes (fourteen), printing and allied trades (nine), and instrument-making (five).[211] This was conceived as a self-financing endeavour; the Industrial Committee of the Board itself advanced to the apprentice's master the indenture fee, which was then recouped from the boy's wages by weekly instalments. Much of the aid to apprentices was made possible by a gift of £500 from Baroness Mayer de Rothschild.[212]

Across all this span of activity, the Board, dominated by the cousinhood, fulfilled a counter-radical role. Its philanthropy had a political ethos which can be reconstituted in broad outline. Paramount was the encouragement of upward mobility. The Board vehemently rejected any notion that it pauperized the poor – rather it claimed that it 'stimulated' the poor to help themselves; promiscuous charity was 'demoralising . . . in order to raise the spirit of the Jewish poor, they must be taught to rely on themselves, and not on almoners, not only for nourishment and for employment, but also for education and for medicine.' The Board combined this policy with concern for the self-reliant family. The workrooms that it operated to train girls and young women as needlewomen and machinists taught a trade 'which would not only secure them against starvation, but would likewise enable them to become an efficient support to their parents'.[213]   The

---

[210] Thirteenth Annual Report, p. 12.

[211] Lipman, *Century of Social Service*, p. 69.

[212] Ibid.; Laurie Magnus, *The Jewish Board of Guardians and the Men who Made It*, London, 1909, pp. 32ff.

[213] Thirteenth Annual Report, pp. 14, 22, 53. The concern for the family must be seen in the context of the phenomenon of 'deserted wives'; in 1870, 105 such cases applied to the Board for assistance. Then there was a decline to 37 in 1874, rising to 161 in 1879 (ibid., p. 14, and 21st Report, p. 10). The wives were in fact not necessarily abandoned – it might be that the husband had left them by agreement, to seek employment elsewhere. In either case, the phenomenon was not only a

aspiration to economic independence was also fostered by the loans that the Board extended both in cash and in the form of tools, equipment and machines. In 1879 the Board hired out forty-three sewing machines, from which 'a large number of families [derived] a comfortable and independent living'.[214]

It is not possible to estimate in any detail the effect of all these vocational and educational policies. Of the period before 1881, the year when the massive influx of Eastern European Jews began, it has been said that the success of the new schools was 'at the very most, a modest one, and possibly of no real consequence at all'.[215] The Board may, however, have had success in diverting boys away from the overcrowded trades of tailoring and cigar-making.[216] For a later period (*c*.1910), at a time when 4,000–5,000 Jewish children were leaving London elementary schools each year, the Board could not have apprenticed under its auspices more than 10 per cent at most.[217] The number of apprentices under the aegis of the Board was 371 in 1908.[218]

This of course disregards the effect of the other activities of the Board and related philanthropic bodies. But it seems likely that the anglicization and embourgeoisement of the poor and the immigrants was very largely the product of their own endeavours. They are certainly not to be regarded as inert raw material, passively submitting to the policies of the cousinhood.

---

function of poverty but also of migration.

[214] Thirteenth Report, pp. 19–20; see also 21st Report, pp. 9–11. The sewing machines were originally donated by Charlotte, Baroness Lionel de Rothschild in 1861 (Magnus, *Jewish Board of Guardians*, p. 71). This policy, and the institutions required to implement it, were reproduced in major provincial congregations. In Manchester, 'a Jews' School founded in 1841, and substantially enlarged in 1869, had the primary objects of introducing these lower orders to the values of English respectability, ridding them of "foreign" and criminal habits and preparing them for entry to more stable occupations than petty hawking. Experiments in poor relief culminated in 1867 with the creation of a Jewish Board of Guardians ... The Board had social as well as material purposes. Its members believed that by close personal contacts with the poor they exercised a "moral influence" which converted potential paupers into "good citizens". A system of free apprenticeships and small loans helped the poor "to relieve themselves – that was, to put them in a fair way of obtaining a livelihood by their own exertions". The objects of the Board were to "Anglicise, educate, alleviate distress and depauperise the people", although without in any way encouraging the settlement of "immigrant paupers"' (Bill Williams, 'The antisemitism of tolerance', in A. Kidd and K. Roberts (eds), *City, Class and Culture*, Manchester, 1985, pp. 76–7). The note of sarcasm is unwarranted.

[215] Endelman, *The Jews of Georgian England*, pp. 244–5.

[216] Magnus, *Jewish Board of Guardians*, pp. 31–2.

[217] Lipman *Century of Social Service*, p. 123.

[218] Black, *Social Politics*, table 3.2, p. 82.

This of course did not endear them to prospective employers, but the ethos of self-help was paramount. Both points of view are expressed in the letter of a certain 'Sabbaticus' to the *Jewish Chronicle* (21 February 1879). 'Jewish workers', he wrote, 'are not so faithful, so obedient, or so capable as the professors of other creeds. But the supreme fault found with them is that they are not satisfied like other men, to drudge all their lives for a moderate salary. They betray too great an anxiety to set up in business for themselves, to the detriment of their master's commercial interests as soon as they have accumulated sufficient experience and capital.'[219]

The cousinhood's policy could not overcome economic conflict – not between the cousinhood and the immigrants, but between the latter and the *immediate* exploiters, their fellow-Jews. A strike in the cigar-making industry (1857–8) pitted Jewish workers against Jewish masters and portended the future;[220] for example, the tailors' strike of 1889 led by Lewis Lyons, secretary of the Jewish Unemployed Committee. Their strike fund enjoyed the modest financial support of such central members of the cousinhood as Samuel Montagu and the newly ennobled Lord Rothschild. Both also mediated between masters and workers lest discontent lead to socialism.[221] Montagu had earlier founded a union, the Jewish Tailors' Machinists Society (1886), which would separate the political from the economic struggle and, even then, forego the strike weapon in the quest for the twelve-hour day. But this venture achieved nothing.[222]

The policy also could not overcome the conflict between the immigrant and his slum landlord, frequently Jewish, in the congested areas of East London where, however, rents showed a substantial and steady increase in the early 1880s.[223]

---

[219] Ber Borochov defines this process as 'the individualisation of industry'. 'A Jew, possessing meagre means, often decides to become a boss "on his own" under circumstances in which a gentile will never dare undertake such a venture . . . He refuses to remain a proletarian . . . This desire to achieve "success" is a deeply ingrained characteristic of the Jewish labouring masses. Tailors, shoemakers and cigar-makers eagerly await the opportunity to rid themselves of their tools and to climb into the higher strata of insurance, dentistry, medicine, law or into an independent business' (*Nationalism*, pp. 61–2).

[220] Pollins, *Economic History*, pp. 123ff; see also H. Pollins, 'Jews on strike', *Jewish Chronicle*, 4 January 1974.

[221] Pollins, *Economic History*, pp. 156–7; Alderman, *Federation of Synagogues*, pp. 27–8; A. Kershen, 'All Out!', *Jewish Chronicle*, 18 August 1989.

[222] L.P. Gartner, *The Jewish Immigrant in England, 1870–1914*, London, 1960, pp. 117ff.; Alderman, *Federation of Synagogues*, pp. 16ff.

[223] J. White, 'Jewish Landlords, Jewish tenants: an aspect of class struggle within the Jewish East End, 1881–1914', in *The Jewish East End, 1840–1939*, London, 1981, pp. 205–15.

'Little use for Learning'

'Prior to the coming of the Russians [that is, before 1880], Anglo-Jewry had but little use for learning and less understanding of, if great respect for, scholars, of which it could boast but few.'[224] This is true – if anything an understatement. The period 'prior to the coming of the Russians' encompasses the whole of the modern history of Anglo-Jewry. The leading rabbis of the eighteenth century left no doubt of their discontent at the neglect of learning. R. Hart Lyon of the Great Synagogue (1756–64) gave repeated expression, in public and in private, to his bitterness. 'Instead of gathering in the houses of learning people go to operas, plays, concerts and clubs . . . I have no pupils, not even a colleague with whom I could pursue my studies . . . I established a Yeshivah but have not succeeded with it . . . There are no Talmud Torahs for children, and what will be the future of Judaism if this state of affairs continues.' Towards the end of his stay in London he exclaimed from the pulpit: 'God Almighty only knows how weary I am of my life here. I can not bear any longer to behold all that you do in public and in your private life.'[225]

Hart Lyon's successor at the Great Synagogue, R. David Tevele Schiff HaCohen (1765–92), also complained of intellectual loneliness: 'I have no colleagues nor pupils to study with', he wrote in 1780 to his brother Meir in Frankfurt on Main. 'You imagine London is a *kehillah*. No! Far from it!'[226] In 1781 and again in 1782 he vainly sought rabbinical appointments at Rotterdam and Würzburg.[227]

It is also instructive that until the latter part of the nineteenth century candidates from abroad took virtually all rabbinical and teaching appointments. This applied both to Ashkenazim and Sephardim. No facilities existed for the local training of rabbis. At a lower level, the little that is known of elementary schools attached to synagogues suggests that their influence was negligible. In 1779, of the sixty-four pupils of the school attached to the Bevis Marks synagogue, scarcely one-eighth could read Hebrew and nearly all were unfamiliar with the daily prayers. The college (*Medrash*) of the synagogue had at this time eighteen students of the Talmud.[228] In 1803 a committee of enquiry feared lest 'the *kahal* become an object of contempt and ridicule', so deficient was the study of the

---

[224] Salaman, 'Whither Lucien Wolf's', p. 17.
[225] Duschinsky, *Rabbinate of the Great Synagogue*, pp. 21ff.
[226] Ibid., p. 225.
[227] Ibid., p. 107.
[228] Picciotto, *Sketches*, pp. 162–3.

Illiteracy among Jewish bridegrooms and brides, 1841–80

Period of years (inclusive)	Percentage of illiterate bridegrooms		Percentage of illiterate brides	
	Bevis Marks	All England	Bevis Marks	All England
1841–50	9.3	32.0	35.8	47.5
1851–60	6.5	28.6	28.8	40.8
1861–70	11.3	22.0	31.8	30.6
1871–80	7.2	18.5	20.1	25.1

Source: Bevis Marks Records, III, p.6.

Torah.[229] Illiteracy, not surprisingly, was a frequent phenomenon amongst the bridegrooms, and particularly brides, who married at Bevis Marks in the nineteenth century. Well-based estimates are shown in the table. Mayhew, enquiring into London life at this time, found that most Jewish streetboys were illiterate, indifferent to religion and knew no Hebrew, and one girl pedlar had neither heard of the chief rabbi nor knew the difference between the Sephardi and Ashkenazi communities.[230]

The *Talmud Torah* of the Ashkenazim, established in 1732 and reorganized in 1788, admitted only orphan boys, and they had to leave within six months of attaining the age of majority (thirteen years). Elsewhere for example, (Fürth and Amsterdam), as Stein has pointed out, promising boys of precisely this age would continue their education till the age of fifteen or perhaps enter a *yeshivah*.[231] Conditions outside London at the important provincial centres of Portsmouth and Brighton were little better.[232] The middle classes and the wealthy, if they acted at all, engaged private tutors, or sent their children to the numerous private schools conducted by Jewish educationalists – at Highgate, Hammersmith and Hackney (for girls). Outside London there were schools of this type at Brighton, Cambridge and Dover.

No change of substance took place in this situation until 1855 when Jews' College was founded, largely at the insistence of the then chief rabbi,

[229] Quoted P.L. Quinn, 'The Jewish schooling systems of London, 1656–1956', Ph.D diss., University of London, 1958, p. 168.

[230] H. Mayhew, *London Labour and the London Poor*, 2 vols, London, 1851, II, pp. 124ff.

[231] S. Stein, 'Some Ashkenazi charities in London', *TJHSE* XX (1964), p. 69.

[232] C. Roth, 'Educational abuses and reforms in Hanoverian England', in M. Davis (ed.), *M.M. Kaplan Jubilee Volume* (Engl. Sec.), New York, 1953, pp. 470ff.

Nathan Adler. Although hostile to the idea that any of his ministerial colleagues attain full rabbinical status,[233] he made education one of his principal concerns. The aims of the proposed new institution were to provide a Hebrew and English education and also to train ministers, readers and teachers in the service of synagogal functions.

But Adler, despite his association with Montefiore, his status as chief rabbi of the Great, and the latter's Laws and Regulations, which gave Adler (together with the Board of Deputies) the power to sanction the formation of any new congregation,[234] still had to reckon with the power of the emancipationists. He himself, like his predecessor Hirschell and like Montefiore, was unsympathetic to the movement.[235] The proposed institution became in fact involved in a struggle akin to that which would shortly surround the controversy over acceptance of 'the law of the land' on divorce.[236] That is why Adler had to argue against the 'gentlemen who tremble at the idea of an exclusive Jewish school and think it injurious to our present or future social position'.[237]

In the case of Adler's plan, controversy centred on the role to be taken by the *Bet HaMedrash* attached to the Great Synagogue. This had been founded in the eighteenth century as a centre for the study of the Hebrew Bible and Jewish literature, but by 1841 was 'virtually ineffective'.[238] It enjoyed a revival in the late 1840s when Adler expounded the Talmud to about thirty adults every Monday and Thursday morning. The reading room was well attended. This revival had no staying power.[239] Even so, as an institution of traditional Talmudic learning the *Bet HaMedrash* was not easily reconcilable with the type of institution sought by such emancipationists as Salomons and Lionel de Rothschild. Moreover, the trustees of the *Bet HaMedrash*, for entirely different reasons, also resisted association with

---

[233] See the comments by R. Apple, 'United Synagogue: religious founders and leaders', in S.S. Levin (ed.), *A Century of Anglo-Jewish Life, 1870–1970*, London, n.d., pp. 18–19; also Singer, 'Orthodox Judaism', pp. 169–70. Williams (*Manchester Jewry*, pp. 212ff.) deals with the conflict this provoked in the case of the Manchester rabbi Dr Schiller-Szinessy, who later became reader in Talmudic and rabbinic literature at Cambridge.

[234] *Laws and Regulations for all the synagogues in the British Empire*, London, 5607–1847, sec. I, art. 5.

[235] Singer, 'Orthodox Judaism', pp. 104ff.; Stein, *Beginning of Hebrew Studies*, p. 7.

[236] See above, pp. 105ff.

[237] *Jewish Chronicle*, 20 February 1857.

[238] P. Ornstein, *Historical Sketch of the Beth HaMedrash*, London, 1905, p. 4.

[239] Ibid., p. 9; J. Mills (*The British Jews*, London, 1853, p. 304) estimates Adler's study circle at 12–15; cf. also S. Singer, 'Jewish education in the mid-nineteenth century', *JQR*, LXXVII (1986–7), nos 2–3, pp. 169–70.

Adler's plan – *they* feared lest it forfeit its character as a study centre for scholarly immigrants.[240]

In the upshot, the college had a character closer to the continental seminary than to a traditional *yeshivah*. It was first headed by the orientalist Louis Loewe (who had both an academic and a *yeshivah* training), and consisted of a day school and the college proper. The former admitted boys between nine and fifteen years of age who could write and read English and read Hebrew. They were instructed in the translation of the prayer book and Bible, grammar, post-Biblical history, religion, an easy commentary on the Pentateuch and some parts of the Shulchan Aruch (the sixteenth-century code of Jewish law). Their secular instruction comprised English grammar, composition and literature, mathematics, ancient and modern history, geography, natural philosophy and Latin, French and German. The school acted as a sort of 'feeder' to the college. Here the curriculum comprised, in addition to the above, instruction in 'the higher branches of theological and scholastic study'. The students acquired secular knowledge in classical literature, logic and elocution at University College, London. These students were required to be British-born or their parents to have resided ten years in the country.[241]

Little more than a year after opening, the school had forty pupils and the college three students.[242] About ten years later the totals were respectively seventy-one and six.[243] Subsequently, the demand for the facilities of the school dwindled and it was closed in 1879. The college, on the other hand, continued to provide ministers and preachers for the pulpits of Anglo-Jewry. But it cannot be said to have redeemed the intellectual status of Anglo-Jewry.[244] Not until the 1880s – a quarter-century after its foundation – did the college possess a library commensurate with its purported responsibilities. In the 1860s Julius Fürst, the German scholar, found the collection 'shaming for wealthy Anglo-Jewry'.[245] No wonder Solomon Schechter could write in 1901:

> the Jewish clergy . . . are rapidly losing touch with the venerable Rabbi of Jewish tradition, whose chief office was to teach and to *learn* Torah. With us the duty of learning (or study of the Torah) seems

---

[240] Steven Singer, 'The Anglo-Jewish ministry in early Victorian London', *Modern Judaism*, V (Oct. 1985), no. 3, esp. pp. 289ff.

[241] R. Isidore Harris (ed.), *Jews' College Jubilee Volume*, London, 1906, pp. viiiff.

[242] A.M. Hyamson, *Jews' College, 1855–1955*, London, 1955, p. 25.

[243] Harris, *Jews' College Jubilee Volume*, p. xxix.

[244] See Black, *Social Politics*, pp. 123–5.

[245] Quoted Ruth Lehmann, *The Library – A History*, London, 2nd rev. ed., 1967–5727, p. 5.

to be of least moment in the life of the minister. As long as he is *in statu pupillari*, most of his energies are directed toward acquiring the amount of secular learning necessary for the obtaining of a University degree, whilst in his capacity as full Reverend he is expected to divide his time between the offices of cantor, prayer, preacher, book-keeper, debt-collector, almoner and social agitator. No leisure is left to him to enable him to increase his scanty stock of Hebrew knowledge acquired in his undergraduate days. Occasionally rumour spreads anent some minister, that he neglects his duty to his congregation through his being secretly addicted to Jewish learning. But such rumours often turn out to be sheer malice.[246]

The 'legal limbo' in which Anglo-Jewry found itself in the initial years of the resettlement eventually yielded to the admission of virtual equality. This was not a painless process. Certainly, nothing was explicitly asked of the Jews as in France or Germany, but Jews certainly felt constrained to conform to English ways. This is as evident in the efforts to care for the poor as it is in Adler's Laws and Regulations. The latter, with their emphasis on 'quiet and decorum, devotion and solemnity', the wearing of 'clerical costume' etc.,[247] irresistibly recall the Anglican milieu.[248] Similarly, the conversion of the deputies into what was in some respects a quasi-agency of the state entailed some degree of limitation on Jewish autonomy.

But this is far from admitting to any derogation from the requirements of Jewish law, above and beyond what was in any case inseparable from the diaspora context. The Torah proved able to assimilate, and accommodate itself to, 'the law of the land' without undue loss, say in respect of marriage and divorce. Even emancipation, which variously alarmed a body of opinion ranging from Joseph Crooll the messianist to Moses Montefiore and Adler, proved harmless. On the contrary, whatever loss it entailed was more than made good by the increased leverage it gave to the community. Autonomy was in fact enhanced by emancipation on balance.

The condition of this achievement was the creation of a community, on a purely voluntary basis, mediated through a range of institutions. It is true that the community, on the way to this achievement, undeniably lost what-

---

[246] S. Schechter, *Studies in Judaism*, 2nd series, repr., Philadelphia, 1945, pp. 195–6.

[247] Intro., pp. iv, 8.

[248] This is a familiar theme in studies of the period. Cf. M. Goulston, 'The status of the Anglo-Jewish rabbinate, 1840–1914', *JJS*, X (June 1968), no. 1, p. 64; S. Sharot, 'Religious change in native orthodoxy in London, 1870–1914', *JJS*, XV (1973), no. 1, p. 58.

ever interest it had ever had in learning. But it successfully accommodated itself to its milieu and withstood the tension generated by messianic hopes. It is not the case, to borrow a phrase from Macaulay, that 'an acre in Middlesex is better than a principality in Utopia' – rather, in Jewish terms, that this juxtaposition is in itself invalid and belongs to another thought-world. With all its shortcomings, defects, aberrations and lapses, 'Middlesex' had, in fact, to be 'Utopia'.

Part II

4

The Other Side

Idols and Images

The first part of this book is intended to make clear certain salient features in the attempt of the laws to gain a purchase on reality; and how this attempt comes to partial fruition in the contrasting communities of Berlin and London. As I understand it, this sort of activity constitutes one grand theme in the history of the Jews – not of course in the sense that the laws are immutable; still less in the sense that London and Berlin typify the organized life of Jews, in the modern period or at any other. It may well be the case that only phenomenologically can Jewish history be understood. Should this be so, what I understand as the control of reality would still remain an abiding aim and theme. And the fulfilment of this aim would still be dependent on a true perception of the real; or, perhaps, what the laws themselves designate as the real. Interaction must certainly be allowed for.

Even in this reciprocal relationship between construction and construct, however, the notion of the real functions as a counterpart to the notion of idolatry in the widest sense. The latter connotes both misperception and, consequently, mistaken action. In its least complex manifestation it takes shape in the guise of artistic imagery, and sometimes as artistic imagery in the form of idolatry. These two fields of activity are by no means identical but they do overlap. Precisely where this takes place is by no means clear. The terminology is itself uncertain. There is no Hebrew term for 'art'[1]; and the term 'idolatry' is inadequate to render the Hebrew expression *avodah zarah*. Literally this denotes 'strange/alien work/service/worship'. It comes to verge on phenomena of wider import than the exclusively material phenomena which the Bible designates as *avodah zarah*; it is expressed, for example, in such negative traits of conduct as arrogance, loss of temper

---

[1] M. Steinschneider, *Allgemeine Einleitung in die jüdische Litteratur des Mittelalters*, Jerusalem, 1938, p. 23.

and wilful destructiveness.[2] Because *avodah zarah* has this wide-ranging connotation, I shall normally use this Hebrew term rather than the comparatively limited 'idolatry'; the latter, though certainly contained in the former, is only one part of it.

Ultimately at stake is the attempt to disenchant the world; alternatively, to avert its enchantment. The idol, as Rosenzweig pointed out, has two faces. Only in retrospect, seen from revelation, is it a substitute for God; in itself, once it has emerged, it is a substitute for reality.[3] But in either case it is the target for the process of disenchantment.[4]

In terms of the Torah, this role is transmuted into an attempt to rid the world of any influence, or source of influence, the effect of which is to impede the Torah's attempt to exert its own influence. Perhaps it can best be grasped through the notion of reification, making out of a sign – whether natural or man-made – some entity to which reality and effectiveness is attributed.[5] By endowing an object, an historical event, a social role, institutions, etc., with ontological status, it changes the way in which reality is experienced from truth to illusion. Rabbi Israel of Rizhin has it that the messianic world will be a world without images, 'in which the image and its object can no longer be related'.[6] This would signify apparently that the temptation to reify the world had been completely overcome and the Torah had achieved its purpose.

Uncertainty remains, of course. A range of artifacts in a range of contexts will always create a penumbra of doubt, but any further attempt at definition would do violence to rabbinic ways of thinking, which choose to work in the empirical mode and treat of specific phenomena rather than operate on any *a priori* basis. The method is inductive and inferential, creating generalities from particulars and then using the generalities to generate further particulars, in a continuous process of ratiocination. Further – historically speaking – Hellenistic notions of decoration, pagan symbols, Islamic aniconism and Christian iconolatry have at different times all affected Jewish custom, practice and theory, in the same way as Jewish teaching has influenced Byzantium, Wycliffites, Lollards, Taborites, Puritans, etc. Jewish practice was born from its own immanent dynamism, qualified by the

[2] TB Shab. 105b.

[3] F. Rosenzweig, *Briefe und Tagebücher 1*, II, The Hague, 1979, p. 770.

[4] See also M. Weber, *Gesammelte Aufsätze zur Religionssoziologie*, Tübingen, 1923, III, pp. 216ff., 240ff.

[5] See also Susan Handelman, *The Slayers of Moses*, Albany, New York, 1982, p. 104; I. Halpérin and G. Lévitte (eds), *Idoles: Données et Débats*, Paris, 1985, p. 138.

[6] G. Scholem, *The Messianic idea in Judaism*, London, 1971, p. 35.

experience of contact with manifold non-Jewish influences, themselves subject to variation over time.[7] The norms of representation have also had to take within their purview the consequences of such technical and artistic innovations as stained-glass windows, portrait painting and photography. All this affected consistency in practice (which does not of course necessarily imply that there will have been any derogation from the necessary standards of scholarly scrutiny). Even extraneous motive may have played a part; it may be that the approval extended to Jewish seamstresses in medieval Spain to embroider dresses with the sign of the cross had economic considerations in mind (although it was also pointed out that the symbol was here not used for the purpose of worship but only as a decoration).[8] Similarly, in Talmudic times, Jewish artisans and craftsmen were only permitted to make ornaments for an idol if they were paid for their work – that is, if it was a source of livelihood and not of belief.[9]

For the moment I shall deal primarily with the status of *avodah zarah* in the narrow physical sense – in the sense of those 'other gods' which the Israelites served beyond the Jordan.[10] The classical example is, of course, the episode of the golden calf at Sinai (Ex. 32), for here there is both a physical man-made object invested with divine power and a specific form of worship. Such practices did not cease with the crossing of the Jordan. The worship of 'the sun or the moon, or any of the host of heaven' (Dt. 17:3) is paralleled by the images and 'the star of your god' denounced by Amos (Amos 5:26). Other, related phenomena include the cult of Baal (for example, I Kings 16:31); the installation of strange gods in the Temple at Jerusalem (II Kings 21); child sacrifice to Moloch (Jer. 7:31; Ezek. 16:36); sacred prostitution (Ezek. 16:17); and the craftsman-made 'calf of Samaria' (Hosea 8:6). Whether the 'other gods' worshipped in these various ways are to be considered as genuine embodiments of power – as Goldberg argued [11] – or whether the worship is purely fetishistic, is immaterial. The fact is that an authentic contest is being waged in which the Torah must eliminate the material means employed in the worship of those 'other gods' and the belief in their existence. Imagery, in whatever guise and in whatever medium, is a genuine enemy. The aniconism characteristic of the Pentateuch and the Prophets is by no means grounded in contempt for the image – rather in a respect for the image that elevates it to the status of rival. The hostility to graven and other images and representations is ambivalent; it derives not only from scorn at their impotence but also from a respectful

---

[7] Boaz Cohen, 'Art in Jewish law', *Judaism*, III (Spring, 1954), no. 2, pp. 165–76.

[8] Quoted B.-Z. Dinur, *Toldot Yisrael*, 2, Bk II, Jerusalem, 1966, p. 226, no. 34.

[9] TB AZ, 19b.

[10] Joshua 24:2.

[11] Oskar Goldberg, *Die Wirklichkeit der Hebräer*, Berlin, 1925.

recognition of their persuasive power. According to Rabbi Moritz Güdemann of Vienna: 'The exclusion of art as a danger already involves the acknowledgement of its bearing, its fascinating effect.'[12] Hermann Cohen spoke of the 'magic powers' of the image.[13]

It is for this reason that in all those passages where the Pentateuch refers to *avodah zarah* it does so in the context of an explicit confrontation between the idol and the one God.[14] This is most notably the case in the first version of the ten commandments. In the first commandment (as customarily known) God identifies and presents himself as that particular *Elohim* (from amongst the others known to the Bible) who rescued the Israelites from servitude in Egypt. This is at once followed by the prohibition of the worship of 'other gods'. 'I am the Lord thy God, who brought thee out of the land of Egypt, out of the house of bondage. Thou shalt have no other gods before Me. Thou shalt not make unto thee a graven image', etc.[15] The same pattern is repeated in the episode of the golden calf;[16] again in Leviticus: 'ye shall make you no idols, neither shall ye rear up a graven image, or a pillar, neither shall ye place any figured stone in your land, to bow down unto it; for I am the Lord your God';[17] and in Deuteronomy, when Moses recapitulates the laws, he recalls: 'the Lord commanded me at that time to teach you statutes and ordinances, that ye might do them in the land whither ye go over to possess it. Take ye therefore good heed unto yourselves – for ye saw no manner of form on the day that the Lord spake unto you in Horeb out of the midst of the fire – lest ye deal corruptly, and make you a graven image' etc.[18] The commandment is reiterated in at least three other passages.[19] The first 'curse' in the Deuteronomic series is reserved for 'the man that maketh a graven or molten image, an abomination unto the Lord, the work of the hands of the craftsmen, and setteth it up in secret'.[20]

This antithesis underlies the view of Maimonides that to reject *avodah*

---

[12] 'Das Judentum und die bildenden Künste' (unpublished lecture given at the Jewish Museum, Vienna, 3 January 1898 – typescript, Hebrew University, Jerusalem).

[13] *Religion der Vernunft aus den Quellen des Judentums*, repr., Wiesbaden, 1978, pp. 65–6.

[14] Carmel Konikoff, *The Second Commandment and its Interpretation in the Art of Ancient Israel*, Geneva, 1973, pp. 25ff.

[15] Ex. 20: 2–4ff.

[16] Ex. 32: 7–8.

[17] Lev. 26:1.

[18] Dt. 4:14–16.

[19] Ibid. 4:25; 5:6–7; 16:21–2.

[20] Dt. 27:15.

zarah constituted a singular criterion of truth. Not only did he argue that the commandments relating to *avodah zarah* equalled in weight all other commandments combined; he also argued that to reject *avodah zarah* was tantamount to the acceptance of the whole Torah.[21] That is why Maimonides also proclaimed that the first aim of the Torah was in fact to extirpate *avodah zarah*,[22] and apprehended the whole course of human history in terms of such ongoing extirpation.[23]

Embellishment and Disturbance

Despite the inseparable association of imagery and *avodah zarah*, the boundaries of both must be appreciated. Aniconism did not of itself exclude access to beauty, still less the production of artifacts. But this did not extend to *ars gratia artis*. Any artifact had to serve a purpose. Maimonides, who was unquestionably amongst the more stringent rabbis in his aesthetic tolerance, nonetheless welcomed 'the satisfaction of the senses' engendered by 'the contemplation of pleasing decorations and objects'; these would refresh the soul for further study.[24] Earlier, in Talmudic times, Rabban Gamliel was held to be justified in his use of pictures of phases of the moon for calendrical purposes, despite the doubt attaching to his representations of the heavenly bodies. He used only sections of the moon, it was argued, and thereby avoided any complete representation, and/or his purpose was pedagogic.[25]

In terms of aesthetic expression the most notable vehicle was derived from the verse: 'This is my God and I will adorn him.'[26] This was understood by the Talmud to signify 'the embellishment of a commandment', and was exemplified in a scroll of the Law, written with a fine pen by a skilled scribe and wrapped in beautiful silk.[27] Other manifestations of the same artistic/creative impulse include, at random, a figured fountain in the courtyard of the synagogue at Palermo (late fifteenth century); or the tombstone to Sabatai Elchanan (d. Bologna, 1546) showing a female figure in the round; or even symbolic representations of the deity in the Sephardi cemetery at Oudekerke and in the synagogues of Ravitsch and Ragozen:

---

[21] MT Laws of Avodah Zarah, 2:4.
[22] *Guide*, III, 29:31.
[23] See E. Schweid, *Ha-Rambam ve-hug hashpa'ato*, Jerusalem, 1973, pp. 15–16.
[24] *Eight Chapters, Introduction to Treatise Avot*, ch. V.
[25] TB RH, 24a–b.
[26] Ex. 15:2.
[27] TB Shab. 133b.

two hands, veiled in cloud, hold aloft the decalogue at the Ark.[28]

In Poland biblical scenes adorned certain synagogues – the binding of Isaac, Noah's Ark, the exiles by the waters of Babylon. This was specifically the case in Renaissance synagogues such as the High Synagogue in Cracow or the Isaac Nachmanowitz Synagogue in Lvov. Anonymous popular artists also depicted the holy cities of Hebron (Cave of Machpelah, Gen. 23:9) and Jerusalem.[29] Such exercises seem to have been less frequent in the synagogues of Spain and Western Europe where, by contrast, the illumination of manuscripts and prayer books proliferated.[30]

In all these instances, however, a balance is required so that the embellishment does not obscure or distort the commandment. The object is certainly not to create an autonomous work of art – merely to enhance a divine commandment to which the embellishment is subordinate. The balance therefore is not equal between the normative and the aesthetic components, because the latter subserve the former.[31] So long as this relationship is maintained, then rabbinical scruples are laid aside and criticism easily dismissed. Thus in the mid-twelfth century R. Ephraim of Regensburg, in response to a query from R. Joel Halevy (see above p. 33), permitted the depiction of birds and horses on synagogue hangings: 'men do not worship the images of birds and horses even when they are depicted separately and all the more so if they are shown on coverings . . . there are therefore no grounds for suspicion.'[32] This was also the view taken by R. Joseph Caro when a questioner asked him whether it was permissible to use as a curtain hanging before the Ark a silk cloth on which had been embroidered a number of figures including birds: 'when the congregation rises to pray they bend towards the Ark and it would seem as if, heaven forfend, they are prostrating themselves before the figures'. Caro followed the arguments of R. Ephraim of Regensburg, extending in fact their permissiveness: 'and even if it were the figure of a man it would perhaps be acceptable'. From this it followed that since there was no suspicion of *avodah zarah* 'the person who bows towards them is as though he bows

[28] A. Grotte, 'Die Kunst in Judentum and das 2 mosaische Gebot', *Der Morgen*, iv (June 1928), no. 2, pp. 176–7.

[29] David Davidowitz, *Omanut V'Umanim b'vatei knesset shel Polin*, Jerusalem, 1982, p. 18.

[30] Ibid., p. 33; cf. also Elkan Adler, 'Jewish art', in B. Schindler (ed.), *Occident–Orient*, London, 1936, pp. 37–49.

[31] See Dr. I. Unna, 'Asthetische Gesichtspunkte im Religionsgesetz', *Jeschurun* (ed. J. Wohlgemuth), I (January 1914), no. 1, pp. 13–19; A. Altmann, 'Zum Wesen der jüdischen Aesthetik', *Jeschurun*, XIV (May–June 1927), nos 5–6, pp. 209–26.

[32] Quoted Kahana, *Mehkarim be-sifrut*, p. 354.

towards a hanging or wall on which there is no figure'.[33]

But at some indeterminate point what is permissible embellishment becomes impermissible. This stage is reached when equilibrium between the embellishment and the commandment is lost, and the former comes to overshadow the latter. At this point a state of disturbance is created, the effect of which is to take the worshipper, student, teacher away from his involvement with God and towards involvement with some sort of image. What Güdemann and Hermann Cohen called 'magic powers', 'fascinating effect', exercise their sway. Some part of the attention that belongs to God is transferred to an artifact which thus itself becomes – to some extent – the object of devotion, and thus – again to some extent – an idol, irrespective of its original purpose. It partakes of a degree of reification. This object is claiming for itself some measure of what is due to God. God is diminished, and an object enhanced. Visual representations are certainly not the sole source of such displacement: the first Mishnah in Berakhoth (chapter V) speaks of intellectual pre-occupation, distress, frivolity, etc. as other such sources. Moreover, a conflict of duties might well emerge should the distraction from prayer actually arise from concern with the performance of some other commandment; for example, in the case of a bridegroom on his wedding night: he is dispensed from the obligation to recite certain night-time prayers.[34] But this is remote from the manufacture of a tangible or visible object deliberately designed to attract attention.

The danger of disturbance is exemplified in the rejection by R. Isaac b. Moses Or Zarua of the trees and birds depicted in the medieval synagogue at Meissen. They would excite admiration and thus betray the worshipper or teacher into the same trap that rendered culpable a certain 'R. Jacob': he interrupted his teaching in order to contemplate a beautiful tree.[35] R. David ibn Abi Zimra denounced without reserve the installation in a Cretan synagogue (sixteenth century) of the coat-of-arms of a benefactor that included a lion in marble bas-relief. Ibn Zimra admitted that rabbinical views were divergent but justified the exclusion of this imagery on the grounds that it smacked of idolatry, that the lion was one of the bearers of the 'heavenly chariot', that it imitated Christian custom, that it would appear as though the congregation were bending to an image and, lastly, that 'in looking at this form they are not directing their heart to their father in

---

[33] *Avkat Rochel*, Leipzig, 1859, no. 66. R. Akiba Eger, however, limited synagogue decoration to representations from the plant world (Davidowitz, *Omanut V'Umanim*, p. 20).

[34] TB Ber. 16a.

[35] Or Zarua, *Piskei Avodah Zarah*, pt 4, ch. 3, no. 203. For 'R. Jacob', cf. *Pirkei Avot* 3:9 and below p. 155, fn. 131.

heaven'.[36] In sixteenth-century Padua, R. Samuel Archivolti protested at 'decorations [that] destroy intent and separate us from our God ... why should our synagogues resemble taverns where people quaff goblets of wine in painted rooms; and why should synagogue walls look like the walls of comedians' theatres'.[37] The same scruples animated R. Meir b. Baruch of Rothenburg when he was asked for his opinion regarding the propriety of decorating prayer books with the coloured figures of animals and birds. This activity was 'certainly not attractive', he replied, 'for in looking at these figures people are not directing their heart to their father in heaven'. Nevertheless, he added, 'there is no prohibition here for these figures are ... of no substance and [*avodah zarah*] is only suspected in the case of a raised seal and not of a sunken seal and all the less so in this case which is neither sunken nor raised but unspecific colour'.[38] Rabbi Moses Isserles, in sixteenth-century Poland, also accepted this view.[39]   It was obviously far more satisfactory if the synagogue could be protected from any decoration at all. This was made clear by Rabbenu Asher b. Yehiel in his Code, the *Tur*: 'and nothing must come between the man [at prayer] and the wall. The Ark and the reader's desk do not intrude but all other things or vessels, etc. do.'[40] Caro, in commenting on this passage of the *Tur*, quotes a responsum by Maimonides. The latter argued that turning in prayer to images, even if they do not project, is undesirable because it bewilders the mind to see them and intent is endangered. 'And we close our eyes in prayer when this happens to us, whether the curtain or the wall is decorated.'[41]

There is also a category of representations that do not disturb so much as suggest or implant false teaching; for example, the chequered history of the zodiac as a decorative motif. Or was it purely decorative? To some authorities the zodiac suggested a belief in astrology. Although it figured in illuminated marriage contracts in seventeenth-century Italy (which also included engravings of Biblical lovers – Abraham and Sarah, Isaac and Rebeccah, Jacob and Rachel), suspicion required that the twelve planets be represented in an untraditional anti-clockwise direction, from right to left; also the signs were arranged in formal pairs, so that the two crustaceans,

[36] R. David ibn Abi Zimra, *She'elot u-Tshuvot*, Livorno, 1652, no. 107. The 'heavenly chariot' is a reference to Ezekiel's vision (Ezek. 1:4ff.); cf. also TB Hag. 13b.

[37] This responsum is reprinted with an introduction in D. Kaufman, 'Art in the synagogue', *JQR*, IX (January 1897), pp. 254–69.

[38] TB Tos. Yoma 54a–b, s.v. cherubim.

[39] 'Darkhei Moshe to the *Tur*', *OH Laws of Prayer*, no. 90.

[40] Ibid.

[41] J. Blau (ed.), *Tshuvot Ha'Rambam*, 3 vols, Jerusalem, 1947–60, II, no. 215.

Scorpio and Cancer, faced each other.[42] In Poland aniconism in the synagogue eliminated from the zodiac the representation of human beings or
human heads. Artists replaced the astronomical sign Virgo by, for example,
a wedding canopy or a hand holding flowers, and Sagittarius by a bow and
arrow.[43] This would not have satisfied R. Eliezer Deitsch of Banihad,
Hungary. In 1900 he was questioned by a congregation of Hungarian Jews
in Newark, New Jersey: was their proposed use of the signs of the zodiac as
a form of synagogue decoration permissible? Deitsch disallowed it entirely. It
was immaterial whether the signs were embossed or sunken – the affair
was in itself ugly. Moreover, they would lend themselves to the possibility
of false teaching. To display the signs of the zodiac would contradict the
notion of prayer with its conviction of divine providence, whereas, pronounced Deitsch:

> Israel has no planet, and even if, heaven forfend, a man's fate points
> to misfortune, he can turn this to good through mercy and supplication
> and if so how can we put before our eyes the form of the planets,
> something that teaches that we also, heaven forfend, are subject to
> the arrangement of the heavens and their governance. . . What a man
> depicts before his eyes makes a great impression on his thought and
> intention. . . Can we not beautify the house of God in a permissible
> way rather than in this?[44]

God and the World

However important the contribution made by the notion of 'disturbance'
and its concomitant, obscuring the word of God, to the understanding of
avodah zarah, it remains a preliminary stage. The degree of reification
involved is indeed small. There is, admittedly, identification, by way of
transference, displacement and association, of what is directed to the Torah
with what is part of the existent, but this remains incidental and arbitrary.
Only when God is in one way or another identified with the world, wholly
or partially, can a full understanding of *avodah zarah* be attained – in other

---

[42] F. Landsberger, 'Illuminated marriage contracts', *HUCA*, XXVI (1955), pp.
502–42. Other forms of marriage contracts to incur censure were those decorated
with pictures of the bride and groom, the sun and the moon. (Cf. the views of R.
Abraham b. Moses di Boton, Salonica, sixteenth century, and of R. Isaac Lampronti,
Ferrara, eighteenth century, quoted in J. Guttmann, *The Jewish Life Cycle*, London,
1987, p. 13).

[43] Davidowitz, *Omanut V'Umanim*, pp. 20–1.

[44] Quoted Kahana, *Mehkarim be-sifrut*, p. 362.

words, when the existent is reified. At this point a crucial barrier has been transgressed. A world which has no sanctity is spuriously transcended. In the background stands the argument that the world is exclusively the creation of God. When the sages of the Talmud debate why man was created last, one answer is this: 'so that the Sadducees would not say that the Holy One, Blessed be He, had a partner in the act of creation'.[45] *Avodah zarah*, however, subverts this in that it denotes an effort by man to bring God into the world. It thereby removes the tension between the fulfilment of the Torah and the attempt at its fulfilment. The fight against *avodah zarah* must therefore take the form of denying any alleged possibility, other than through the Torah, of communication and mediation between man and God. Any such alleged possibility in effect precludes genuine communication.

The crucial prohibition is contained in Maimonides's exposition of the seventh in his version of the 613 commandments: 'whoever couples God's name with anything else is uprooted from the world.'[46] He is echoed across the centuries. R. Moses Isserles (Poland, sixteenth century), declared that man, 'by making an intermediate between himself and God will bring down the whole Torah for this is the causative factor of unbelief in God, and if man says that this is only an intermediary it is as though through this *avodah zarah* proliferated in the world'.[47] Likewise R. Judah Loew b. Bezalel (Prague, sixteenth century): an image, even if made only in order to serve God, eventually becomes an intermediate entity, 'and everything that is intermediary between man and the one he serves is *avodah zarah*'. Such an image can only be subjective for, argues Judah Loew (referring to Dt. 4:12), 'you saw no manner of form . . . and you make a form to Him who has no form and if so this is absolute idolatry.'[48]

Now the notion of 'absolute idolatry' is exemplified above all in the three-dimensional reproduction of a man. There are two inter-penetrating reasons for this. The first arises from the fact that it was in the vision of a man that God appeared to the prophets.[49] Any such reproduction would therefore suggest the attribution of human form to that which is formless and thus constitute a falsification of the reality of God and, further, a barrier to the understanding of God.[50] This would apply even if the sculptor, say,

---

[45] TB San. 38a. (The Sadducees are at this time considered heretics, unbelievers.)

[46] *Sefer Ha-Mitzvot*, p. 158.

[47] R. Moses Isserles, *Torat Ha'Olah*, ed. D. Elbaum, Tel Aviv, 1983, pt 1, ch. 16, pp. 18b–19; Halpérin and Lévitte, *Idoles*, p. 146.

[48] *Tiferet Yisrael*, repr., Jerusalem, 1970, ch. 46, p. 14.

[49] See Caro's commentary ('Beth Yosef') to the *Tur, Yore Deah, Laws of Avodah Zarah*, no. 141 (referring to TB Rosh Ha'Shana, 24b).

[50] See Güdemann, 'Das Judentum', p. 6.

were explicitly to foreswear any such intention or even suggestion. As any man is formed 'in the image of God', the sculptured representation of any man, even for adornment, must bear that image and point to his maker.[51] Obviously, the argument would apply *a fortiori* should the sculptured man actually be intended, as it were, to be a god. The second argument that founds the prohibition of a sculptural representation arises from a deficiency inherent in the very product of the sculptor's craft: he cannot reproduce in his physical medium that spirit that alone makes a man what he is. In other words, his task is impossible and his statue again a falsification.[52] The only way to render a human sculpture acceptable and permissible was by disfiguring it so that it would no longer be complete ('the principle of incompleteness').[53] Caro writes: 'there are those who say that the figure of a man or a mythical animal was prohibited only in the case of a complete figure with all his members, but the figure of a head, or a body without a head is not prohibited at all.'[54] *Per contra*, that is why R. Moses Schreiber (the Ḥatam Sofer, Moravia, nineteenth century) required a sculptor to deform two silver figures of Moses and Aaron which he had fashioned as adornments for a scroll of the Law. He demanded that the tips of the noses on the two figures be removed. In another case Schreiber prohibited prayers at a grave marked by a tombstone bearing the statue of a man in relief – unless and until the figure was removed or 'squashed'.[55]

---

[51] Cf. the Ḥinukh, commandment no. 39.

[52] See S. Schwarzschild, 'The legal foundations of Jewish aesthetics', *Journal of Aesthetic Education*, IX (January 1975), no. 1, pp. 29–42, esp. pp. 33ff.; cf. also D. Novak, *Law and Theology in Judaism*, New York, 1974, ch. 6 ('Fine art in the synagogue').

[53] Schwarzschild, 'Legal Foundations'.

[54] Shulhan Arukh, *Yoreh Deah*, 141:7 ('And this is the custom', comments Isserles, ad. loc.).

[55] *Sefer Ḥatam Sofer*, pt vi, New York, 1958, nos. 6, 4. These cases are discussed, though in an unsympathetic spirit, by L. Löw in his *Beiträge zur Jüdischen Altertumskunde*, Leipzig, 1870, pp. 39, 209. The opposition of 'incompleteness' or 'distortion' to what Goux terms 'le régime sémiotique représentatif' is demonstrated in the work of Delauney, Kandinsky, Malevitch, Mondrian (painting); in Schönberg, Berg, Webern (music), (Goux, *Les Iconoclastes*, p. 133). See also Schwarzschild, 'Legal foundations'. J. Sabil ('Les juifs dans la peinture française moderne', in Finbert, *Aspects du Génie*, pp. 274–86), referring to the work of Pissarro, Modigliani, Chagall, Soutine et al., points to 'a meeting' between modern art and the Jewish condemnation of 'the image as an arbitrary fixation of appearance outside time, as a blasphemous attack on the majesty of time'. Bruno Zevi ('Ebraismo e concezione spazio-temporale nell'arte', *Rassegna mensile d'Israel* [June 1974], pp. 207–22) makes the same point when he speaks of a Jewish preference for becoming over being and formation over form, whereas it is 'the consciousness of space that feeds idolatry'.

Other teachers took a more stringent approach and even to one-dimensional representations applied 'the principle of incompleteness': thus the eyes in the wall paintings at the famous synagogue in Dura-Europos were scratched out.[56] The same criterion was applied when portrait-painting and photography developed as modes of human representation. R. Zvi Hirsch Ashkenazi, the 'Haham Zvi' of Hamburg and Amsterdam, father of the famous R. Jacob Emden (1697–1776), refused to sit for a portrait which an appreciative Sephardi congregation in London wished to present him with. The congregation had to resort to a subterfuge and employ an artist who performed the task in the absence of his subject.[57] In the late nineteenth century a photographic portrait was challenged by the noted Polish rabbi, Malkiel Zvi Halevi Tennenbaum, and, more recently, by R. Menashe Klein of New York.[58] R. Abraham Kuk (Palestine, twentieth century) took a middle stance: a photographic portrait of the human face was permissible provided that it did not extend to the whole body.[59]

But if a complete human representation in the round is, without qualification or dissent, the object most redolent of *avodah zarah*, it is of course not the only one. The golden calf is another example, and in principle there is no object that is not susceptible to reification, as religious history abundantly attests (compare the recently established journal, *Visible Religion*: Leyden, 1982, and after). In the light of the Torah these all denote spurious attempts to supplant its own task as the sole and true medium of communication with God. That is why I would like to argue that all objects used in this manner lie along the same continuum in that all partake of a common capacity to alienate their respective protagonists from the Torah.

[56] E. R. Goodenough, *Jewish Symbolism in Dura*, New York, 1964, pp. ix–a, 23–4; see also E. Bevan, *Holy Images*, London, 1940, p. 59. It is also significant that no human representation appeared on the Jewish coins issued in Hasmonean times (U. Rappaport, 'The emergence of Hasmonean coinage', *AJSR*, I [1976], p. 183).

[57] R. Jacob Emden, *She'ilot Yavetz*, Altona, 1739, pt 1, no. 170. Hirsch Ashkenazi had visited London in 1704–5 in order to adjudicate in a theological dispute at the Bevis Marks congregation.

[58] Cf. She'elot Divrei Malkiel no. 58, 1897; She'elot Mishne Halakhoth no. 114, 1977. (I owe these references to the kindness of the late Judge Bernard Meislin of New Jersey.)

[59] R. Louis Jacobs, *Theology in the Responsa*, London, 1975, p. 327. It is significant, however, that attempts to validate photographic portraits attributed to them quasi-magical influence: David Zvi Katzburg in his introduction to Avigdor Katzburg, *Tmunot Ha'Gedolim im Me'orot v'Korot Ḥayehem*, New York, 1925, argued that the photographic portrait of a great teacher 'would awaken healthy emotion in the heart of the viewer' and could be compared in its effect to 'the vision that the righteous Joseph' had of his father, Jacob. (According to tradition this vision enabled Joseph to resist seduction at the hands of Potiphar's wife [Gen. 37:7ff.].)

More – when Hermann Cohen writes of 'the contradiction, the antithesis to art that necessarily arises in prophetic monotheism' and of an art that 'ascends from sensuous objects to the gods',[60] he is drawing attention to the ontological identify of art and *avodah zarah*. Conversely, he is confirming Feuerbach's defence of polytheism as 'the basis of science and art'.[61] The distance from a marble lion in a Cretan synagogue to the golden calf of the Sinai desert may not be all that great. It is at least sufficient to justify rabbinic suspicion and reserve. Pygmalion was an object-lesson to the rabbis as much as to the Greeks.

Against Nature

What applies to the artifacts of man applies also to the artifact of God; that is, nature. This is no more the abode of divinity than is a statue or an idol. This again does not exclude appreciation for visual beauty: 'Blessed art you, O Lord our God, King of the Universe, who has made the creation.'[62] There is a beauty that, as attaching to the creation, can legitimately be admired. But admiration (and the stewardship of nature) remains the limit of response, for only this can preserve the crucial distinction between the creator and the creation. Should this limit be transgressed, then nature has played the role of the commandment that has been 'over-embellished', and the admirer will have succumbed to the disturbance thereby created. It was precisely to this sort of reaction that Maimonides traced the inception of *avodah zarah*, in the form of star-worship. He located this in the days of Enosh. It was then that men said,

> since God has created these stars and planets to guide the world and has placed them in the firmament and given them honour and they are servitors who serve Him they are deservedly praised, glorified and honoured. And it is the will of God, blessed be He, that men aggrandise and honour those whom He aggrandised and honoured . . . when this idea entered their heart they began to build temples to the stars to offer sacrifices to them, to praise and glorify them in words and to bow down before them in order, through their evil thinking, to win the favour of the Creator.

Such people, Maimonides continues, 'do not say that there is no God

---

[60] Cohen, *Religion der Vernunft*, p. 62.

[61] L. Feuerbach, *Das Wesen des Christentums*, 2 vols, Berlin, 1956, VI, p. 191.

[62] See also the more specific occasions evocative of appreciation (e.g. mountains, seas) in *Singer's Prayer Book*, 14th edn, London, 1929, pp. 287ff.

save this star'. But in course of time the star comes to be represented by an image and this image then becomes invested with divine attributes so that, save for a few individuals, the true notion of God is lost; 'and they did not know Him and all the ordinary people, the women and children knew only the figure of wood and stone'.[63]

But if nature is conceived of as amoral and inert,[64] then it is impossible to deify it. What is amoral cannot also be, in any sense at all, divine. This, in its turn, follows from the proclaimed nature of God as transcendent teacher, and is a most powerful deterrent to the reification of nature. This was precisely understood by Hegel. 'The divine exists as unity and universality, essentially only for thought and – being in himself imageless – is withdrawn from the forming and structuring of the fantasy; so it is then also forbidden to Jews and Mohammedans to form for themselves an image of God for closer contemplation in the sensuous world. There is no room here therefore for plastic art which absolutely requires the most concrete vitality of the shape.'[65] Thus, to conceive of God as a teacher, writes Hegel, was tantamount to removing Him from the world, nature etc.;[66] God conceived as pure abstract spirit left the natural world 'without spirit'; it became 'prose', 'undeified'.[67]

Isaiah is a strong, perhaps the strongest, case in point, proclaiming that the same wood used to create an image for worship lends itself indifferently to the making of bread, the roasting of meat or the heating of one's house: 'shall I fall down to the stock of a tree?', Isaiah asks contemptuously.[68] Of course, it is not necessary to be Jewish to agree with Isaiah: compare Epictetus's question: 'What work of art has in itself the faculties of which it gives indication in its structure? Is it not stone or bronze or gold or ivory?[69]

It is in this light that the scriptural injunction to construct an altar of

---

[63] MT Book of Knowledge, Laws of star worship, I, 1–2; cf. also Rashi's comments on Gen. 4:26, where he points out that it was at the time of Enosh that men began 'to call the names of men and the names of images by the name of the Holy One blessed be He to make them objects of worship and to call them divine'.

[64] See above p. 8.

[65] *Aesthetik I*, Berlin-Weimar, 1965, pp. 175–6.

[66] *Der Geist des Judentums, Frühe Schriften I*, Frankfurt on Main, 1971, pp. 277–9, 298–9, 304.

[67] *Philosophy of History*, Eng. trans., New York, 1944, pp. 195ff.

[68] Is. 44:9–19; for a discussion of the identical views of Elijah and the Psalmist, see Jose Halevi Faur, *Iyunim ba-Mishneh-Torah le-ha-Rambam*, Jerusalem, 1978, p. 205.

[69] *Discourses*, trans. P. E. Matheson, Oxford, 1916, II, Bk 2, 8:19–20; cf. also Bevan, *Holy Images*, pp. 64ff.

earth, or, if of stone, that the stones remain unhewn, is understood (Ex. 20:21–2). In both cases, the material is not identifiable with the presence of God. Both are designedly anonymous and undistinguished, in such a way as to avert any temptation to locate God in any particular place.[70]

So out go the sacred shrines, grottos, groves, relics, effigies, images etc. dear to the pagan and Christian worlds and certain Jewish circles. There are no Shakespearean 'tongues in trees, books in the running brooks, sermons in stones'; no Blakean 'Holy Word, that walked among the ancient trees'. Caught in the same trap are many of the folk-religious aspects of Ḥassidism: the belief in angels, spirits (good and evil), saintly human intermediaries between man and God and even a sort of pantheism: during the penitential period preceding the New Year and the Day of Atonement, the very fish in the streams tremble; on the scholars' festival (Lag ba-Omer) between Passover and Pentecost all the trees rejoice.[71] The Ḥassidic notion that a man could 'transmit/transfer' his prayer to a human intermediary was condemned as 'absolute idolatry' by their opponents.[72]

What, then, is left of nature? Its indispensable function as the source of man's sustenance and wellbeing, and the raw material, so to speak, for the performance of the *mitzvot*. Natural phenomena are evaluated in terms of their halakhic properties. This is the *modus operandi* whereby God is brought into the world; it is not through the deification of a grotto or a tree. When Soloveitchik's 'man of law' encounters a spring, he asks: 'does it meet the legal requirement demanded of this or that norm', such as immersion? When he sees trees, plants, animals, fruits etc. 'he classifies them according to their species and genera' and their degree of ripeness, for these criteria will determine their eligibility for religious purposes; sunrise, sunset are calls to the performance of specific time-bound commandments; mounds, hilltops are evaluated in the perspective of their legal standing.[73]

There *are* attempts, such as that of the Jewish Hegelian, Dr Salomon Formstecher, to create some sort of conciliation. In contrasting natural religion, with its dependence on plastic art, and Judaism, which must disavow such art, Formstecher writes: 'no plastic symbol must arouse the thought of God, no statue make Him present; only the contemplation of the divine creation and of divine rule shall cause the Israelite to feel the nearness of his God.'[74] But such a view is isolated amongst the multitudin-

[70] See E. Shohat, 'Magamot Politiyot be-sipurei ha'avot', *Tarbitz*, 24, 1955, pp. 252–67, esp. p. 266; also R. Judah Loew b. Bezalel, *Tiferet Yisrael*, pp. 140–1.

[71] A. J. Heschel, *The Earth is the Lord's*, Torchbook edn, New York, 1966, p. 19.

[72] M. Vilensky (ed.), *Ḥassidim u-Mitnagdim*, 2 vols, Jerusalem, 1970, p. 236.

[73] R. Joseph Soloveitchik, *Halakhic Man*, Engl. trans., Philadelphia 1983, pp. 20–1.

[74] Dr S. Formstecher, *Die Religion des Geistes*, Frankfurt on Main, 1841, p. 68.

ous denunciations of pantheism, which, in Hegel's terms, reduce nature to 'prose'.[75] Overwhelmingly, Jewish thought emphasized the utter transcendence of God and thus sought to ensure that no pantheistic obstacle hampered man's communication with the divine.[76] This is a crucial aspect of that revolt against the given to which I referred in Part I. It is the very condition of that revolt. It is only through iconoclasm and the refusal to enchant nature that the Torah can be implemented.

Preserving the Word

The ideal mode of communication between God and man would be immediate and unmediated. It would coincide with the deconstructionist ideal whereby thought is contemplated directly, linguistic signs are regarded as impediments and language must therefore be made as transparent as possible.[77] A cautionary model, should at least part of this ideal not be implemented, is found in Mendelssohn's argument that 'the first cause of idolatry' arises from the very signs used for language, whether written characters or hieroglyphics. The characters are seen not as 'mere signs but [as] the things themselves', and thus become objects of worship. Their role as symbols is disregarded and overlooked in favour of a process that leads to fetishization.[78]

I would certainly not wish to present Maimonides as a deconstructionist *avant la lettre*. But his argument that the greater the prophet, the less his need to have recourse to image and metaphor and, further, that the voices

---

[75] 'Clearly', as Hans Jonas writes, 'the very idea of Jewish monotheism implied a certain demotion of the world compared with pagan nature worship, and much of prophetic energy had been expended on hammering home the truth that no part of the world was divine' (H. Jonas, 'Jewish and Christian Elements in Philosophy', in Jonas, *Philosophical Essays*, repr., Chicago, 1980, p. 29); cf. also Henri Frankfort: 'the absolute transcendence of God is the foundation of Hebrew religious thought . . . Consequently every concrete phenomenon is devalued. . . . To Hebrew thought nature appeared devoid of divinity' ('Kingship under the judgement of God', in M. R. Konvitz (ed.), *Judaism and Human Rights*, New York, 1972, p. 97), and K. Löwith, *Wissen, Glaube und Skepsis*, 2nd edn, Göttingen, 1962, pp. 68–9. Lévinas writes: '[Judaism] has demystified the universe. It has disenchanted nature' (*Difficile Liberté*, Paris, 1963, p. 259).

[76] See also Cohen, *Religion der Vernunft*, pp. 50–1.

[77] J. Culler, *On Deconstruction – Theory and Criticism after Structuralism*, London, 1987, p. 91.

[78] Mendelssohn, *Jerusalem*, pp. 107ff.; see also A. Funkenstein, 'The political theory of Jewish emancipation', in W. Grab (ed.), *Jahrbuch des Instituts für deutsche Geschichte, Beiheft 3*, Tel Aviv, 1979, pp. 18ff.

seen by all the people at Sinai (Ex. 20:15) connote not action and speech, but an 'overflow', as in prophecy, are consonant with a deconstructionist outlook.[79] Indeed, it would also be impossible for God to communicate in any other way, for that would entail the ascription of some physical equipment to that which is by definition immaterial. Elsewhere Maimonides maintains that 'a voice from nature' was specially created for the revelation to Moses, and reports the view of others that the soul of Moses was 'possessed' in such a way as defies understanding.[80]

An earlier midrashic version of the theory of 'overflow' also dematerialises the revelation: at Sinai, 'the utterance itself went in turn to each Israelite, saying to him, "do you undertake to keep me? Such and such rules are attached to me, so many penalties, so many precautionary measures, so many relaxations and stringencies; such and such a reward I contain"'.[81]

If, however, communication by verbal means is in fact ascribed to God, this is the consequence, according to Maimonides, of the transference by man to God of his own characteristics. Save through the instrumentality of speech, men cannot conceive of the transference of notions amongst themselves. This mode of communicative activity is therefore attributed also to God when He wishes to communicate with man.[82] In this human sense, the revelation is verbal. God chose to reveal his doctrine of human history not through a vision, which indeed is expressly denied to Moses (Ex. 33:20), but through the verbal medium. The word is thus exalted in human terms as the closest approximation to the original. But if it is an admission of the unbridgeable division between God and man, a sort of *pis aller*, it nevertheless possesses a strength of its own that equips it for its task and elevates it far above the image. The word alone possesses the power to recall, and lends itself to discursive handling in a way denied to the image.

The word of God stands in opposition to the image. The positive obverse to the injunction that the pillars, altars, graven images etc. of the idolaters must be destroyed is 'not to do so unto the Lord your God' (Dt. 12:3–4). This was extended to include any object bearing any part of the word of God. This is the only relationship that can preserve an object from the category of actual or potential idol and in fact endow that object with a sort of divinity: if it should contain or bear the word of God (and only when so

---

[79] *Guide*, I:46, II:12; cf. also Schweid, *Ha-Rambam*, p. 79.

[80] Letter to R. Hasdai Halevi, in A. Lichtenberg (ed.), *Kobetz Tshuvot Ha-Rambam*, Leipzig, 1859, II, p. 23b.

[81] MR Song of Songs I:2, 2; see also the discussion of this passage in Jose Faur, *Golden Doves with Silver Dots*, Indiana, 1986, pp. 118ff.

[82] *Guide*, I:46.

doing), as do phylacteries, *mezuzah* or scrolls of the Law.[83] It was to avert such destruction that R. Meir b. Baruch of Rothenburg forbad the use of the names of God (such as 'the merciful one') to decorate children's cakes, whilst permitting the names of kings.[84] The indirect erasure of the words and names of God also incurred prohibition. The case arose in connection with a room, formerly used as a village synagogue, on the walls of which were inscribed prayers and supplications. Could such a room, long after it had ceased to be used for worship, be converted into a bath-house and distillery, R. Samuel Landau was asked. 'No', he answered: 'it seems, in my humble opinion, forbidden to distill spirits in this room on the walls of which are written names which must not be eradicated because the fumes which regularly accompany the distilling of spirits will blacken the walls and bring about the removal of the name.'[85]

If indirect causation must be prevented, how much more so direct causation? Suppose, then, that the internal walls of a synagogue bearing one or the other of the divine names and/or a Biblical passage needed redecorating. In such a case, R. Eleazar Fleckeles (Goitein, Moravia) required that 'a piece of linen or paper or something similar be taken and fixed over the walls where the writing was and then painted over in such a way that the letters beneath continue to live'.[86]

Preserved in this and other ways the word can, for later generations, retain, recapitulate and renew the original experience of revelation and manipulate concepts. The contrast is clear. Accepting, as recently argued, that the paintings in the third-century Dura-Europos synagogue form a cycle 'carrying the spectator to the Messianic idea of Return, Restoration and Salvation',[87] it would be ludicrous to suggest that these paintings can

---

[83] See G. Blidstein, 'The Tannaim and plastic art: problems and prospects', *Perspectives in Jewish Learning*, V (1973), p. 15.

[84] R. Meir Mi'Rothenburg, *Tshuvot Psakim u'Minhagim*, ed. Y. Z. Kahana, 2 vols, Jerusalem, 1960, II, No. 217; see also S. Back, *R. Meir b. Baruch aus Rothenburg*, Frankfurt on Main, 1895, p. 97.

[85] *Noda bi'Yehuda, Mahadurah Tinyana, II*, Jerusalem, 1969, no. 17.

[86] Kahana, *Mehkarim*, p. 387, n. 273; p. 392, n. 318. I cannot refrain from noting the contrast with an episode recorded in the history of the Church of Great St. Mary's at Cambridge. 'Expenditure is recorded in 1552 for "painting the Scriptures" on the walls, and in 1556 for "washing out the Scriptures". The reference is to the painting in and out of the Decalogue (and other texts) in the English churches, during the Reformation and the Catholic revival under Queen Mary. Under Elizabeth they were once more restored' (I. Abrahams, 'The Decalogue in art' in *Studies in Jewish Literature in honour of Kaufmann Kohler*, Berlin, 1913, p. 49).

[87] R. Wischnitzer, *The Messianic Theme in the Paintings of the Dura Synagogues*, Chicago, 1948, p. v.

in any way at all match in power and wealth of communication the multitude of rabbinic discussions of these themes. A picture can certainly 'speak' and convey a mood, an impression (for example, a horror of war, as in Picasso's 'Guernica'), but beyond these limits it cannot teach and remains inarticulate. It typifies 'wordless symbolism', (as Suzanne Langer says), in contrast to which the word stands as follows:

> Language in the strict sense is essentially discursive; it has permanent units of meaning which are combinable into larger units; it has fixed equivalences which make definition and translation possible; its connotations are general so that it requires non-verbal acts like pointing, looking or emphatic voice inflections to assign specific denotations to its terms. In all these salient characters, it differs from wordless symbolism, which is non-discursive and untranslatable, does not allow of definitions within its own system, and cannot directly convey generalisations.[88]

The word therefore is justified not only in terms of its utility but also in terms of fitness for purpose. In the case of contact between spirit and spirit, the neo-Kantian, Salomon Ludwig Steinheim, juxtaposes word and image.[89] He was certainly permissive in the qualified welcome he gave to ornamentation and historical painting in the synagogue and to the use of prayerbooks with painted initials. Steinheim even favoured the introduction of instrumental music into the synagogue – which did not, apparently, have to be Jewish in inspiration, since he singled out the melodies of Bach and Handel, *inter alia*. 'Why', he asked rhetorically, 'do people still cling to the convoluted street-singing of the late middle ages?'[90] But none of this leniency obscured Steinheim's perception that 'only in the spirit, circumscribed by no figure, and only in the word, the tone-product – its appropriate external, can the spiritual, the morally good find its approximate expression in our sensuous human nature; every picture is inadequate, a diminution or even a distortion of its expression. And this is precisely the sublime meaning of that prohibition of image worship.'[91]

This established a paradigmatic antithesis to the pagan worship of Phidias's statue of Zeus, the highest example of such worship,[92] and brought

[88] S. Langer, *Philosophy in a New Key*, Mentor edn, New York, 1952, p. 78.

[89] For a general view of Steinheim's philosophy, see H. Graupe, 'Steinheim und Kant', *LBYB*, V (1960), pp. 140–76; also A. Shear-Yashuv, *The Theology of Salomon Ludwig Steinheim*, Leiden, 1986.

[90] *Die Offenbarung nach dem Lehrbegriffe der Synagoge*, Leipzig, 1856, II, pp. 446–7.

[91] Ibid., III, pp. 202–3.

[92] Ibid., III, pp. 203, 207, 438.

the iconoclastic followers of the second commandment also into opposition to the Christian world. Steinheim acknowledged to the full the contrary efforts made by Clement of Alexandria, Tertullian and Origen.[93] He also appreciated the iconoclastic impulse stemming from Arianism in the pre-medieval period and from Protestantism in the post-medieval world.[94] But all such efforts had struggled in vain against the 'image worship [which was] a natural consequence to the apotheosis, the belief in the God-man'.[95] He was also acutely sensitive to the degeneration wrought by Solomon, who built 'for himself and his God a temple after the model of the surrounding pagans'.[96]

All this reinforced his argument that only the word, a sound-utterance, could fittingly convey the revelation of spirit to spirit.[97] The word alone could serve as the bond between the eternal and the temporal; but to serve images was 'the sure characteristic sign of a confusion of the temporal and the eternal, the physical with the spiritual and the most reliable proof that the doctrine of divine revelation had either not made a complete break-through or that it had fallen below its level and come close to paganism'.[98]

Abusing the Word

But even the word can be abused. The Bible knows of *avodah zarah* only through material objects, occult practices and natural phenomena. This range of manifestations later shows itself to be incomplete. In the same way as a piece of wood, that might be used for heating or cooking etc., is abused when fashioned into an idol, so too can the word be abused when employed as a metaphor or image. This form of idolatry eventually comes to create a spurious reality that competes with, and seeks to displace, genuine reality. Certain forms of literature and *belles-lettres* create a simulacrum of the real and thereby impede communication with and from the latter, which,

---

[93] Ibid., III, p. 214; see also Bevan, *Holy Images*, p. 107.

[94] Steinheim, III, *Die Offenbarung*, p. 220.

[95] Ibid., III, p. 209.

[96] Ibid., p. 211.

[97] Ibid., ch. XXIV, pp. 434ff.; cf. also Lévinas: 'Dieu voilant la face et reconnu comme présent et intime – est-il possible? S'agit-il d'une construction métaphysique, d'un salto mortale paradoxal dans le goût de Kierkegaard? Nous pensons que là se manifeste, au contraire, la physionomie particulière au Judaisme: le rapport entre Dieu et l'homme n'est pas une communion sentimentale dans l'amour d'un dieu incarne, mais une relation entre esprits, par l'intermédiaire d'un enseignement, par la Thora. C'est précisément une parole, non incarnée de Dieu qui assure un Dieu vivant parmi nous' (*Difficile Liberté*, p. 174).

[98] Steinheim, II, *Die Offenbarung*, p. 445.

ultimately, remains impervious. Lévinas rightly draws attention to the naked-ness, sobriety and distrust of rhetoric characteristic of Talmudic and rab-binic style.[99] There is, in short, a sort of 'linguistic iconoclasm', as J.-J. Goux writes. The supreme example of this is the self-concealment of God through the withholding of His name. 'Strictly speaking', writes Goux, 'remaining radically iconoclastic, also in language, no metaphor, no image is appropriate for Him: He is the nameless one.'[100] God, 'the Absolute', Horkheimer points out, is not to be represented even by a word.[101] Baeck also has a passage in which he writes of the Biblical struggle both for and against language. When Moses asks God for His name he is answered: 'I am that I am' (Ex. 20:4). Baeck comments: 'that means He for whom no word or name is sufficient. The fight for language here becomes the fight *against* language.'[102] This deliberate namelessness of God is a parallel to the prohibition of the human image. In both cases the intent is to avert the supreme danger that God might, as it were, be reified and become subject to human attempts at domination. Only to cattle, birds etc. might man give names.[103]

There is one exception to this 'linguistic iconoclasm', accepted on grounds of expedience. 'The Torah speaks in the language of man',[104] that is, it is couched in such terms as to make itself comprehensible to all. It must therefore lend itself to transmission at different levels of receptivity. This exemplifies Nietzsche's dictum that the more abstract the truth to be taught 'the more you must seduce the senses towards it'.[105] Clearly, the ideal would be direct apprehension of the thought, but since this is impossible, language, thereby made indispensable, needs to be as unobtrusive and as transparent as possible, lest it hinder access to the thought.

The fight against language and for the ineffable must at times, therefore, yield to the need for mass comprehension, and on these grounds the use of figurative, metaphorical and pictorial mimetic language is justified. The sensuous is a concession to the undeveloped intellect and God has taken

[99] E. Lévinas, *Du Sacré au Saint*, Paris, 1977, pp. 7–8.

[100] J.-J. Goux *Les Iconoclastes*, p. 25.

[101] M. Horkheimer, *Die Sehnsucht nach dem ganz Anderen*, Hamburg, 1970, pp. 57–8.

[102] Leo Baeck, *God and Man in Judaism*, Engl. trans., London, 1958, pp. 18–19. Michael Guttmann (*Yesodei Kiyuman Shel Mitzvot*, Breslau, 1930, p. 36) points out that despite the freedom of language in the use of anthropomorphisms exercised by the sages, this never went so far as to suggest any corporeality on the part of God.

[103] Gen. 2:20.

[104] TB Yeb. 71a; BM 31b.

[105] *Jenseits von Gut und Böse*, no. 128.

account of these human differences in the conveyance of His teaching to His creatures: 'for some', writes Isaac Israeli, the Neo-Platonist of the ninth-century,

> are animal-like and foolish, who will never allow anything to enter their minds and to occupy their thoughts save what they have perceived with their senses and seen with their own eyes. Others are intelligent, of an enquiring mind, keep their eyes open to the truth of words, and distinguish between their spiritual and corporeal meaning. . . . The creator, blessed be He, put His message in spiritual, unambiguous words to serve as guide and true teacher to those endowed with intellect and understanding so as to enable them to reach an understanding of the meaning of those messages which are couched in corporeal and ambiguous terms for the benefit of those who are dull, deficient in intellect, and bereft of understanding in order that it might impress their imaginative faculty on account of the coarseness and corporeality thereof, and because of the proximity thereof to the sense.[106]

Judah Halevi is another to stress the utility – not to say the indispensability – of the use of images in the instruction of the masses.[107] A special category and a special difficulty in the use of the sensuous arises from the anthropomorphic language of the Bible. But in general this was treated as another demonstration of the necessity of the sensuous for the comprehension of the unlearned. Bahya ibn Pakuda, for example, sees this manifested in the anthropomorphic terminology which will enable the unlearned to fix in their minds the existence of God, whereas the thinking man will discard such expressions and seek out the abstractions.[108] R. Isaac Arama took a similar view, seeing in certain 'spatial' expressions referring to God a means to make God's immateriality comprehensible to an individual who could only conceive of God in material terms.[109] But the most determined and articulate of those philosophers who refer the sensuosity of language to the

---

[106] A. Altmann and S. M. Stern (eds and trans.), *Isaac Israeli*, Oxford, 1958, pp. 139–40.

[107] *Kitab Al Khazari*, trans. H. Hirschfield, London/New York, 1905, I, 97; cf. also ibid., IV, 3: 'We speak also of the devouring fire on the top of the mount [Ex. 24:17] which the common people saw, as well as of the spiritual form which was visible only to the higher classes.'

[108] D. Kaufmann, 'Die Theologie des Bachya ibn Pakuda', in Kaufmann (ed.), *Gesammelte Schriften*, II, Frankfurt on Main, 1910, pp. 74ff.

[109] *Akedat Yitzhak*, Pressburg, 1849, II, serm. 48, pp. 136a–7b; C. Pearl, *The Medieval Jewish Mind*, London, 1971, pp. 25–6.

needs of mass comprehension is Maimonides.

It is impossible to take Biblical anthropomorphism literally, on logical grounds alone. How, asks Maimonides, are phrases such as 'beneath His feet' (Ex. 24) or 'written with the finger of God' (Ex. 31:18) or 'the hand of God' (Ex. 9:3) to be understood? All the more so as they contradict those passages that speak of God being both 'in heaven above, and upon the earth beneath' (Dt. 4:39) – 'and a physical body is not in two places at one time'. Moreover, any 'manner of likeness' (Dt. 4:15 and Is. 40:25) is denied to God. Maimonides therefore explains all these expressions by virtue of their being 'in accordance with the understanding of mankind who can only know bodies and the Torah speaks in the language of men. These phrases are metaphorical terms such as, "if I whet my glittering sword" (Dt. 32:41). So has God a sword and does He kill with a sword? No, these are metaphors . . . all is in a prophetic vision and spectacle.[110]

The limits of what is verbally permissible are set by the pedagogic intent and must not be overstepped. In any case, to avert possible danger Maimonides forthrightly insisted that children, the multitude etc. must also be taught that 'there is absolutely no likeness in any respect whatever between Him and the things created by Him.'[111] This follows the Maimonidean doctrine of negative attributes, which at this point converges with his aesthetic. The more this doctrine is disregarded and the more predications are made of God, the more He will be likened to other things.[112]

Anthropomorphism and other forms of fantasy-language remain legitimate only so long as they remain pedagogic and do not extend to the creation of a world of metaphor. They would otherwise become nothing more than *belles-lettres*. It may be that there is a hint of this suspicion in the contrast made by Maimonides between rabbinical enumeration of the 613 commandments and their enumeration in poetic form (as was widely practised, to Maimonides's distress, in contemporary Spain). In the introduction to his own compilation he criticizes both rabbis and poets for their unquestioning adherence to the traditional enumeration. But the poetic compilations 'are not to be held culpable, for their composers were poets and not rabbis and performed their appropriate task to perfection with well-mingled expressions and beauty of arrangement'.[113] But more than this – namely, the questioning of tradition – should be expected of rabbis, Maimonides seems to be saying.

Be that as it may, it seems that many centuries passed before the need to demand any sort of 'literary iconoclasm' was seriously entertained. The

---

[110] MT Book of Knowledge, I, 8–9.
[111] *Guide*, I, 35.
[112] Ibid., I, 59.
[113] Introduction to *Sefer Ha'Mitzvot*.

reading of 'external' books and of the works of Homer provoked conflicting views amongst the teachers of the Talmud.[114] Not until the sixteenth century did Joseph Caro actually equate the reading of fiction with the practice of *avodah zarah* and bring them under a common rubric. His authoritative legal compendium, the *Shulhan Aruch*, prohibited the reading of allegories, tales of profane discourse, books of delight (such as the poems of Emmanuel of Rome) and stories of wars – not only because of 'not sitting in the seat of the scornful' (Ps. 1:1) but also because of 'turn not unto the idols, nor make to yourselves molten gods' (Lev. 19:4).[115] This Levitical prohibition was formerly taken to refer to physical images.[116] But Caro extended its applicability to the verbal realm. He established an equivalence between a literary romance, say, and a plastic figurative work of art.

Behind this lies the ability of literature to take the content of what is to be communicated and create a disjunction between this and the actual teachings, which are relocated into another world of non-commitment and contemplation. This displaces man's concern from its rightful abode with the normative to a concern with aesthetic contemplation. Side by side with the real world of man's being lies in waiting an imaginary world that devalues the real and turns it willy-nilly into an aesthetic spectacle.[117] In terms of our framework the literary work embodies a reification of the real. It purports to signify a certain situation with all the claims and demands that follow from this situation – but without in fact signifying anything real. There is an antithesis between what would rightly lend itself to the scrutiny, betterment etc. exercised by the laws, and that situation where scrutiny is redundant because the situation itself is a mere fiction. Nietzsche, in his self-proclaimed role as 'teacher', had again and again to hold himself aloof from what a recent critic calls 'the uncommittedness of the only-aesthetic'.[118]

---

[114] See the material cited in H. Cohn, *Human Rights in Jewish Law*, London/ New York, 1984, pp. 130ff. The sages of Palestine had a far more indulgent attitude to the reading of light literature than had the sages of Babylon (A. Kohut, 'Talmudical Miscellanies', *JQR*, III (1891), pp. 546–8).

[115] *Shulhan Aruch*, Orech Hayim 307:16.

[116] Cf. TB Shab. 149a.

[117] Adorno has a valuable passage in which he dismisses as 'null' all moral judgements on the personages of novel or drama, even if they are rightfully incurred by the original; and the reason he gives also illustrates the transformatory literary mechanism at work: 'form acts like a magnet which orders the elements of the empirical world in a way that alienates them from the context of their extra-aesthetic existence' (T. Adorno, *Aesthetische Theorie*, Frankfurt on Main, 1972, p. 336).

[118] M. Bindschedler, *Nietzsche und die poetische Lüge*, Basle, 1954, pp. 53–4.

As it happened, this particular form of *avodah zarah* was never widespread – to judge, at least, by the paucity of criticism. The reality principle of the Torah has largely inhibited the emergence of what Moritz Lazarus called 'a second world', created by epic and dramatic poetry. The 'almost exclusively lyric-didactic' poetry of the Jews rejected 'what has never and nowhere happened'. Not 'the products of a free fantasy, the images of a completely unreal world [are] its object, but the given, the real phenomena of nature, the figures, characters and actions and religious movements of history'. Where fantasy does enjoy free play is in the *midrashim*, and even there its role is limited: it is 'not architectonic but only ornamental'. There is nothing comparable to the depictions of the Homeric heroes.[119] It is precisely to 'the exclusivity of its monotheism' that Hermann Cohen attributes the absence of drama in Israel; and makes the contrast between a genuine solution to the problem of suffering and that to be found 'in the illusory feeling of the spectator'.[120]

The same concern with the blurring of the division between the reified uncommitted world of literary art and the normative world can also be detected in rabbinic discussion of David. He deservedly suffered retribution, according to the rabbis, when he declared: 'Your statutes have been my songs in the house of my pilgrimage' (Ps. 119:54). He degraded 'statutes', with their normative authority, to the status of *belles-lettres*, to 'songs', and thus diminished 'words of Torah'.[121] The same sort of distinction was also made in connection with the Song of Songs. To treat this as a secular air, to take away its meaning as a medium of divine communication and instruction, 'brings evil to the world', declared the rabbis. The personified Torah in this passage laments that it is not 'a harp upon which [men might] frivolously play'.[122] The same reasoning justified the alarm felt lest the Song of Songs be translated into the vernacular and thereby become part of the literature of love-songs.[123] To take another example: those rabbis who denounced Moses Mendelssohn's translation of the Bible into German did so not only because it made the Torah into a mere instrument for language teaching, but also because it would encourage readers to look, for

---

[119] M. Lazarus, *Die Ethik des Judentums*, Frankfurt on Main, 1904, pp. 34–5. The book of Job is an inexplicable exception to this argument. Job never existed (see TB BB 15a), yet his story is accepted as part of the canon. His 'second world' is taken seriously.

[120] Cohen, *Religion der Vernunft*, p. 166.

[121] TB Sotah 35a.

[122] TB San. 101a.

[123] R. Louis Jacobs, *Theology in the Responsa*, p. 264; cf. also D. Novak, *Law and Theology*, 2nd series, New York, 1976, p. 131.

example, on the books of the prophets as mere 'literature'.[124] 'Woe to the man who says the Torah is just a story-book', exclaims the Zohar, the mystical classic.[125]

At a lower level of seriousness, literary and musical artistry also had the power to interpose itself between the text and its recipient, the aesthetic element procuring the degeneration of the normative. On these grounds for example, R. Isaac Arama (of Tarragona and Catalayud, fifteenth century) sought to exclude from the liturgy of the Day of Atonement a poem by Solomon ibn Gabirol. Arama feared lest the poet's skilful use of the acrostic form, spelling out his name, disturb religious devotion.[126] Similarly, were a cantor to repeat certain words of public prayer that they might better fit his melody, then he would, *inter alia*, be treating the Torah as a song to be sung for pleasure.[127] Closely related to this was the view that instrumental music in the synagogue must accompany only those songs that do not form part of 'the established liturgy', and none of the liturgical prayers.[128] If the latter were to be accompanied by instruments, or if a cantor, rather than merely leading the congregation in prayer, were to exploit his status, voice etc., then he would be guilty of diverting attention from the content of the prayers to his performance of their rendering. But where the music was meaningless then it was perfectly acceptable.

Indeed, this attribute was the criterion of its acceptability and perfection. Hermann Cohen's study of Mozart's libretti exalted music for signifying nothing other than 'what it itself says. . . That is its advantage through which it surpasses all arts.'[129] Even in Schönberg's opera, *Moses and Aron*, there is still an attempt to preserve, amidst the spectacle, an ethical commitment. Moses, 'the proclaimer of thought', *speaks*, whereas Aaron, 'the builder of fantasy', expresses himself through song, 'the medium of the sensuous'.[130]

[124] See the controversy in Altmann, *Moses Mendelssohn*, pp. 486ff.

[125] Commenting on Num. 8:1–12:16.

[126] Sarah Heller-Wilensky, *R. Yitzhak Arama u-mishnato*, Jerusalem/Tel Aviv, 1956, p. 201.

[127] See the responsum (1875) of R. Moses b. Joseph Schick (Moravia) quoted in R. Louis Jacobs, *Theology in the Responsa*, p. 225; also S. Simonsohn, 'Some disputes on music in the synagogue in pre-reform days', *PAAJR*, 34 (1966), pp. 99–119.

[128] H. Pollack, *Jewish Folkways in Germanic Lands (1648–1806)*, Cambridge, Mass., 1971, p. 155.

[129] H. Cohen, *Die dramatische Idee in Mozarts Operntexten*, Berlin, 1915, p. 25; cf. also Altmann, 'Zum Wesen', pp. 213–14, and R. Scruton, *The Aesthetic Understanding*, Manchester, 1983, p. 59.

[130] K. H. Wörner, *Gotteswort und Magie – die Oper 'Moses und Aron' von Arnold Schönberg*, Heidelberg, 1959, p. 70. See also R. Craft, 'Moses and Aaron in Paris',

Normally, however, the word (or its musical equivalent) is misused in order to create an effect of such a nature as to devalue the message purveyed by the word. It has taken the communication from the world of action to that of uncommitment, creating a fictitious world, impervious and irrelevant to the commandments. In the same way as the idolater fancies that his artifact is indeed an intermediary to a primary source of power and influence, perhaps even a source of power in its own right, so too does that person err who takes seriously a work of fiction, making it into a norm for human conduct and enlightenment. He has reified the drama, say, by attributing to a mere sign the status of being, and on this fallacious union constructed an edifice of meaning.

If the principal effect of iconolatry, whether in visual or verbal form, is thus to blur contact with the source of instruction, action as such is impeded and the desired reproduction by man of God's attributes distorted to some greater or lesser extent. This is tantamount to saying that man's effort towards the acquisition of God-like attributes – his prescribed aim – is arrested or at least diverted.

In one respect, the views of Plato and the rabbis coincide. Athens and Jerusalem are at one in their condemnation of appearance, as an appeal purely to the lower and less discriminating part of the soul.[131] But the divergence is equally striking in that the rabbis, unlike Plato, are not in search of a timeless idea – God is not an idea – but in search of a mode of action in the here and now. Thus their attack on the artist is diversely founded. Plato asks rhetorically: 'must we not infer that all these poetical individuals beginning with Homer, are only imitators; they copy images of

---

New York Review of Books, 13 December 1973, pp. 24–7. A recent critic writes of this work as 'a kind of anti-opera, one that utilizes "operatic" elements precisely in order to undercut them and to assert the triumph of a higher spiritual force'; and the words 'I am striving to flee from matter' in Schönberg's unfinished oratorio, *Die Jakobsleiter*, are said to 'encapsulate the longing for transcendence that informs the whole piece' (H. Lindenberger, 'Schönberg, the transactions of aesthetics and politics', *Modern Judaism*, IX (1989), no. 1, pp. 55–70, esp. pp. 63ff.; cf. also, p. 139, fn 55 above, and S. Beller, *Vienna and the Jews, 1867–1938*, Cambridge, 1989, pp. 232ff.

[131] Socrates and an otherwise unknown R. Jacob would also have understood each other. The former says to Phaedrus: 'I am a lover of knowledge, and the men who dwell in the city are my teachers, and not the trees or the country . . . only hold up before me in like manner a book, and you may lead me all round Attica, and over the wide world' (Plato, *Phaedrus*, 230). R. Jacob has it that 'he who walks by the way and teaches and interrupts his teaching to say "how beautiful is this tree, how beautiful is this field", Scripture counts it to him as though he were guilty against himself' (*Pirkei Avoth* 3:9).

virtue and the like, but the truth they never reach?'[132] They blend knowledge by acquaintance with knowledge by description.[133] The crux of the rabbinical case against the artist, however, is grounded in his ability to bewilder the senses with his artifact and thus divert man from effective and purposeful communication with God.

There is also an analogy with the aesthetic of Kant, for whom there was 'perhaps no more sublime passage in the lawbook of the Jews than the commandment: you shall make no image nor yet any likeness, neither what is in the heavens, nor on the earth, nor under the earth, etc.'[134] Kant makes the comparison between this aversion to representation and his own argument concerning the notion of 'the moral law and the disposition to morality within ourselves'. Now these entities are certainly differently conceived from the God of the Bible, but the comparison with the rationale of Biblical aniconism still holds good; for Kant goes on to argue (in terms that recall the rabbinic admonitions against mediation, the intellectual harm in giving form to the formless etc. – see above pp. 138ff.), that there is in fact less danger in the exercise of unbridled fantasy concerning ideas of morality, where the senses have nothing before them, than from the fear that these ideas will be impotent and can be strengthened by 'images and childish apparatus'. 'Therefore', Kant continues, 'governments have willingly allowed religion to be richly supplied with additions of the latter, and thus sought to spare the subject the trouble of, but at the same time to remove the capacity for, extending his spiritual powers beyond the limits which are arbitrarily set for him, whereby he is more easily handled, being purely passive.'[135]

This argument of course is perfectly reproduced in the Talmudic prohibition of an image or statue bearing any symbol of sovereignty, such as staff, orb, bird, sword, crown, ring etc.[136] In our terminology, these symbols are all modes of reification, attributing meaning to objects and thereby befuddling the intellect.[137] Taking this argument a stage further, affiliation has been found between the iconoclastic consequences of what one Jewish philosopher calls 'the Kantian negation of a metaphysical cognition of

[132]   *The Republic*, X, 600e.

[133]   Iris Murdoch, *The Fire and the Sun*, Oxford, 1977, p. 32; see also p. 65.

[134]   *Kritik der Urteilskraft*, pt I, bk 2, sec. 29.

[135]   Ibid. See also Kant's *Critique of Practical Reason*, Engl. trans. T. K. Abbott, London, 1948, p. 233.

[136]   TB AZ, 40b–41a.

[137]   See also Goux, *Les Iconoclastes*, p. 19; J. F. Lyotard, *The Post-Modern Condition*, Engl. trans., Minneapolis, 1984, pp. 78–9.

God',[138] and what others have variously referred to as the (Biblical) rejection of pantheism and the identification of God with man or nature, or 'the Jewish reverence for the divine' as defence against anything 'that claims to be absolute and is not. . . . The reverence for the absolute as negation of idolatry'.[139] In both the Jewish and the Kantian aesthetic there is a correlation between the unknowability of the absolute (or God) and the negation of *avodah zarah*.

But the danger in the reificatory process in the Jewish case is deeper, in that the notion of God, appropriately purified by philosophy and the norms of thought of all human or material likeness, is also accompanied by the notion of God as teacher. If the prophet has visions of God, he is also, as Hermann Cohen writes, 'an ethicist of practice, a politician and a jurist, because absolutely he wishes to put an end to the sufferings of the poor'.[140] The work of art, like the idol, must therefore be at best indifferent, at worst harmful, to human interest by reason of the fact that, because both introduce man to fiction, they offer no purchase to that process whereby suffering may be relieved. In that the idolater makes an object that he considers capable of meeting his wishes; and in that the artist creates some world, irrespective of the particular medium employed, that serves as the repository of his own hopes, dreams, fears etc.; then both idolater and artist fall by the same standard of the real and the effective enunciated in the Torah.

At one level, the world of art offers an illusory solution to the demands of the alienated condition. At another it projects itself as a world removed from the discipline of history. In such a world of discontinuity anything can happen – suffering, for example, can be effortlessly removed. The deception thereby practised is akin to that practised by the idol worshipper who attributes divine power to the work of his own hands. In the end the idol worshipper comes to resemble his creation by virtue of their joint participation in deception. Both Isaiah and the psalmist couple their denunciation of *avodah zarah* with a pointed awareness of the stultification that overcomes those who mistake illusion for reality.[141]

The translation of this argument into historical terms exposes its importance. *Avodah zarah* deprives man, to a greater or lesser degree, of his mode

---

[138] A. Lewkowitz, 'Kants Bedeutung für das Judentum', *MGWJ*, 68 (1924), p. 124.

[139] H. Cohen, 'Innere Beziehungen der Kantischen Philosophie zum Judentum', in *Jüdische Schriften I*, Berlin, 1924, p. 295; M. Horkheimer, 'Nachwort', in T. Koch (ed.), *Porträts deutsch-jüdischer Geistesgeschichte*, Cologne, 1961, pp. 264–5.

[140] H. Cohen, *Religion der Vernunft*, p. 166; Samuel Hirsch, *Die Religionsphilosophie der Juden*, Leipzig, 1842, p. 479, argues on similar lines.

[141] Is. 44:18ff.; Ps. 106:36ff.; 115:8.

of communication with God. Both the communicator – God – and the communicand – man – suffer. In the first case the nature of God is subjected to misunderstanding by any attempt at representation; in the second, the intellect is befuddled. At the historical level, therefore, counsel is lost. What begins as a theologico-intellectual error terminates in a loss of direction. McLuhan used to say, 'the medium is the message', but if the former is constituted of wood or stone or iron etc., then for all the artistry expended on the shaping of the material medium, it cannot transcend its inherent limitations as a non-signifying signifier. To the monotheist, as distinct from the adherents of 'visible religion', there is only one world in which, say, the poor and the afflicted can be comforted. It is that world in which they actually live and to which the Torah directs their actions.

This is what brings together an illuminated prayerbook, a tale of romance, the statue of a man, a portrait painting, a drama, an idol. In the same way, though of course to very varying degrees, they all claim for their reified existence a direct, an unmediated relationship to reality such as would endow them with an actual existence. The 'alien worship' – *avodah zarah* – they represent fallaciously re-creates the real, thereby obscuring it and impeding the operation of the Torah. To make the point in a different way: these phenomena create a world which contravenes a cardinal demand of the Torah, in that they break the bond uniting commitment and action. Whatever should happen to the statue that depicts a man is to the man himself indifferent and irrelevant. It is akin to striking an idol. No censure is incurred by those who, in a drama, perpetuate acts of cruelty. The undoubted emotion generated by such a spectacle is dissipated in the recognition of its discontinuity from the real. It is, after all, only an act. It is wholly within the logic of the Torah that it must reject the catharsis theory of tragedy. On the contrary, it will see in drama, far from a purgation of the emotions, a surrogate for catharsis.[142]

Rousseau has some comments that are remarkably apposite:

> in weeping over these fictions, we have satisfied all the rights of humanity, without having to add anything further of our own, whereas the unfortunate people in themselves would demand from us care, comfort, consolation, effort which could associate us with their hardships; which would at least make demands on our indolence and from which we are indeed happy to be exempt. . . . That is more or less all that all these grand sentiments and all these brilliant maxims praised with such bombast are good for – to be relegated for ever to the stage, to show us virtue as a stage trick, good to divert the public but which it would be madness to wish to transport seriously into

[142] Cf. Zevi, 'Ebraismo e concezione spazio-temporale', p. 210.

society. Thus the most advantageous impression of the best tragedies is to reduce all the duties of man to some passing affections, sterile and without effect, to be applauded for our own courage by praising that of others, for our humanity by pitying the evils that we could have cured.[143]

This distinction is not between theory ('the duties of man') and the inadequacy of practice ('passing affections'), but between commitment and contemplation. This is the distinction that monotheism finds unacceptable and why it must insist that it speaks without intermediary to the protagonists of the real.

---

[143] 'Lettre à D'Alembert sur les Spectacles', pt I. Kant also remarks on those who imagine themselves 'improved by a tragedy' whereas they are merely gratified at having 'happily diverted a period of boredom' (*Kritik der Urteilskraft*, pt I, bk 2, sec. 29).

5

The Idolater and the Messiah

Preamble

In the same way as the Torah gives rise to the forming of settled communities (as I have tried to show in regard to Berlin and London), so does its counterpart – *avodah zarah* – seek fulfilment in certain types of messianic movement, their adherents and expositors. These complement those other manifestations of *avodah zarah* mentioned earlier, but they do so in a far more dramatic way. The call of the messianic figure for an end to the exile and the restoration of Israel to its Land – perhaps to an altogether unprecedented glory – is frequently accompanied by dependence on this or that aspect of *avodah zarah*. The call has been reinforced and even inspired by the observation and calculation of planetary conjunctions etc.; and/or by the signs of the times derived from current events ('the activation of history'); and/or by aspects of the material world (normally the soil). These are all held to convey some divine message, such as the idolater also holds when contemplating or consulting the object of his worship or his oracles. The material world is animated with an allegedly divine message.

A messianic figure is comparable to the artist in that it is precisely his diminished sense of the real that equips him to animate the real and people it with his own fantasies and possibilities. He is engaged – unlike the Torah – not in transforming the existent through grappling with its particular problems, but in reading into the existent his own aspirations. Through these he perceives the existent and through them his own conduct is prescribed.

It is immaterial whether the media of reification are the stars, a war, the soil or a figure regarded as the bearer of a particular insight relevant to the future, allegedly imparted to him by God, who has selected this particular individual as a channel for the divine.[1] In their different ways all these varied phenomena satisfy the call for some visible embodiment of the divine and earnest of its concern. They are all forms of pantheism. But this lies

---

[1] For examples and references, see below, pp. 167ff.

of course at the very heart of *avodah zarah*, for it purports to bring God into the world and so obliterate the distinction between the other and the real. This negates the Torah which, other than itself, rejects absolutely all forms of mediation between God and man. But it is not paradoxical to say that the Torah itself helps to generate messianic thinking and figures: the burden of immediacy, reality and the rejection of reification is at times intolerable. Messianism is frequently an index of the failure of the Torah. In other words, it is to be understood in terms of the Torah and not as the emanation of some autonomous contrary principle.

As part of his disregard for the existent, the messianic figure also diminishes the present. For him, as for Alice, it is 'jam yesterday, jam tomorrow, but never jam today'. But this is an example of 'the inauthentic present'.[2] Through the devotion to an idealized past (such as the Davidic monarchy) or an idealized future (the renewal of that past) or something entirely new, the present goes by default. This is precisely exemplified through the views of those philosophers who relegate Jewish history to a waiting or defiance of time. Hess, for example, in the expectation of a restored Jewish state, sees this as the sequel to a 'winter-sleep . . . [during which] the Jewish people has not in vain for two thousand years defied the tempest of world history';[3] Fackenheim, in similar mood, in reference to the establishment of the State of Israel, writes of 'the precise and historic moment when after nearly two thousand years, this people . . . has returned into history'.[4]

Scholem has perceived the antithesis between 'winter-sleep' and statehood in terms of the capacity of the messianic idea, though itself unable to achieve realization, 'to enforce a *life lived in deferment*, in which nothing can be done definitively, nothing can be irrevocably accomplished. . . Precisely understood, there is nothing concrete which can be accomplished by the unredeemed.'[5] He writes also of 'the endless powerlessness in Jewish history during all the centuries of exile, when it was unprepared to come forward on to the plane of world history'.[6] Taubes perceives the conflict between the here and now, lying at the centre of the aspiration of the Torah, and messianic movements, in terms of a rabbinically enforced 'retreat from

---

[2] J. Gabel, *False Consciousness*, Engl. trans., Oxford, 1975, esp. pt 2.

[3] From the foreword to Hess's *Rom und Jerusalem*, repr., Tel Aviv, 1935 (first published 1862); see also below p. 000.

[4] E. Fackenheim, *To Mend the World*, New York, 1982, p. 8; cf. also p. 92. Another example: 'only since the establishment of the State of Israel have Jews re-entered history' (M. Wyschogrod, *The Body of Faith*, New York, 1983, p. 235). So where were the Jews before re-entry?

[5] G. Scholem, *The Messianic Idea in Judaism*, Engl. trans., London, 1971, p. 35. (Italics in original.)

[6] Ibid.

history', a life 'outside of history'; by contrast, 'every attempt to actualise the messianic idea was an attempt to jump into history, however mythically derailed the attempt may have been'.[7]

Now it may readily be agreed that the accomplishment of the unredeemed can indeed only be partial and faulty. But this sounds like a tautology, if the terminology is sufficiently precise to warrant any judgement at all. The cloudiness of the language does not, however, obscure the agreement with which the history of the Jews is relegated to a sort of limbo. In the one case it is unprepared, incomplete; in the other, it is likened to 'retreat', 'derailment'.

Rabbinical Reserve

A man, says Polak, 'can live simultaneously in the here and now and in another world of his own creation'.[8] But this is unquestionably a difficult stance, and earlier I tried to show how the Torah sought to mitigate the difficulty and to combine acceptance of the 'here and now' with its simultaneous critical rejection. In short, it confined the attempted realization of the hopes it generated within a certain network of normative acts. It was not always successful, and Maimonides attributed this lack of success to the length of the exile and its attendant persecutions.[9]

The fear of untoward consequences already showed itself in the reluctance of the Talmudic sages to discuss the messiah, particularly the conditions of his advent. Save for two passages of doubtful authenticity, the figure of the messiah is, in the Mishnah, not mentioned at all.[10] When the Gemarah takes up the theme, it does so in an inconclusive and speculative spirit. Chapter XI of Tractate Sanhedrin is the principal repository of Talmudic thinking on the messianic idea. Although there is a general thrust in favour of the idea that Israel must submit to the Torah in order to merit messianic rule, it is also true that no consensus emerges. At the lowest level of expectations stands the view of R. Hillel, for whom the messiah had already come in the reign of king Hezekiah.[11] Otherwise the rabbis ask:

[7] J. Taubes, 'The price of messianism', Proceedings of the 8th World Congress of Jewish Studies, Division C, Jerusalem, 1982, p. 103.

[8] F. L. Polak, 'Utopia and cultural renewal', in F. E. Manuel (ed.), *Utopias and Utopian Thought*, London, 1973, p. 282.

[9] 'Epistle to Yemen', in A. Halkin, (ed.), *Crisis and Leadership: Epistles of Maimonides*, JPSA, 1985, p. 96.

[10] S. Zeitlin, 'The Essenes and messianic expectations', in L. Landman (ed.), *Messianism in the Talmudic Era*, New York, 1979, pp. 511ff.

[11] TB San., 98b.

will the advent be heralded by the deepest suffering? Or will the process of redemption not take the form of a seven-year cycle of events, marked at one extreme by famine and the decline of learning and, at the other, by the advent of the son of David? What will be the respective part of man and God in this process? Will Israel's suffering and/or its good deeds be the determining factor?[12]

These discussions are not only inconclusive but also incompatible with each other. As Funkenstein writes, 'the long array of so-called calculations of the end . . . seem to have been gathered merely to prove their extreme divergence and unreliability.'[13] What, however, does stand out from these and other Talmudic discussions, and from other contemporary sources, is the extreme suspicion attaching to any attempt to accelerate the messianic advent through militant action. Their attitude is epitomized in the reported saying of R. Johanan: 'if there were a plant in your hand and they should say to you: "look the messiah is here!" go and plant your plant and after that go forth to receive him.'[14] In retort to those who sought to determine the time of the advent, R. Samuel b. Nahmani (in the name of R. Jonathan) exclaimed: 'cursed be the bones of those who calculate the end.' Any other attitude would only lead to disillusion – rather should Israel wait, trusting in the Isaianic promise: 'happy are all they that wait for him' (30:18).[15] If R. Jonathan's contemporary, Ḥanina b. Harna, did calculate the end, then it was only to determine a date some two centuries in the future (470 CE) when it would lack all contemporary significance. The context is in any case a calendrical discussion.[16]

This cast of mind was inevitably reinforced by the experience of the Bar Kochba revolt against Rome in 132 CE, with its pronounced messianic accompaniment. Even in its time R. Torta repudiated R. Akiba's support for Bar Kochba with the derisive comments: 'the grass will be growing out of your cheeks, Akiba, and the son of David will still not have come.'[17] Similarly, the author of the apocalyptic work, 'The Assumption of Moses',

---

[12] TB San., 97a–8a; cf. also the discussion of these passages in E. Lévinas, 'Temps messianiques et temps historiques', in E. Lévinas, *La Conscience Juive*, Paris, 1963, pp. 268ff.; and in J. Neusner, *The Messiah in Context*, Philadelphia, 1984, ch. 4.

[13] A. Funkenstein, 'Maimonides: political theory and realistic messianism', *Miscellanea Medievalia*, xi (1977), p. 83; see also E. E. Urbach, *Hazal-Emunot ve-De'ot*, Jerusalem, 1969, p. 585.

[14] *The Fathers According to Rabbi Nathan*, ed. and trans. A. J. Saldarini, Leiden, 1975, ch. 31.

[15] TB San., 97b.

[16] TB AZ, 9b.

[17] MR Lam. 2:2.

of c.140 CE, condemned those Jews who accepted Bar Kochba as the messiah and took to open warfare against the Romans. These were the people to whom he attributed responsibility for the subsequent sufferings of the Jews.[18] The revolt itself generated an enduring admonition in the concept of 'the four oaths', educed from the Song of Songs: 'R. Halbo said, "there are four adjurations here [that is, in the Song of Songs]. God made Israel swear not to rebel against the powers; not to force the end; not to reveal their mysteries to the nations of the world; and not to go up from the diaspora [that is, to the land of Israel] en masse. If so, why should the king messiah come to gather the exiles of Israel?"'[19] The 'four oaths' never came to enjoy binding legal force, but did constitute an enduring caution, to be invoked as occasion required.

These arguments did not of themselves rule out the possibility of messianic thinking. But it had to take account of the evident danger inherent in the very theme. Maimonides, for example, developed a doctrine that so rigorously eschewed all 'messianic' elements as entirely to invalidate them. Here is a doctrine without apocalypse or eschaton. The messiah and his age must either be historical or they must be a delusion. Maimonides made full use of the 'reality principle', irrespective of other criteria: after all, he writes, 'no one is in a position to know the details of this and similar matters until they have come to pass'. The prophets are not specific and the rabbis have no traditions. There was 'a divergence of opinion'. In any case, 'neither the exact sequence of those events nor the details constitute religious dogmas', and nor did they warrant much attention, for they conduced 'neither to the fear of sin nor to the love of Him'.[20]

Maimonides himself lived at the time of the Crusades which, for the Jews of Yemen and North Africa, was also a time of forced conversion, despair and impoverishment. On all accounts he was encouraged to think of the present in terms of 'the travails of the messiah'. In his own family there was such a tradition, he wrote to the beleaguered Jews of Yemen in 1172.[21] But Maimonides combined the expectation of imminent redemption with a doctrine rooted in the continuum of history. To the three sources of certain belief – mathematical demonstration; sense data; traditions of the

[18] Zeitlin, 'The Essenes', pp. 497, 511.

[19] MR Song of Songs, 2:7. The number of 'oaths' varies in different sources but not their general purport; cf. TB Ket. 111a and the discussion in M. Breuer, 'Ha-Diyun beshalosh ha-shevuot be-dorot ha-aharonim' in *Ge'ulah u-medina*, Jerusalem, 1979, pp. 49–57.

[20] MT Laws of Kings, 12:2.

[21] 'Epistle to Yemen', Halkin, *Crisis and Leadership*, p. 96; see also below p. 169 for the general messianic atmosphere generated by the Crusades; and H. H. Ben-Sasson, *Ha-Ishiyut ve-doro*, Jerusalem, 1964, p. 95.

prophets or sages – Maimonides now added historical evidence. The messianic days had already existed in the time of independent Jewish statehood. Thus all that the present condition of exile requires is 'the liberation from servitude to foreign powers', quoting Samuel, the third century Babylonian teacher.[22] The days of the messiah are this world and the world follows its customary path, except that sovereignty will be restored to Israel. Clearly, the 'customary path' of the world is at variance with prophetic vision, so that Maimonides naturalizes this also. Immediately preceding his reference to Samuel, he explains that 'the words of Isaiah [11:6]: "and the wolf shall dwell with the lamb and the leopard shall lie down with the kid"', are to be understood figuratively:

> meaning that Israel will live securely among the wicked of the heathens who are likened to wolves and leopards... They will all accept the true religion, and will neither plunder nor destroy, and together with Israel earn a comfortable living in a legitimate way, as it is written: and the lion shall eat straw like the ox [Is. 11:7]. All similar expressions used in connection with the messianic age are metaphorical. In the days of king-messiah the full meaning of these metaphors and their allusions will become clear to all.[23]

It proved difficult to sustain the argument that prophetic language is only figurative and metaphorical, thus making it possible to allow the world to continue on 'its customary path', for Maimonides also seems to maintain that in some situations prophetic discourse must be understood in a literal sense: for example, 'in that [messianic] era there will be neither hunger nor war, neither jealousy nor strife. Blessings will be plentiful, comforts available to all.'[24] In what sense, then, are the strong and the weak to continue to exist, or 'the poor not to cease from the land' (Dt. 15:11)?[25] Similarly, when he quotes Micah (4:3) to the effect that 'nation shall not lift up sword against nation, Neither shall they learn war any more', he seems to be taking this in a literal, non-metaphorical sense.[26]

For all that, Maimonides's resolve to integrate the messianic era into the historical continuum is unmistakeable; as Novak puts it, to make 'the messianic reign a political possibility in human history'.[27] Nowhere is this

[22] MT Laws of Kings, 12:2.
[23] Ibid, 12:1.
[24] Ibid, 12:5.
[25] 'Commentary on Mishnah, Intro. to Sanhedrin', ch. x (*Perek Ḥelek*).
[26] Ibid.
[27] D. Novak, 'Maimonides's concept of the messiah', *Journal of Religious Studies*, ix (1982), no. 2, p. 50.

more apparent than in his presentation of the messiah himself. He too belongs to the restorationist scheme by virtue of his human, Davidic descent. Moreover, though an altogether exceptional person, he remains recognizably human and is not required 'to perform signs and wonders, bring anything new into being, revive the dead or do similar things'.[28] He is required to prove himself, however, by meditating on the Torah, observing the commandments and prevailing on Israel to follow the Torah and fight the battles of the Lord against his enemies.[29]

At this point he is still on trial, as it were, on the analogy of Bar Kochba, who was first acknowledged as messiah but from whom messianic recognition was withdrawn when he was killed in battle. But if the presumed messiah, having succeeded and survived thus far, now goes on to rebuild the Temple on its site, and gathers the dispersed of Israel, then 'he is', Maimonides concludes, 'beyond all doubt the messiah'. 'He will prepare the whole world to serve the Lord with one accord, as it is written: "for then will I turn to the people a pure language, that they may all call upon the name of the Lord to serve him with one consent" [Zeph. 3:9].'[30] This is the condition that warrants and justifies Israel's longing for the messiah – not that they might exercise rule, or be glorified or eat, drink and be merry, but that they will now 'be free to devote themselves to the Law and its wisdom, with no one to oppress or hamper them, and thus make themselves deserving of life in the world to come'.[31]

This whole process also finds room for the historical contribution of Christianity and Islam. Though religions of falsity, the latter founded by a 'madman' and the former interpreting the Torah 'in a fashion that would lead to its annulment',[32] they none the less help 'to prepare the whole world to worship God'.[33]

But in messianic days the world still 'follows its customary path'. Maimon-

---

[28] 'Miracles and wonders' are, however, a mode of proof in the 'Epistle to Yemen' (Halkin, *Crisis and Leadership*, p. 125).

[29] This is elsewhere contrasted favourably with reliance on astrology, to which Maimonides attributed the destruction of the first Temple: 'our fathers sinned and are no more because they found many books dealing with these themes of the stargazers, these things being the root of idolatry. . . They did not busy themselves with the art of war or with the conquest of lands, but imagined that those studies would help them' (A. Marx [trans.], 'The correspondence between the rabbis of southern France and Maimonides about astrology', *HUCA*, 3 [1926], p. 350).

[30] MT Laws of Kings, 11:3–4.

[31] Ibid., 12:4/5.

[32] 'Epistle to Yemen', Halkin, *Crisis and Leadership*, pp. 98ff.; also above p. 000.

[33] MT Laws of Kings, 11 (end) (following the translation of I. Twersky [ed.], *A Maimonides Reader*, New York, 1972, p. 226).

ides is at pains to stress that although increased longevity will be one fruit of the general beneficence of life and 'the absence of cares and sorrows' in the messianic age, yet the messiah will die, his son and grandson likewise. It is again not strange therefore that although the messianic age 'will endure thousands of years . . . [and] not easily disintegrate', the unspoken implication is that it will disintegrate.[34] Kraemer has here identified a Platonic reference, mediated through Averroës's Commentary on *The Republic*: 'a city which is thus constituted can hardly be shaken; but, seeing that everything which has a beginning has also an end, even a constitution such as yours will not last for ever, but will in time be dissolved.'[35]

In keeping with this sobriety, Maimonides also considers the possibility that the messiah will not come in the lifetime of any particular individual. And in one perspective at least the consequence is not striking. If the messiah should come, so much the better – 'life will be more pleasant', he wrote in the Epistle on Martyrdom (*c.*1165). 'If he does not come we have not lost anything: on the contrary we have gained by doing what we had to do.'[36] This diminution of the advent is qualified by the argument that even in the pre-messianic conditions of exile and its inseparable hardships, it still remained possible for individuals, in proportion to the degree with which they directed their intellect and in accordance with their capacity, to seek to acquire a knowledge of God, and thus to anticipate the bliss of the world to come. In this sense that world already exists and, as the true aim of human endeavour, is already accessible.[37]

The Messiah and the Stars

But only to the elite is this stance available, and to the many it would be sustainable only so long as the gap between the existent and the desirable/ expected does not widen beyond a certain point. This is a dynamic structure that allows for elasticity of desirability and expectation. At some variable point, however, dependent on particular historical circumstances, it will cease to be possible to tolerate the gap and recourse will be had to a flight

---

[34] *Perek Ḥelek.*

[35] *The Republic*, viii, 546; cf. J. Kraemer, 'On Maimonides' messianic posture', in I. Twersky (ed.), *Studies in Medieval Jewish History, II*, Cambridge, Mass., 1984, p. 112.

[36] 'Epistle on Martyrdom', Halkin, *Crisis and Leadership*, p. 33.

[37] MT Laws of Repentance, 8:8; see also Novak, 'Maimonides's concept of the messiah', p. 47; Kraemer, 'On Maimonides' messianic posture', p. 141; A. Ravitsky, 'K'fi ko'ah ha'adam – Yemot ha'meshiah be-mishnat ha-Rambam', in Ts. Baras (ed.), *Meshihiyut ve-eskatalogiya*, Jerusalem, 1984, p. 200.

from the existent. A more satisfying meaning will be wrested from history.

The form of such flight is not predetermined and will vary with attendant circumstances. When confidence in the efficacy of the praxis required by the Torah is, for one reason or another, dissipated; alternatively, when the *modus operandi* has seemed too protracted and exigent to satisfy the urgency of the demand for redemption; in either case the Torah then displays its vulnerability to some sort of redemptionist messianic movement. This represents an alternative model of redemption that caricatures, however, the halakhic model through the inadequacy of its means in relation to the obstacles that impede its fulfilment, or through its immoderate confidence in divine aid or through a combination of both. The quest for the re-establishment of integrity will have been satisfied, through accelerating what is in any event considered no more than inevitable. A precipitate means will be sought, and ostensibly found, to transform the 'here and now' into 'another world'. At this point antinomianism is likely to make its appearance, embracing forms of activity allied to, or incorporating some form of, *avodah zarah*, attributing to persons, planets, occult forces etc. an influence that properly belongs only to the Torah. It is made clear in a responsum of R. Judah b. Asher that belief in astrology, in some entity other than God to determine the present and reveal the future, is ontologically bound up with sorcery, divination, necromancy, soothsaying etc. These are, of course, all denounced as spurious sources of power and foreknowledge. Spurious but not impotent: R. Judah would not otherwise have attributed to the sway of astrology the loss of the first Temple and the exile – a view shared by Maimonides.[38]

These efforts to suppress the messianic idea and/or to cleanse it of its supernatural or idolatrous elements and associations did not succeed. At least since the end of the first millennium CE, almost no decade has passed that has not been identified as pregnant with the messiah.[39] A stream of strange figures passes before us – a 'mixed multitude' of military adventurers, astrologers, numerologists, *exaltés*, 'calculators of the end', antinomian thinkers and charismatic personalities. Of course, if that is all they were, their views and activities would be of negligible interest. But these same people also include scholars, astronomers, statesmen, geographers. Even so, they cherished visions that encompassed both violent aspirations and the passivity of historico-literary reflection and analysis. The movements or influences were localized and marginal but could never be disregarded.

---

[38] *Zikhron Yehuda*, Berlin, 1846, no. 91; see also TB Yoma 9b. It is no less necessary to disenchant the future than the present. See, on this point, W. Benjamin, *Illuminationen*, Frankfurt on Main, 1961, p. 279.

[39] See the short sketch in L. Zunz, *Gesammelte Schriften*, *III*, Berlin, 1876, pp. 224–31.

In many cases an element of violence occasioned the movements and/or the theories, elements such as the Mongol invasion of the west, the wars of religion, the supposed discovery of the lost ten tribes of Israel (sixteenth–seventeenth centuries), Napoleon's summoning of the Parisian Sanhedrin (1806), Mehemet Ali's invasion of Palestine (1832), the First World War and the Six Day War of 1967.[40] This is what I understand by 'the activation of history'.

For the sake of simplicity I shall touch by way of illustration on only certain of these phenomena; in the late medieval period, the seventeenth century and the twentieth century. I will be highly selective but not, I hope, unrepresentative.

The period of the Crusades, in the eleventh and twelfth centuries, and the century following the expulsion from Spain and Portugal (1492, 1496) were marked by widespread messianic ferment.[41] It could not be otherwise, during the Crusades, given that the fate of the Promised Land itself was at stake. The international situation matched the ancient criterion: 'When you see the powers fighting amongst themselves, look out for the footsteps of the messiah.'[42] 'Wars are part of the beginning of redemption.'[43] In his *Scroll of the Revealer* (published in or shortly before 1129), R. Abraham b. Hiyya (1065–1136, a celebrated astronomer of Castile) expounded a messianic prophecy, based on the Biblical text, supplemented with data drawn from the movement of the planets. The earliest date when the messianic era might be expected to begin was 1136 CE; certainly by 1206 he foresaw 'wars in the land showing signs of the signs of redemption' and two decades later 'the head and beginning of our salvation with the help of the Lord'.[44] In a similar vein, R. Abraham ibn Daud, of twelfth-century Toledo, adapted the traditional exegesis of Daniel's Four Empires (Persia, Babylon, Greece, Rome) in his *Sefer Ha'Kabbalah* – Book of Tradition, *c.*1160 – so as to deduce that the return of the rule of the house of David 'is imminent in

---

[40] See A. Z. Aescoly and Y. Even-Shmuel (eds), *Ha-Tenuot ha-meshihiyot be-Yisrael*, Jerusalem, 1956; A. H. Silver, *A History of Messianic Speculation in Israel*, repr., Gloucester, Mass., 1978; J. Schapira, *Bishvilei Ha'Geulah*, 2 vols, Tel Aviv, 1947.

[41] See the material assembled in B.-Z. Dinur, *Yisrael Ba'Golah*, vol. II, pt 3, Jerusalem, 1968, ch. 13.

[42] MR Gen. 42:4.

[43] TB Meg. 17a.

[44] For detailed references, see L. Kochan, *The Jew and his History*, London, 1977, pp. 23–4. A. Marx, 'The correspondence between the rabbis of Southern France', gives an idea of the prevalence of astrological beliefs at this time.

our day'.[45] Towards the very end of the thirteenth century hopes such as these, further excited by the Moslem capture of Acre (1291), inspired the Jewish community of Cesena in north-central Italy to set out for the Promised Land.[46]

The events of the late fifteenth and sixteenth centuries generated perhaps an even greater degree of messianic ferment.[47] Again the Jewish and international situation took a vital role. The temptation to activate history was irresistible. The fall of Constantinople, the expulsion from Spain and Portugal, the emergence of Luther, the Reformation, the conflict between the Pope and the Emperor – all seemed to presage a violent overthrow of the established order in favour of the Jews. At least to the Sephardi world this seemed so.[48] Ashkenazim, as in the period of the Crusades and again in the sixteenth century, remained largely immune.[49] Josel of Rosheim, appointed 'Commander of German Jewry' by the emperor Charles V, had none of the admiration for Luther manifested by some of his Sephardi contemporaries and certainly shared none of the messianic expectations that they attached to the Reformation.[50]

Amongst the Sephardi exiles from Spain, Don Isaac Abrabanel, former finance minister to the rulers of Portugal and Castile, was one of the first to invest contemporary events with messianic meaning. In three works of Biblical and Talmudic commentary composed at the turn of the fifteenth century, he interpreted the contemporary Turkish advance into Europe and the disarray of the Christian world to signify the coming redemption of Israel. It was the time foreseen by Ezekiel when 'every man's sword shall

[45] Kochan, *The Jew and his History*, p. 26.

[46] See Sylvia Schein, 'An unknown messianic movement in thirteenth century Italy: Cesena 1297', *Italia*, V (1985), nos. 1–2, pp. 99–103.

[47] See Rivka Shatz, 'Kavim l'demuta shel ha'hitor'rut ha'politit-meshihit l'achar gerush Sefarad', *Da'at*, XI (summer 1983), pp. 53–66; and I. Tishby, *Meshihiyut b'dor gerushei Sefarad u'Portugal*, Jerusalem, 1985; J. Hacker, 'Links between Spanish Jewry and Palestine, 1391–1492', in R. Cohen (ed.), *Vision and Conflict in the Holy Land*, Jerusalem, 1985, pp. 111–39.

[48] Yerushalmi writes: 'Italian Jewry was particularly susceptible to every messianic tiding and, perhaps because of its geographic location, often served as an eschatological news-agency for other parts of the Jewish world' ('Messianic impulses in Joseph ha-Kohen', in B. Cooperman [ed.], *Jewish Thought in the Sixteenth Century*, Cambridge, Mass., 1983, p. 468).

[49] See also below pp. 172ff. This difference has never been satisfactorily explained, but see G. D. Cohen, 'Messianic postures of Ashkenazim and Sephardim', LBI, New York, 1967; and S. Sharot, 'Jewish millenarianism: a comparison of medieval communities', *Comparative Studies in Society and History*, XXII (1980).

[50] H. Fraenkel-Goldschmidt (ed.), *Joseph of Rosheim, Sefer Ha-Miknah*, Jerusalem, 1970, intro., pp. 40, 67.

be against his brother' (38:21) – 'and these brothers are Edom and Ishmael' (that is, Rome and Islam), commented Abrabanel.[51] Their clash and mutual annihilation would leave the path clear for the redemption of Israel as a sort of *tertium gaudens*.

The later sixteenth century produced a multitude of predictions in which this paradigm was reproduced and current convulsions understood in terms of a cosmic clash, Israel's humbled state being the prelude to its restoration. In 1525 R. Abraham b. R. Eliezer Halevi (*c*.1460–after 1528, Kabbalist and wandering scholar in Italy, Greece, Turkey and Jerusalem) perceived a fourfold unfolding of redemption – 1520 and 1524 had already witnessed pre-messianic 'visitations'; in 1530 the messiah was to appear; and in 1536–7 the Temple to be rebuilt.[52] This process he associated with, and attributed to, Lutheran activity, for whose onslaught on Rome he expressed deep appreciation. But the process, in Halevi's view, was taking place not only through Lutheran iconoclasm and the unmasking of 'the falsity of their [that is, the Catholic] faith',[53] but also through Luther's success in attracting a mass following 'with his wisdom and the sweetness of his discoveries' – and, emphasizes Halevi, 'he will gradually draw them closer to the religion of Moses and have no doubt that the hand of the Lord has done this'.[54] Halevi could also draw comfort from developments at the military-diplomatic level where, for example, 'the Lord has already begun to destroy the glory of Rome [in 1522], for then there began the war in Rhodes, the honoured daughter of Rome and when the daughter was violated, the mother began to lose her honour'.[55]

R. Abraham Farrissol (*c*.1451–*c*.1525, Bible commentator and geographer, of Ferrara and Mantua) occupied something of an intermediate position. In Daniel 12:7 he saw 'the shattering of the power of the holy people' as a reference to the humiliated and dispersed condition of Israel; and in the recent expulsions from Spain, France, Savoy and Lombardy further blows which, however, were 'signs and portents that the desired end foreshadowed by Scripture is approaching. Happy is he who awaits its

[51] *Ma'ayenei Ha'Yeshuah*, Stettin, 1860, p. 50b; for other details, see Kochan, *The Jew and his History*, pp. 28ff.

[52] Ira Robinson, 'Two letters of Abraham ben Eliezer Halevi', in I. Twersky (ed.), *Studies in Medieval Jewish History and Literature, II*, Cambridge, Mass., 1984, pp. 403–22.

[53] Ibid., p. 444.

[54] Ibid.

[55] Ibid., p. 448. There is an account of these predictions in their wider context in H. H. Ben-Sasson, *The Reformation in Contemporary Jewish Eyes*, Jerusalem, 1970, pp. 17ff.

coming; may our eyes behold it!'[56] On the other hand he denounced specific predictions and individual pretenders, of whom at least three came his way, namely Bonet de Lattes, Asher Lämmlein and David Reubeni.

The first was a physician from Provence who engaged in scientific pursuits at the pontifical court of Alexander VI. He also served as rabbi of the Roman community. He combined exegesis of Daniel with the conjunction of Jupiter and Saturn in 1504 to predict the messiah's arrival the following year. Writing after the event, apparently, de Lattes provided easy meat for Farrissol, who accused de Lattes of deception and invoked the ancient anathema 'may all the calculators of the end be destroyed'.[57]

Asher Lämmlein came from Germany to north-east Italy, Istria and Venetia at the turn of the sixteenth century. Lämmlein did not represent himself as the messiah, only as his prophet.[58] Even so, he and his followers were able to mislead large numbers of Italian Jewry into undertaking fasts and other ascetic exercises in preparation for the coming end of days. Farrissol denounced Lämmlein for his lack of wisdom and for his secretiveness – 'and in the end it was all vanity and emptiness of mind', he concluded.[59]

Some twenty years later, in 1523, Farrissol evinced a similar scepticism in regard to David Reubeni. Self-proclaimed son of a king Solomon and brother of a king Joseph who supposedly ruled the lost tribes of Reuben, Gad and half-Manasseh in the desert of Habor in the Arabian peninsula, Reubeni claimed to be animated by the holy spirit to lead the Jewish people to the Promised Land. There they would rebuild Jerusalem and the Temple of Solomon; 'the time was approaching to bring about this great cause.'[60] In 1524, Reubeni was received by Pope Clement VII, to whom he proposed an alliance between the Jewish 'state' and the Christian world against the Moslem invaders. Reubeni did enjoy much Jewish support but Farrissol remained cautious.[61] R. Azriel Dayiena of Sabbionetta and R. Abraham b.

[56] Ben-Sasson, *Reformation*, p. 18. For a comprehensive analysis of Farrissol's importance as geographer and polemicist, see D. Ruderman, *The World of a Renaissance Jew*, Cincinnati, 1981; pp. 137–8 deal with his messianic contacts.

[57] H. Vogelstein and P. Rieger, *Geschichte der Juden in Rom, II*, Berlin, 1895, pp. 81–2.

[58] See Aescoly and Even-Shmuel, *Ha-Tenuot*, pp. 249, 307–8; and D. Tamar, 'Al R. Asher Lämmlein', *Zion*, 52 (1987), no. 3, pp. 399–401.

[59] R. Abraham Farrissol, *Magen Avraham*, ch. 24, ed. S. Löwinger, *REJ*, NS V (1939), p. 35.

[60] Cf. Reubeni's statement to Gianbattista Ramusio, a Venetian senator, in Aescoly and Even-Shmuel, *Ha-Tenuot*, pp. 381ff. There is a translated extract from Reubeni's diary in Elkan Adler (ed.), *Jewish Travellers*, London, 1930, pp. 251–328.

[61] *Iggeret Orhot Olam*, Venice, 1586, ch. 14.

Moses Cohen of Bologna both sought to discredit Reubeni by depriving him of his rabbinical title – they feared lest popular enthusiasm pass beyond control.[62]

It is certainly testimony to the unbroken rejection of despair that these individuals and their programmes could gain credence. But it is also bewildering to hear that these visionary movements gave benefits to a suppressed people, 'in inspiring them to activity, revitalization, and a sense of sacrifice'.[63] In fact, the messianic urge and its capacity to bring about the degeneration of cosmic optimism, mediated through the Torah, into messianic movements, generated as many calls for sobriety as there were calls for enthusiasm. Critics seized on the association with astrology. This, *eo ipso*, condemned the prediction. Abraham ibn Ezra in his commentary to Daniel 11:31 denounced the calculations of R. Abraham b. Ḥiyya and of Solomon ibn Gabirol, who sought 'to bind together the end to the great conjunction of two supreme stars ... and all who calculate words and letters through reference to their numerical value – it is all vanity and empty-headedness, for Daniel did not know the end, and nor do those who follow him.'[64] R. Isaac Arama of Barcelona (*c*.1420–94) pointed out that nothing of R. Abraham b. Ḥiyya's predictions had been fulfilled, and that belief in astrology prolonged the exile and denied providence – 'may the souls perish of those who calculate the end'.[65] R. David ibn Abi Zimra applied to R. Abraham Halevi the derisive words of R. Torta to R. Akiba at the time of Bar Kochba: 'already the grass has grown on his cheeks and the son of David has not yet come.'[66]

The historical critic and essayist of the sixteenth century, R. Azariah de Rossi, singled out for censure R. Mordecai Dato (1525–91/1601), an Italian Kabbalist, who had predicted the rebuilding of the Temple in 1575, the ingathering of the exiles in 1605 and the resurrection of the dead in 1645. Rossi also referred to R. Abraham b. Hiyya and Don Isaac Abrabanel and spoke of their 'confusion'. They 'imagined in their souls to bring the hidden to light with the help of the decrees of the stars and the great conjunctions of the heavenly hosts'. Rossi affirmed as a principle that 'the destiny of Israel or any hope of their salvation did not depend on the conjunction [of the planets] but God alone is our salvation and He knows its time – perhaps

---

[62] D. Kaufmann, 'Azriel b. Solomon Dayiena et la seconde intervention de David Reubeni en Italie', *REJ*, 30 (1895), pp. 304–9.

[63] H. -H. Ben-Sasson, *Trial and Achievement*, Jerusalem, 1974, p. 208.

[64] Abraham ibn Ezra on Daniel 11:31.

[65] R. Isaac Arama, *Ḥazot Kashah*, Pressburg, 1849, p. 33b.

[66] R. David ibn Abi Zimra, *Magen David*, Amsterdam, 1713, p. 39b, where he also writes: 'in the matter of the messiah there is no tie or bond to the observance of the Torah.'

even today "if you hearken to His voice" (San.98a).' He quoted with approval Ibn Ezra's commentary on Daniel 11:31 denouncing astrological predictions as 'all vanity and empty-headedness'.[67]

R. Jacob Sasportas and Sabbatai Zvi

The ontological bond between this type of messianism and *avodah zarah* is not confined to the resort to astrology. It appears also in the threat posed by an individual who purports to bear a divine message, that will conduce perhaps to the revelation of a 'second' Torah, as it were. He embodies that aspect of *avodah zarah* that I have tried to explain through the notion of mediation.[68] This was the issue created by the emergence of Sabbatai Zvi and his prophet Nathan of Gaza. This seventeenth-century charismatic figure undoubtedly inspired greater enthusiasm than any of his predecessors, especially among Sephardi communities in the Ottoman Empire and among former Marranos.[69] By now an intimidating armoury of weapons had accumulated and stood ready to deploy against any pretender to messianic status. But the appeal to history was still paramount.

Nathan of Gaza, sometimes also known as Nathan Ashkenazi, began his career as a preacher summoning individuals to repentance, prescribing various spiritual exercises as a means of redemption from sin.[70] He predicted Sabbatai's messianic career in a letter of 1665 to Raphael Joseph Chelby in Eygpt:

> now I reveal how the matter will be. After a year and some months from today he will take dominion from the king of Turkey without war, solely by songs and hymns of praise, in that he will declare all peoples subject to his rule, and he will take with him solely the king of Turkey to all the places that he will subdue and all kings will tender tribute to him and the king of Turkey alone will be his servant and there will be no massacre of the uncircumcised save in the lands of Ashkenaz. At that time there is yet no ingathering of the exiles and

[67] A. de Rossi, *Me'or Eynayim*, ch. 43, pp. 368ff.; cf. also pp. 276, 376, 382.

[68] See above p. 138.

[69] The degree of support claimed by G. Scholem (in his *Sabbatai Zvi – The Mystical Messiah*, Engl. trans., London, 1973), needs to be qualified; see, for Germany and Poland, B. D. Weinryb, *The Jews of Poland*, Philadelphia, 1973, pp. 216–21, and the notes on pp. 368–9; also S. Sharot, *Messianism, Mysticism and Magic*, Chapel Hill, North Carolina, 1982, ch. 7, passim; and G. D. Hundert, 'No messiahs in paradise', *Viewpoints*, II (1980), no. 2, pp. 28–33.

[70] I. Tishby, *Netivei Emuna u-minut*, Jerusalem, 1964, pp. 30ff.

the Jews will have greatness, each in his own place. The rebuilding of our holy temple and our glory will not take place at that time, save that the rabbi [that is, Sabbatai Zvi] will reveal the site of the altar, will offer sacrifices and the ash of the heifer [Nu. 19:2ff.], and this will last four or five years.

After this the rabbi will go to the river Sambatyon and in one way or another will entrust rule to the king of Turkey and give him command over the Jews. After three months he will rebel through the wiles of his counsellors, and at that time troubles will multiply but he will stand firm and I will try them as gold is tried and will refine them as silver is refined [adapted from Zechariah 13:9] and no man will escape save those dwelling here [that is, in Gaza] where stands the head of the government... And at the end of this period there will be the signs from the Zohar and this will last until the coming year of sabbatical release [1672] and this is in the seventh year and the son of David comes and in the seventh year a sabbath which is of Sabbatai Zvi the king.

This is the year that marks the culminating triumph of the messiah's career – universal acceptance by kings and peoples, the ingathering of the exiles in the Land of Israel, the rebuilding of the Temple and the resurrection of the dead, first in Palestine, forty years later those buried outside.[71]

In actual fact the acts of the supposed redeemer amounted to certain antinomian decrees, such as the annulment of the Fast of the Ninth of Av (commemorating the destruction of the first and second temples), the annulment of the Fast of the Tenth of Tebeth, and the utterance of the ineffable name of God. Towards the end of 1665 he appointed kings from amongst his followers, each allegedly a reincarnation of one of the ancient kings of Israel and Judah.[72] Sabbatai's career culminated in 1666 in his apostasy to Islam. This did not discredit the redeemer entirely but it did of course provide his opponents with a further powerful weapon.

R. Jacob Sasportas of the Portuguese Sephardi community at Hamburg was the most articulate and best informed of these opponents. He had left London in 1665 on account of the plague – 'the destroying hand of the Lord'[73] – and reached Hamburg by way of Amsterdam. After undergoing with his family a period of quarantine,[74] he found in Hamburg a divided

---

[71] This is taken from Isaiah Tishby's edition of R. Jacob Sasportas's dossier on Sabbatai Zvi – *Tsitsat Nobel Zvi*, pp. 10–12 – first published in full, Jerusalem, 1954. (Later referred to as Tishby, *Tsitsat Nobel Zvi*.)

[72] Scholem, *Sabbatai Zvi*, pp. 427ff.

[73] *MJHSE*, III (1937), p. 11.

[74] 'Aus dem ältesten Protokollbuch der Portugiesisch-Jüdischen Gemeinde in

community. An influential and dominant majority certainly accepted the claims made for Sabbatai by Nathan of Gaza, though not without a certain caveat. The *pinkas* of the community records its 'thanksgiving to the Lord of the World for the news from the Levant, confirmed from Italy and other regions that He in His divine grace and mercy has given us a prophet in the Land of Israel in the sage R. Nathan Ashkenazi and an anointed king in the sage R. Sabbatai Zvi . . . chosen to redeem His people from exile. . . May the God of Israel cause the truth of these tidings to be confirmed and grant us the inheritance of our land.'[75] This was in December 1665, but in March 1666 the community leaders required their rabbi, R. Moses Israel, to proclaim in the synagogue an immediate prohibition on 'all wagers on the coming of our salvation'. Offenders had to pay a fine of five reichsthaler if the wager was laid with a fellow Jew (ten reichsthaler if with a Christian) and also forfeit the sum wagered.[76] There is no direct evidence, to the best of my knowledge, of any such bets, but if they had not existed there would have been no need to prohibit them. Now, we know that Jews are prone to gambling and a gambler was not to be trusted.[77] Even so, to bet on the redemption requires an uncommon degree of scepticism or frivolity and certainly illuminates the evolution of opinion amongst the Hamburg Sephardim.

But Sasportas still had to write with circumspection, all the more so as he was in receipt of foodstuffs (meal, butter, cheese) and firewood from the community, to alleviate his hardship.[78] Moreover, he was himself for a time a believer in the pretender, and this led Sasportas to doctor and edit some of his original writings in order to present an unblemished picture of unremitting disbelief.[79]

Even so, the personal motives that were to turn R. Sasportas from acceptance to scepticism and ultimate rejection conform to rabbinic tradition in the face of a messianic pretender. There were formal arguments; sociological arguments; and arguments *ad hominem* (naturally, with some overlap). To the first category belongs R. Sasportas's argument that 'the coming of

---

Hamburg', (trans. J. Cassuto from the original Portuguese, since destroyed), *Jahrbuch der Jüdisch-Literarischen Gesellschaft*, X (1913), p. 289.

[75] Ibid., pp. 292–3.

[76] Ibid., XI, pp. 12–13.

[77] See above, p. 50, fn 57; and L. Landman, 'Jewish attitudes to gambling', *JQR*, nos. 58–9 (1967–9), pp. 34–62.

[78] 'Aus dem ältesten Protokollbuch', X, 1913, pp. 290, 294; for a sketch of Sasportas's 'difficult' character and outsider position in the Hamburg community, see Tishby, *Tsitsat Nobel Zvi*, pp. 27ff.

[79] See the comparison of earlier and later versions in Rivka Schatz's review of Tishby's book in *Behinot*, X (1956), pp. 50–67.

the messiah does not need a prophet, and after his coming this is not astonishing for is it not written that "I will pour out my spirit in all flesh?"'(Joel 3:1).[80] 'I will never accept that the sages of the Land of Israel confirmed [a man] as an anointed king and as a sprig of the tribe of Jesse at the word of a prophet and not at the word of the man himself', he declared.[81]

The sociological argument deployed by R. Sasportas revolved around the consequence of what would now be known as 'cognitive dissonance'. What other reaction could be expected, once Sabbatai's falsity were made manifest, than disillusion with the messianic idea itself? Only in this way could belief be reconciled with reality. Thus Sasportas wrote to the rabbis of Amsterdam – where Sabbatian enthusiasm was rife – and gave cautious voice to the fear that sin might result

> when the time comes and he will not fulfil the decree of that prophet and he will find room to say that his promise and his prophecy were conditional and he will leave room to argue against him . . . and it is likely that for some light or heavy transgression the prophet will find room to exculpate himself and the name of the messiah will become despised and the prophet a dreamer of dreams and we become a reproach to our neighbours;

and again to Amsterdam

> it seems to me that doubt is preferable to certainty. For in the future if all the principles and details connected to the coming of the redeemer prophesied by the man of God are not fulfilled the consequences will be catastrophe for all the mass of the people and some of their leaders who have become convinced that he is the king-messiah . . . and will later see that his truth is not confirmed [and] will say that there is no messiah in Israel, that they have already consumed him in the days of the prophecy of Gaza.[82]

'In these matters,' R. Sasportas wrote to Vienna, 'it is better to move gradually and to see the affair as a distant possibility and to help it with reversion [to God] but they [the supporters of Sabbatai] on the contrary make a heretic of him who is sceptical and they make the matter dependent on the word of a prophet and from an infirm premise draw a firm conclusion.'[83] To this fear of disillusion, Sasportas added, in a letter to the

---

[80] Tishby, *Tsitsat Nobel Zvi*, p. 39; cf. also p. 88.
[81] Ibid., p. 13.
[82] Ibid., pp. 14–15, 18 (adapted from TB San., 99a; see also ibid., 97b).
[83] Ibid., p. 119.

rabbis of Izmir, the further fear that 'the faith of the Christians would be strengthened in saying that their messiah had already come'.[84]

This forms a transition to Sasportas's third and most far-reaching cluster of arguments – those *ad hominem*. The failure of Sabbatai to manifest his status at the historical level would entail his acceptance on mere faith on the model of the Christian acceptance of Jesus, and thus perhaps create the danger of a new heresy, or at least the transvaluation of existing, accepted values that demanded proof at the level of the real, the historical, the manifest.[85]

Nathan of Gaza firmly grasped this central issue at the outset of the redeemer's career, and made of Sabbatai a man whose 'grievous sufferings ... on behalf of Israel' were a sort of atonement that entitled him to unquestioning acceptance without further demonstration: 'and because of this', said Nathan, 'he has the power to deal with the Israelite people as he sees fit, to declare [a man] guiltless or burdened with guilt and even to pardon the most burdened man in the world, even though he be as Jesus he has the authority to pardon, and he who murmurs against him, even though he be the most pious man in the world he has the power to impose on him grievous sufferings ... there is no life to Israel if they will not believe in these matters without sign and demonstration.'[86]

This was precisely what Sasportas had to reject. At one level, the lower, as it were, the pretender needed to make a 'negative' show of power. He had at least to punish sceptics and unbelievers, 'for', he writes, 'the Lord does not delight in those who transgress His teaching and His prophets'.[87] It was veritably incumbent on Sabbatai to give a sign; otherwise he was, in effect, conniving in the views of the sceptics and rendering them 'liable to death at the hands of heaven if they do not heed his word'. Referring to Maimonides's Mishneh Torah (Laws of the Foundation of the Torah 9:3, and to a comment thereon by Caro), Sasportas maintained that in default of 'sign and demonstration' there was no obligation to heed the prophet and disregard incurred no penalty.[88]

But a 'positive' demonstration of authenticity was also imperative, and this demand Sasportas repeated in a variety of nuances and formulations. He referred, for example, to Maimonides, who had specified the tasks of the messiah in such a way as to make them commensurate with his qualifying characteristics. To repeat:

[84] Ibid., pp. 166–7.
[85] See above p. 173.
[86] Tishby, *Tsitsat Nobel Zvi*, pp. 9–10.
[87] Ibid., p. 117.
[88] Ibid., pp. 142–3.

and if there shall arise a king from the house of David, reflecting on the Torah and observant of the *mitzvot* like David his father in accordance with the written and oral Torah and compel all Israel to go in its path and maintain it whole and fight the wars of the Lord, then this man is presumed to be the messiah and if he succeeded in rebuilding the sanctuary in its place and gathered the scattered ones of Israel, then he is certainly the messiah.[89]

Sasportas quotes this passage and is provoked to comment: 'it seems that his deeds prove him and establish the presumption that he is the king-messiah.' But otherwise, 'all was dependent on faith in the prophecy'.[90]

Rabbi Sasportas's emphasis on the crucial need for manifest proof through successful action was justified in the light of the 'new Torah' or 'two Torahs' that he feared;[91] more particularly, he was sensitive to the Christological trends that characterized Sabbatianism, as exemplified in the importance attached to faith, and the threat of a schism that this posed. He feared 'a new Torah', as proclaimed by Jesus;[92] he feared a certain divinization of the redeemer;[93] and he saw analogy between the apostasy of Sabbatai and Jesus, who had suffered on account of his generation in order to save them from their sin and from the sin of the first man. 'But how is it possible', Sasportas asked, 'that in order to atone for one sin it is necessary to commit a second?'[94] Sabbatai in fact was more heretical than Jesus, for the latter had never at least denied the Torah, never declared 'I am the messiah', whereas Sabbatai had done all this and more.[95] A campaigner sympathetic to Sasportas, R. Joseph Halevi of Leghorn, also made the contrast between 'the principle of Torah and good deeds' which rewarded their practitioners with the promise of life in the world to come, and those whose faith is not as ours, for 'they believe that a man can save souls'.[96]

These were no empty fears. Disillusioned Sabbatians took a prominent place in conversions to Christianity in the later seventeenth and eighteenth centuries.[97] And amongst those who remained faithful, Christological doc-

---

[89] Maimonides, MT Laws of Kings, 11:4.

[90] Tishby, *Tsitsat Nobel Zvi*, pp. 18–19; cf. also p. 320.

[91] Ibid., pp. 113, 115, 212; see also p. 123.

[92] Ibid., p. 131.

[93] Ibid., p. 93. It may be that Sabbatai himself acknowledged Jesus as a true prophet (Scholem, *Sabbatai Zvi*, p. 399).

[94] Ibid., p. 298.

[95] Ibid., p. 315.

[96] Ibid., p. 170.

[97] H. M. Graupe, *Die Entstehung des modernen Judentums*, Hamburg, 1969, pp. 75ff.

trines did develop in the form of heretical semi-underground sects. The sect led by Baruchiah in Salonika in the early eighteenth century propounded a doctrine that emphasized a unity formed of the first cause, the God of Israel and the messiah. It believed in the descent of God to the material world as saviour; in the annulment of the Torah of Creation in favour of the establishment of the Torah of Emanation, the messianic or spiritual Torah; and in the saviour's ascent to the world of the divine, whence he governed all the worlds; and it expressly denied that Sabbatai Zvi was merely flesh and blood, created and not creator.[98] This is to say nothing of the links between Sabbatianism and the later Frankist movement, with its syncretistic if not positively Christian outlook.[99] The inability of Sabbatai Zvi to manifest his alleged status at the historical level laid bare a breach that only antinomian concepts could, vainly, attempt to make good.

The Zionist Messiah

In 1958 Werblowsky discerned two types of religious Zionism: a pietistic variety that saw in the movement a means towards the observance of the divine commandment to live in Eretz Israel, as the only country where the totality of the commandments can be performed; and an eschatological, religious Zionism that invested the movement with 'messianic significance'.[100] But he concluded on a note of qualified optimism, suggesting that 'Zionism may well turn out to have not only established this Jewish State, but also to have led Israel back into the history of the Covenant by liquidating its messianism.'[101]

Three decades later this prospect looks more and more remote. On the contrary, in contemporary Israel a Sabbath prayer, composed by the chief rabbinate, identifies the present state of Israel with 'the beginning of the flowering of our redemption'.[102]

From its inception, Zionist thinking was conditioned by its exposure to

---

[98] G. Scholem, 'Baruchiah – Rosh ha-Shabbataim be-Salonika', *Zion*, VI (1941), p. 190.

[99] See the article by G. Scholem, *Enc. Jud.*, VII, cols. 55–72; also G. Scholem, 'Die Metamorphose des häretischen Messianismus der Sabbatianer in religiösen Nihilismus im 18. Jahrhundert', in *Zeugnisse – Theodor W. Adorno zum 60. Geburtstag*, Frankfurt on Main, 1963, pp. 20–32.

[100] R. J. Z. Werblowsky, 'Crises of messianism', *Judaism*, VII (Spring 1958), no. 2, p. 119.

[101] Ibid., p. 120.

[102] See Bernard Casper, 'Reshit Zemichat Ge'ulatenu', in Jonathan Sacks (ed.), *Tradition and Transition: Essays presented to Chief Rabbi Sir Immanuel Jakobovits*, London, 1986, pp. 107–16.

the process of modernization and the special form taken by that process in nineteenth- and twentieth-century Europe. What I have in mind is the idea of nationalism as a contemporary historical phenomenon. Obviously, Zionism, in the sense of settlement in the Land of Israel, did not have to wait on the emergence of European nationalism – its rootedness in earlier Jewish history was far too deep for that – but it is also true that Zionism assimilated to itself certain nationalist elements. This again must be qualified, for this assimilation operated only in respect to certain strands in Zionist thought and activity. It is completely absent from Herzlian Zionism, for example.

But where assimilation does operate, the result is a powerful amalgam of Jewish and gentile elements, inextricably fused together. This was all the more the case given the transcendent values ascribed to the nation as the bearer of the messianic future and the natural affinity between secular and Jewish messianism.[103] The nation as such is reified.

Modernization and its political expression, nationalism, moved through Europe at a varying pace. They struck first in east-central and south-eastern Europe in the Jewish perspective, and the consequences made themselves evident in the work of R. Zvi Hirsch Kalischer and R. Judah Alkalai. The first was born in 1795 in the border province of Posen, part of western Poland later under Prussian rule, where Germans and Poles fought for supremacy. Alkalai was born in 1798 in Sarajevo and later held rabbinical office at Semlin in Serbia, a centre of Balkan nationalist strivings. In the case of both thinkers, their advocacy of a return to Zion that could be initiated by human agency (but only completed by divine) was encouraged by comparison with the redemptive activity of their neighbours. 'Shall we fall behind all other peoples', asked Kalischer,

who accounted their blood and property as nought by comparison with the love of their land and their people? Pay heed to what the men of Italy, the people of Poland, the state of Hungary have done, who threw away their lives and possessions . . . for the inheritance of their land, and we, the children of Israel, whose land is more glorious than all, our heritage, more holy than all parts of the earth . . . are silent like a man of no spirit. Are we not despicable in our own eyes, for all peoples have acted only for their own glory whereas we act not

---

[103] See M. Graetz, 'Ha-Meshihiyut ha-hilonit ba-meah ha-tesha-asarah kederekh shiva la-yahadut', in Ts. Baras (ed.), *Meshihiyut ve-eskatalogiya*, pp. 401–18; also Anita Shapira, 'Zionism and political messianism' in *Totalitarian Democracy and After*, Jerusalem, 1984, pp. 354ff.

only for the glory of our forefathers but for the glory of God who chose Zion.[104]

Alkalai, whose proto-Zionist writings preceded those of Kalischer by some two decades, shared the same presuppositions and hopes, which he formulated, however, in greater detail.[105] He was also more emphatic in his references to the nationalist spirit of the time. 'Certainly every man of heart yearns with all his soul for the holy land. And it is natural that every man yearns for the land of his fathers', Alkalai wrote in 1848.[106] In a pamphlet of 1866 he seems to assimilate 'the new heart and new spirit' of which Ezekiel spoke (36:26) to the spirit of the time; after quoting this passage Alkalai continues: 'the spirit of the time asks of all peoples/states to set up their land, to establish their language and it also asks of us to set up the temple of our life and to establish our sacred language and bring it back to life.'[107] In 1869, on the morrow of the establishment of an independent Rumania and Serbia, Alkalai asked: 'why are we less than the Wallachians and Serbs?'[108] In Corfu R. Judah Bibas, a similar enthusiast for the resettlement of the Promised Land, was influenced by the Greek struggle against the Turks; the Jews too must train in the use of arms to conquer their patrimony from the same usurper, he argued in the 1830s.[109]

The 'spirit of the time', in its common summons to the Jews and the peoples of Europe, found in the work of Moses Hess, *Rome and Jerusalem* (1862), its fullest and most sophisticated expression. Hess, born in Bonn in 1812, had very little of the rabbinic background shared by Alkalai and Kalischer, and developed an interest in Spinoza, left-Hegelianism and socialism. He lacked a formal education, Jewish or otherwise, and as a young man became estranged from Judaism. This was never absolute, but not until early middle age did Hess identify himself with his origins.[110] In later life he was active as a socialist journalist and militant in the International Working Men's Association.[111]

On his return to Judaism, Hess embraced Jewish messianic teaching as

---

[104] Z. H. Kalischer, *Drishat Ziyon*, ed. I. Klausner, Jerusalem, 1964, p. 179. (First published 1863).

[105] See the analysis of Alkalai's views in J. Katz, *Le'umiyut Yehudit*, Jerusalem, 1979, pp. 308–56.

[106] *Kitve La-rav Yehudah Alkalai*, ed. I. Raphael, Jerusalem, 1974, I, p. 279.

[107] Ibid., II, p. 696.

[108] Ibid., p. 708.

[109] I. Klausner, *Be-Darkhei Zion*, Jerusalem, 1978, pp. 110–14.

[110] M. Graetz, 'Le-shivto shel Moshe Hess le-yahadut', *Zion*, 45 (1980), pp. 133–53.

[111] The most recent and comprehensive study of Hess's life and ideas is S. Avineri, *Moses Hess: Prophet of Communism and Zionism*, London/New York, 1985.

an imminent reality, as part of 'the present age which began with Spinoza and reached its world-historical existence in the great French revolution'.[112] He drew his confidence from the most profound force animating the nineteenth century – that of nationalism – as the bearer of messianic tidings. He saw it as 'a healthy reaction ... against the levelling tendencies of modern industry and civilisation', which threatened to destroy the 'organic life impulse by an inorganic mechanism'.[113]

Hess held that Judaism had inspired that 'rebirth of the nations' which the French revolution had initiated.[114] This was the result of an enduring and immanent messianic consciousness, unprecedented since the days of Bar Kochba; Sabbatai Zvi was its false prophet and Spinoza its true prophet.[115] But although the Jews had precipitated this mighty movement, they themselves had now – in Hess's view – fallen behind, as it were. As it happened, however, their hour had now struck, and Hess built the return of the Jews to Zion into his general messianic interpretation of European history in the nineteenth century. He was writing on the morrow of the Italian war of unification of 1859, and he foresaw that with

> the liberation of the eternal city on the Tiber also begins that of the eternal city on Mount Moriah, with the rebirth of Italy also the resurrection of Judah ... the springtime of peoples began with the French revolution; 1789 was the spring equinox of the historical peoples. The resurrection of the dead is no longer alienating at a time when Greece and Rome are re-awakening, Poland breathes again, Hungary arms for the final struggle ... To those peoples believed dead, which, in the consciousness of their historical tasks, must assert their national rights belongs unquestionably the Jewish people which has not in vain defied the storms of world history ... and always directed its gaze, and still does, towards Jerusalem.[116]

As token of this consummation Hess enthusiastically welcomed the emergence of a modern Jewish literature couched in Hebrew for the most part, and, even more enthusiastically, Kalischer's plans for the resettlement of Palestine. 'Pious Jews', he wrote, 'stretch out their hands to the enlightened on the common soil of our nationality.'[117]

Hess showed remarkable percipience into the enduring force of national-

---

[112] *Rome and Jerusalem*, p. 102.
[113] Ibid., p. 87.
[114] Ibid., p. 102.
[115] Ibid., p. 49.
[116] Ibid., pp. 5–6.
[117] Ibid., pp. 137–9.

ism; and his argument for the predominance of national over class struggle as a historical phenomenon has been vindicated a thousand times over, in contradistinction to the reverse position propounded by Marx. But he rejoins Marx through their common confidence in the ability of strife to generate lasting harmony. A prophet cannot complain if his predictions are examined; and Hess must suffer accordingly when he is found to argue that 'the danger that the various national types will sharply segregate themselves against, or ignore, each other is today as little likely as the other that they will mutually fight and enslave each other'.[118]

This failure is directly related to the reification of a changing historical conjunction. For this reason the idolization of the nation as a source of value became the focus of later rabbinical conflict. The association between Kalischer's messianic aspiration, the resettlement of the land of Israel and the proposed resumption of sacrifices in Jerusalem had already aroused disquiet in rabbinic circles at the time of their first advocacy in the mid-nineteenth century.[119] By the end of the century disquiet had crystallized into denunciation. At stake was not so much settlement *per se* – after all, Jews of unquestioned piety had been migrating to the Promised Land for centuries – but rather the auspices under which settlement was now to take place, as a secular movement coloured and impregnated by notions of European nationalism. From this *point de départ*, it was easy to decry the new movement as pseudo-messianic and to fit it into the traditional categories of rejection, either explicitly, or by way of juxtaposing the Torah to Jewish nationalism. Restoration at these hands must be false *ex definitione*.

There were also, of course, sociological factors at work. The process of modernization by means of a movement that combined the nationalist with the messianic was doubly abhorrent. It threatened, if successful, to render rabbis redundant and in any case, during the period of struggle, their position of authority would necessarily be challenged.[120]

But this is subordinate to the issue of principle: could a secular nationalist movement be entrusted with the divine task of settlement in the Land? It was not necessary to be a rabbi to deny all validity to such an enterprise. Dubnow, for example, the great secular historian and protagonist of diaspora autonomy, denounced 'political Zionism [as] merely a renewed form of messianism that was transmitted from the enthusiastic minds of the religious kabbalists to the minds of the political communal leaders'. And he ques-

---

[118] Ibid., p. 87.

[119] Jody Myers, 'Attitudes towards a resumption of sacrificial worship in the nineteenth century', *Modern Judaism*, vii (February 1987), no. 1, pp. 29–49.

[120] See below p. 185.

tioned whether 'the results of political messianism [will] be happier than those of mystical messianism'.[121]

The protagonists of Zionism were fully alive to the likely odium aroused by any association with messianic ideas, and did their utmost to distance themselves from any such taint. Joseph Samuel Bloch, the Viennese parliamentarian and polemicist, warned Herzl in 1895: 'if you should come forward in the role of messiah, you will have all Jews against you.'[122] Rabbi Jacob Reines, himself one of Herzl's religious allies and founder of the religious-Zionist Mizrachi party, claimed positive merit for the absence from the Zionist idea of 'any trace at all of the idea of redemption'. The whole aim of the Zionists was 'to better the condition of Israel'.[123] When Herzl had an audience with the king of Italy in 1904 he foreswore any connection between the 'purely national' Zionist movement and religious-messianic ideas.[124]

These efforts failed in so far as Zionism was identified by its rabbinical opponents as both nationalist and messianic. This theme stood out in the famous symposium published at Warsaw in 1900, *Or La'Yesharim* (*A Light for the Upright*).[125] The contributors found their inspiration in Psalm 27:11: 'except the Lord build the house, they labour in vain that build it.'[126] They frequently emphasized their denunciation by associating Zionism with false sectarian messianism. R. Eliezer Ḥayyim Meisel of Lodz castigated the Zionists as '*worse for Israel than all the false messiahs who have arisen in our people*; they did not try to force the people away from their belief in the principles of the Torah and the commandments, only falsely made themselves out to be messiahs. Not so the new false messiah under the name "*Zionist*" which comes and disguises itself beneath the mask of *nationalism* and concern for the grave needs of our people.' Interestingly enough, Meisel also saw the conflict in terms of a struggle for power. He accused the Zionists of intending to take 'the whole government of the people into their hands, all the societies for education, all the organs of welfare'.[127] To

---

[121] S. Dubnow, *Nationalism and History*, ed. K. S. Pinson, Philadelphia, 1958, p. 157. This was written around the turn of the century.

[122] Ch. Bloch, 'Theodor Herzl and Joseph S. Bloch', *Herzl Year Book, I*, New York, 1958, p. 158.

[123] Quoted A. Ravitsky, 'Ha-Tsefui ve-ha-Reshut ha-netuna', in Col. Har'even (ed.), *Yisrael le'krat ha-me'ah ha-21*, Jerusalem 1984, p. 135; see also R. Samuel Jacob Rabinowitz, *Ha-dat ve-ha-leumiyut*, Warsaw, 1900, pp. 127-9.

[124] T. Herzl, *Diaries*, IV, Engl. trans., New York/London, 1960, p. 1,599.

[125] Ed. R. Shlomo Zalman Landau and R. Joseph Rabinowitz.

[126] J. Salmon, 'Meshihiyut masortit u-leumiyut modernit', *Kivunim*, xxi (1983), pp. 97–102.

[127] *Or La'Yesharim*, p. 51.

R. Shalom Dover, the Zionists' 'whole desire and objective' is 'to throw off the yoke of the Torah and commandments and to hold fast only to nationalism and this will be their Judaism ... only nationalism will be their banner'.[128]

'The corner-stone of their system', wrote another contributor to the symposium, is that 'only through language [modern Hebrew] and history will the people arise to a rebirth ... and what is their message now? To give life to the people like all peoples, subject only to their retaining the name Hebrew in their heart ... is not their system to remove all holiness from Israel to make the Torah into history and the words of the prophets a lyre for poets to play on. . . ?'[129] R. Elijah Akiba Rabinowitz repeated the Talmudic warning against 'forcing the end', and also decried the Zionist appropriation of religious symbols and ceremonies.[130] In other contexts, R. Hirsch Hildesheimer of Berlin and the Brisker (Brest-Litovsk) Rav, R. Joseph Soloveitchik, and his son, R. Ḥayyim of Volozhin, explicitly compared Herzl and/or the Zionist movement to Sabbatai Zvi, the ultimate embodiment of the false messiah.[131]

I have mentioned already the protean nature of the messianic idea and its ability to absorb confirmation from the most disparate elements – natural phenomena, wars, invasions, disasters, triumphs. All is grist to the messianic mill. One of the most striking efforts in this sense was certainly the incorporation of secular nationalism into the messianic schema developed by R. Abraham Kuk (1865–1935), the first Ashkenazi chief rabbi in mandatory Palestine. There was an earlier intimation of this notion in the *raison d'être* advanced by the religious Zionists (rabbis Reines, Mohilever etc.) and their party, the Mizrachi, namely that they would help to bring their secular colleagues back to Judaism.[132] But R. Abraham Kuk went much beyond this. A genuine messianic conviction moved him; in, for example, regarding Herzl as an authentic messianic figure.[133] The age, he held, was one of incipient redemption, and in 1909 he wrote: 'Behold we see eye to eye that

[128] Ibid., pp. 58, 59.

[129] Ibid., pp. 98, 99, 103. The significance of the last phrase is discussed above p. 153. See also Yigal Elam, 'Gush Emunim – a false messianism', *Jerusalem Quarterly*, no. 1 (Fall 1976), pp. 65–6.

[130] R. Elijah Akiba Rabinowitz, *Tsyon b-Mishpat*, Warsaw, 1899, pp. 10, 65–6; cf. also E. Don-Yehiya and C. Liebman, 'The symbol system of Zionist socialism: an aspect of Israeli civil religion', *Modern Judaism*, I (1981), no. 2, pp. 121–48.

[131] S. R. Ben-Horin, *Ḥamishim Shnot Tsiyonut*, Jerusalem, 1946, p. 107; A. Druyanov, *Ktavim le-toldot Ḥibbat Ziyon*, Tel Aviv, 1925, II, no. 925.

[132] Salmon, 'Meshihiyut masortit', pp. 99ff.

[133] Cf. the material cited in Chaim Waxman, 'Messianism, Zionism and Israel', *Modern Judaism*, VII (1987), no. 2, p. 190, n. 56.

its time is coming [a reference to Is. 60:22]. The hope of Israel and its rebirth are growing in shape and form;'[134] and in 1913: 'the time is a time to act with the help of the Lord, may His name be blessed, for God has visited His people and from the east and the west, from the north and the south our oppressed brethren are coming, "they shall enquire concerning Zion with their faces hitherward" (Jer. 50:5) and there is no doubt that this great movement is the beginning of redemption.'[135]

The First World War, the latter years of which Kuk spent in London, fitted into this activation of history. This was the traditional 'birth-pangs of the messiah', for which, of course, ample precedent had been found in the Talmudic and the Renaissance–Reformation periods.[136] But this must smack of *avodah zarah* by virtue of its reification of a contingent, relative and ephemeral conjunction of historical events, particularly when these events are marked by violence. It invests nature with a transcendental meaning.

Thus Kuk, in traditional fashion, conceived positively of war in the framework of its association with the messianic advent: 'when there is a great war in the world the power of the messiah is stirred . . . and afterwards, when war ceases, the world is renewed with a new spirit and the footsteps of the messiah are more evident than ever. . . The present world war has in it an anticipation, terrible, great and profound.'[137] Kuk gave his support to the political Zionists led by Weizmann as against the spiritual Zionists led by Ahad Ha'am – 'woe betide us if we abandon the stormy vessel of our people without guide or pilot.'[138] On the eve of the issue of the Balfour Declaration, in an appeal to the leaders of Anglo-Jewry, who were unsympathetic in the main to Zionism, Kuk saw 'with magnificent clarity the hidden ways of the hand of God'.[139] In the Declaration itself he discerned 'the first step in the growth of the horn of the salvation of Israel'.[140]

His reinforced commitment is manifest in his adaptation of a midrashic dictum (commenting on Dt. 12:29). The original reads: 'The duty of

---

[134] *Igrot Ha-Ra'ayah*, Jerusalem, 1943, I, p. 214.

[135] Ibid., II, 1946, p. 176.

[136] See above, pp. 163, 170 ff.

[137] *Orot*, 3rd edn, Jerusalem, 1963, p. 13 (first published 1921); cf. also Ravitsky, 'Ha-Tse'fu, p. 163.

[138] R. Abraham Kuk, *Ḥazon Ha-Geulah*, Jerusalem, 1941, p. 128; A. Eisen, *Galut*, Bloomington, Indiana, 1986, p. 113, has a valuable exposé of Kuk's linkage of 'holiness and heroic valour'.

[139] *Igrot Ha-Ra'ayah*, III, 1965, p. 113.

[140] See R. Kuk's letter to Lord Rothschild (recipient of the Declaration in his capacity as chairman of the English Zionist Federation), ibid., p. 130.

dwelling in the Land of Israel is equivalent to all the other commandments of the Torah.'[141] This was frequently quoted by religious Zionists, such as R. Mohilever in his message to the first Zionist conference at Basle in 1897.[142] Kuk rephrased the dictum, however, and replaced 'dwelling' by 'conquest'. This brought him to consider the possibility of war for the land, even though the commandments were given for a man 'to live by', whereas in war, 'in the nature of things, there is always a danger to life'. In the meantime, however, every effort must be made through purchase.[143]

In the same way as the policy of the British government could be interpreted as divinely inspired, so too could the secular, even irreligious Jewish settler. Kuk was in fact unable to conceive of a secular Jewish nationalist.[144] Such settlers' views were, of course, utterly repugnant to Rav Kuk and much of his writing was devoted to recalling their adherents to religious truth.[145] But the conduct and beliefs of such Zionists did not *eo ipso* disqualify them as partners in the enterprise of redemption. Kuk drew comfort from the way in which the cunning of history had operated in the past. 'Already in the days of Ezra', he wrote in 1910 to one of his rabbinical opponents, R. Jacob David Wilowsky of Safed,

> many great men did not desire the establishment of a settlement in Israel, but preferred to remain in Babylon. Ezra was thus obliged to take with him the least desirable elements of the Jewish people, who were far from attractive and who desecrated the Sabbath even in the Land of Israel. Yet the result was that from these very people sprang forth salvation. The second Temple was built, and from it there proceeded the dissemination of the Oral Law and the spread of Torah in Israel. And so it will be in our days. By strengthening the Yishuv and increasing the number of our brethren in the Holy Land, we shall ensure the shining forth of the light of redemption and salvation.[146]

It cannot be my intention to criticize these views in detail; only to note that the kernel of Kuk's teaching, the notion that providence can fulfil its

[141] Sifre on Deuteronomy, Piska 80.

[142] A. Hertzberg (ed.), *The Zionist Idea*, Philadelphia, 1960, p. 402.

[143] From a speech in 1934 to the Jewish National Fund, in *Hazon*, p. 222. Precisely the same issue – whether the occupation of the land can justify the inseparable risk to life – is current at the time of writing (see the *Jerusalem Post*, 18 August 1989).

[144] R. Kuk, *Orot*, para. 9, pp. 63–4.

[145] M. Nehorai, 'The state of Israel in the teachings of Rav Kook', *Da'at*, nos. 2–3 (1978–9), pp. 46ff.

[146] *Igrot*, I, p. 348.

purposes through wrongdoers, recalls the notion of 'a commandment (mitzvah) fulfilled by means of a transgression'.[147] Kuk drew support from the distinction made by the mystics between those of the pre-messianic generation who are 'good within and evil without'.[148] But this was precisely the argument presented by those who justified Sabbatai Zvi's antinomianism and his apostasy to Islam.[149]

In fact, the experience of cognitive dissonance proves intolerable and the person afflicted in this way resorts to what is effectively an artistic reconstruction of reality. In the case of Kuk, so much sympathy had been invested in his redemptionist Zionist vision that those engaged in the task of fulfilment had to be metamorphosed in such a way as to bring them into conformity with the vision. Earlier, it had been impossible for the followers of Sabbatai Zvi to do otherwise than devise 'rational' explanations for his apostasy.

Kuk was not successful in his lifetime.[150] He did provide, however, material for a later messianic revival, under mixed religious and secular auspices. The reference is to the Bloc of the Faithful – Gush Emunim – and their views as proclaimed by R. Zvi-Yehudah Kuk, son of R. Abraham Kuk. The Bloc, or rather its young forerunners, were 'believers in search of a dogma',[151] and this they found in the 1960s in Kuk's works.

It seems clear that events that the elder Kuk (d. 1935) did not live to see encouraged this development – the Holocaust, the establishment of the state, 'the ingathering of the exiles' and – above all – the war of 1967 that brought Judea and Samaria under Israeli rule.[152] One sympathizer has identified the wars of 1948, 1956 and 1967 as the wars of Gog and Magog, predicted by Ezekiel.[153] Be that as it may, this succession of events crystallized, if it did not engender, a movement and mood of messianic expectation. It brought nearer, to all appearances, the completion of a

[147] For a discussion of this point cf. Ravitsky 'Ha-Tsefui', p. 149; also the discussion in TB Sukkah, ch. 3.

[148] *Igrot*, I, p. 370.

[149] See G. Scholem, 'Redemption through sin', in Scholem, *The Messianic Idea in Judaism*, London, 1971, pp. 78–141, esp. pp. 99ff.

[150] E. Don-Yehiya, 'Religious leaders in the political arena: the case of Israel', *Middle Eastern Studies*, xx (1984), no. 2, p. 163; see also S. Sharot, *Messianism, Mysticism and Magic*, Chapel Hill, NC, 1982, p. 227.

[151] G. Aran, 'The roots of Gush Emunim', *Studies in Contemporary Jewry*, II, Bloomington, Indiana, 1986, p. 138.

[152] See Ravitzky, 'Ha-Tsefui', pp. 153–4; Amnon Rubinstein, *Mi-Herzl ad Gush Emunim*, Tel Aviv, 1980, pp. 91, 112.

[153] M. M. Kasher, *Ha-Tekufah ha-gedolah*, Jerusalem, 1972, p. 444; see also ibid., pp. 14, 17.

process – the prerequisites to fulfilment were falling into place. History itself, as tradition and doctrine required, was taking on the dimensions of a genuine cosmic drama. Rabbi Zvi Yehudah Kuk maintained at this time: 'our reality is a reality of repentance and it is a messianic reality'.[154] 'We must know that the Kingdom of Heaven is being revealed in this kingdom, even in the kingdom of Ben-Gurion.'[155] The same voice came also from the secular leaders of Gush Emunim.[156]

As in earlier instances, the cloven hoof of *avodah zarah* shows through the messianic garb. The idolization of history is accompanied by an idolization of the land – 'the living Torah faith . . . determines the Jewish attitude towards the hills and dales, the fields and meadows, the rocks and dunes of every inch of the Promised Land. . . Divinely implanted in Israel, the Torah continues to pour forth that life-giving substance that invests the very stones and dust of Eretz Israel with a sacred beauty.'[157] There is here a parallel to the romantic nationalist cult of 'the soil', endowing particular manifestations of nature with sacral and divine qualities.[158] The land is indeed 'holy', but this is only in relation to, and by virtue of, the commandments whose performance is dependent on the land; if the land *per se* is regarded as 'holy', as an absolute value, then it degenerates into a golden calf and its worship into what has been called 'a territorial fetishism, i.e. where territory is the god'.[159]

But again, echoing the challenge to earlier messianic movements, countervailing arguments have made themselves heard: 'no internal upheavals have wrought greater havoc in Jewish history than pseudo-messianic expectations.'[160] In Israel itself, the response to the claims of meta-history has been to emphasize the value of moderation, territorial compromise, the

---

[154] Quoted Ravitsky, 'Ha-Tsefui', p. 162; see also R. Zvi Yehudah Kuk's view that 'this is already the middle of redemption' (quoted Eisen, *Galut*, p. 127).

[155] Quoted U. Tal, 'The land and the state of Israel in Israeli religious life', Proceedings of the Rabbinical Assembly of America (76th Annual Convention), xxxviii (1976).

[156] Ehud Luz, 'The moral price of sovereignty', *Modern Judaism*, vii (1987), no. 1, pp. 84ff.

[157] Z. -Y. Kuk, 'Torah loyalty and the land', in *Contemporary Thinking in Israel*, IV (1978), pp. 185–6.

[158] See the discussion of this point in U. Tal, 'The nationalism of Gush Emunim in historical perspective', *Forum*, Jerusalem, (Fall/Winter 1979), no. 36, p. 12.

[159] J. Shilhav, 'Interpretation and misinterpretation of Jewish territorialism', in D. Newman (ed.), *The Impact of Gush Emunim*, London/Sydney, 1985, p. 120; see also G. Aran, 'A mystic-messianic interpretation of modern Israeli history', *Studies in Contemporary Jewry*, IV (1988), p. 274.

[160] Rabbi I. Jakobovits, 'Israel, Religion and Politics', *L'Eylah*, (Autumn issue 5741 – 1980), p. 2.

need for political realism, the distinction between promise and fulfilment, the warning that protracted rule over a hostile minority of Arabs cannot but jeopardize humane values.[161] Isaiah Leibowitz, conceiving of Zionism purely in instrumental-utilitarian terms, has called for the complete severance of religion and state – 'one must not affix a religious halo to a political-historical event.'[162] What is significant, of course, is that these challenges emanate from circles that share many of the same religious presuppositions as their opponents. The struggle against the messiah continues to be waged though the setting is now a sovereign state. This, however, only adds a fresh dimension to the traditional conflict.

---

[161] See the material assembled by Tal, 'The land and the state of Israel', pp. 11ff.; also U. Tal, 'Totalitarian democratic hermeneutics and policies in modern Jewish religious nationalism', in *Totalitarian Democracy and After*, Jerusalem, 1984, pp. 146–50.

[162] I. Leibowitz, 'State and religion', *Tradition*, xii (1972), nos 3–4, p. 10; cf. also I. Leibowitz, *Emunah, Historiya ve-arakhim*, Jerusalem 1982, pp. 128ff., where Leibowitz talks of Zionism as an instrument to remove Jews from the rule of non-Jews.

Excursus: The Messiah and the Utopian

Bloch has drawn an analogy between messianism and utopianism:

> Messianism in religion is utopia which causes the wholly other of the content of religion to be transmitted in that form in which no danger of the anointment of the Lord and theocracy is contained. . . Judaism froze in the armour-cladding of cultic law, but messianism kept itself alive through all codified epigonism: it was misery, it was above all the promise in Moses and the prophets, refuted by no empiricism, which kept it alive. 'He who denies messianism, denies the whole Torah', says Maimonides and it is the greatest Jewish teacher of the law who says this, a rationalist and no mystic. The joyful tidings of the Old Testament run up against Pharaoh and on this conflict sharpens its enduring utopia of liberation.[1]

This analogy not only gives unwarranted emphasis to one aspect of Maimonides's thought but is also seriously misleading. The same Maimonides also argued that in the days of the messiah 'the world proceeds on its customary path' – the very antithesis to utopia.[2] Moreover, the Jewish messiah – and especially so in the Maimonidean version – deserves better than to be equated with the utopian thinker or activist. For all his extravagance, antinomianism, resort to astrology etc., he appears in a far more favourable light when see from the utopian viewpoint than when seen in that of the Torah.

First, neither the prophets nor any of the pretenders indulge in detailed visions of the future, still less do they depict a functioning society. They are silent on the subject or limit themselves to generalities. It is certainly possible to project an ideal in the future.[3] But this is couched in terms not

---

[1] E. Bloch, *Das Prinzip Hoffnung*, 2 vols, Frankfurt on Main, 1959, V, ch. 53, p. 1,464.

[2] See above p. 165.

[3] See, e.g. M. Higger, *The Jewish Utopia*, Baltimore, 1932; S. Schwarzschild, 'A

of institutions, only of features: 'economic abundance, economic equality, the abolition of private property in land and of the market-economy, the universal rule of Jewish monotheism, theocratic democracy, universal truth, justice and peace'.[4] Isaiah, writes Buber, knows that 'a dominion of justice' will come – 'but he knew nothing and said nothing of the inner structure of that kingdom'. He had no idea; he had only a message.[5] In a word, it is less necessary, as a corrective to alienation, for prophets and pretenders to construct an alternative world to complement or compensate for the present.

This caution is epistemologically bound up with and reinforced by an aversion for the unknown, the absolute, the wholly other – manifest not only in the reserve to be exercised in using the term for 'God', but also in the prohibition of images, as prefiguring the unknown.[6] Here too, even in the tempting context of the future, reification is rejected. To construct a utopia is to reify the future.

This striking absence of detail from the Jewish messianic visions is in marked contrast to the wealth of detail supplied by the utopians. The latter normally depict a whole society in operation. This, however, does not add to the verisimilitude of the vision. Rather, this is dependent on the location of the detailed ideal being a distant island, a remote continent, a territory situated beyond impassable seas or unclimbable mountains, or in some other temporal dimension altogether, to all of which an extraordinary accident is normally required to afford access.[7] Should this status alter, then the location is at once dislocated. Now that the moon has become accessible, it has 'suffered the fate of Tahiti', the Manuels wisely remark.[8] There will be no more voyages to the moon with Cyrano de Bergerac or H. G. Wells. In other words, there must be a disjunction, preferably absolute, between the existent and the ideal. This, paradoxically, is the condition of credibility. Were a rapprochement possible, then the unreality of the enterprise would become apparent. Were the utopia to be located in a familiar environment, then its unreality would be all too obvious. The

---

note on the nature of ideal society – a rabbinic study', in A. H. Strauss and H. F. Reissner (eds), *Festschrift for Curt Silbermann*, New York, 1969, pp. 86–105.

[4] Schwarzschild, 'A note on the nature of ideal society', p. 96.

[5] M. Buber, *Israel and the World*, New York, 1948, p. 109.

[6] M. Horkheimer, *Die Sehnsucht nach dem ganz Anderen*, Hamburg, 1970, pp. 57–8; cf. also E. G. Reichmann, 'Max Horkheimer the Jew – critical theory and beyond', *LBYB*, XIX (1974), p. 194.

[7] F. Graus, 'Social utopias in the Middle Ages', *Past and Present*, no. 38 (December 1967), pp. 3–19, especially p. 9.

[8] F. E. and F. P. Manuel, *Utopian Thought in the Western World*, Oxford, 1979, p. 78.

names of these societies – Oceana, Icaria, Freeland, Bensalem, New Atlantis, Erewhon – are in themselves evidence of their contrived and imaginary 'existence'.

It is typical of the genre that More's informant should be an intrepid sailor, Raphael Hythloday, who, after participating in Vespucci's voyage to America, leaves the expedition and finds himself in the heavily fortified and all but inaccessible island of Utopia; Bacon's sailors are shipwrecked on New Atlantis; Cosmoxenus Christicanus in Andreae's Christianopolis actually sets sail on a ship named *Fantasy* which is duly wrecked on an island; Campanella's City of the Sun relies for its information on the word of a Knight Hospitaller of Jerusalem and a sea captain from Genoa, etc.

The utopian society not only lacks a spatial location; in respect of the temporal dimension also it is defective. It is a society without change or growth. Its past is nebulous and its future non-existent. All processes follow recurrent patterns and lack 'structurally generated conflicts' – there is a persisting, sustained and universal consensus.[9] Time comes to an end. The utopian is a Rousseau, discarding his watch lest he be reminded of the time: 'thank heaven, I cried out in a passionate outburst of joy, now I shall no longer find it necessary to know what time of day it is!'[10] In More's Utopia, Fourier's Phalanstery and Cabet's Icaria the clocks no longer strike, Duveau points out. For St. Simon, whereas the theocratic and military states of society are transitory, the industrial state knows no future beyond itself; similarly for Marx: whereas the class struggle is for millennia the motive force of history, no sooner does the proletariat come to power than this ceases to be so.[11] The contrast with Maimonides, for whom time is inextricably part of the messianic polity, could not be more striking. The messiah and his descendants are all mortal men; and one day their realm also comes to an end, as do its progenitors themselves.[12]

---

[9] Cf. R. Dahrendorf, *Essays in the Theory of Society*, London, 1968, pp. 107ff.; R. Nozick, in *Anarchy, State and Utopia*, Oxford, 1974, pp. 328–9, writes in a similar strain: '[utopians] describe a static and rigid society, with no opportunity or expectation of change or progress and no opportunity for the inhabitants themselves to choose new patterns ... utopians assume that the particular society they describe will operate without certain problems arising, that social mechanisms and institutions will function as they predict, and that people will not act from certain motives and interests. They blandly ignore certain serious problems that anyone with any experience of the world would be struck by or make the most wildly optimistic assumptions about how these problems will be avoided or surmounted.'

[10] 'Rousseau juge de Jean-Jacques', 2nd dialogue, quoted E. Cassirer, *Rousseau, Kant, Goethe*, Engl. trans., Princeton, NJ, 1945, pp. 56–7.

[11] G. Duveau, *Sociologie de l'Utopie*, Paris, 1961, pp. 9–10.

[12] See above p. 167.

Lastly, and here I cannot do better than quote Ricoeur: 'no connecting point exists between the "here" of social reality and the "elsewhere" of the utopia'.[13] From the viewpoint of the Torah this is the crucial factor, for it must challenge and ultimately deny credibility to any enterprise whose attainment lacks attachment to the existent and is beyond human experience. As it is, the Torah can only wonder at the credulity of those who take seriously a society removed in space and time from common experience. How could one ever even begin to construct an Oceana, an Icaria, a Freeland, a Bensalem, a New Atlantis, an Erewhon? A sympathetic expositor and critic of More's *Utopia* writes:

> although in his book More displays immense skill at devising specific and practical methods to attain envisaged ends within the Utopian commonwealth (as a planner More is way out in front of Plato and Marx) on one problem – the most practical of all – he has nothing whatever to say. He offers no suggestion on how the corrupt Christian commonwealth, whose rottenness his probings into the social disorders of the time lay bare, can be transformed into the Good Society . . . here there is only silence. His very last words in the published version of *Utopia* point to the abyss that he had left in the original version: 'many things be in the Utopian weal public which in our cities I may rather wish for than hope after'.[14]

It is necessary, therefore, that utopias have to be discovered ready-made. They dare not be shown *in statu nascendi* because then both time and means would destroy the illusion.

It is argued in defence of such schemata, however, that they serve to deny the coincidence of reality and possibility, or even that they give to history its point. Mannheim, whose analysis of 'the utopian mentality' is unsurpassed, even maintains that 'whenever the utopia disappears, history ceases to be a process leading to an ultimate end'.[15] Bloch himself gave this notion a special application by seeing in the accounts of utopian societies, and in art and music, not illusion but intimations of the 'not yet',

---

[13] P. Ricoeur, *Lectures on Ideology and Utopia*, New York, 1986, p. 17.

[14] J. H. Hexter, *More's Utopia – the Biography of an Idea*, New York, 1965, pp. 58–9. No wonder Hexter cannot determine the precise ontological status of the *Utopia*. At one point it is described as the first example of the genre of 'imaginary societies'; but a few lines later Hexter writes: 'More's land of Nowhere is down to earth' (Introduction, *The Complete Works of St Thomas More*, IV, New Haven, 1974, p. cvi).

[15] K. Mannheim, *Ideology and Utopia*, pb. edn, Engl. trans., London, 1960, p. 227.

in the form of 'a laboratory and also a festival of fulfilled possibilities . . . an intimation of future freedom'.[16] These intimations and visions of the 'not yet' demonstrate that the real is not exhausted by the immediate; that utopia is a means to the exploration of possibilities; that it is a stimulus to action;[17] or that it is a pure critique of 'the absolutisation of actual development' and thus that its purpose would be thwarted should it in fact be realized.[18]

Now it is certainly true that certain forms of music and poetry, say, do have the power to create a world of serenity and beauty and do point to the presence of another realm, but they do not indicate the means to the creation of such a world, still less do they indicate how such a world might be made accessible. And of course participation in this other world is short-lived and dependent on a particular set of circumstances. The curtain falls, the musicians lay down their instruments, the voices are silent, all that remains is the recollection of serenity. Marcuse writes: 'there is no work of art . . . which does not in its very structure evoke the words, the images, the music of another reality, of another order repelled by the existing one and yet alive in memory and anticipation, alive in what happens to men and women, and in their rebellion against it.'[19] This may well be true – even so, the experience of art, however intense, is transitory and fragile, outside any framework of action, and cannot, for this reason, rank with the Torah as a means to the realization of that state of serenity.

Over and beyond this, it is clear that any reference back from any utopian society to any existing society must be inauthentic: the two games take place in obedience to different rules. In the one, space and time are inescapable dimensions of existence; in the other, both dimensions are arbitrary. The man who steps into his time-machine *à la* Wells to experience the future or sets sail on the *Fantasy* to unknown climes *à la* Andreae is venturing into a world that knows none of the normal constraints. What is said and described there can have no relevance to the world left behind. There is

[16] See p. 7 above.

[17] See P. Furter, 'Utopie et Marxisme selon Ernst Bloch', *Archives de la Sociologie de la Religion*, (1966), pp. 9ff.; W. Hudson, *The Marxist Philosophy of Ernst Bloch*, London, 1983, pp. 172ff.

[18] P. Sergius Buve, 'Utopie als Kritik', in *Säkularisation und Utopie – Ebracher Studien*, Stuttgart, 1967, p. 33. Ricoeur makes the same point when he writes 'the field of the possible is now open beyond that of the actual; it is a field, therefore, for alternative ways of living' (*Lectures on Ideology*, p. 16).

[19] H. Marcuse, *Counter-Revolution and Revolt*, London, 1972, p. 92; see also S. E. Bronner, 'Between art and utopia: reconsidering the aesthetic theory of Herbert Marcuse', in A. Pippin, A. Feenberg and C. Webel (eds), *Marcuse – Critical Theory and the Promise of Utopia*, London, 1988, pp. 107–40.

here a misleading use of the imagination. The rules of one game have no relevance to the rules of another. A game of cricket in the Elysian fields can teach nothing to the players at Lords. The so-called possibilities that are opened up may not in fact be genuine possibilities at all, because they are subjectively created and determined in advance by the author of the particular utopia. It is he who decides what can or cannot take place.

Supposing, however, that the apologist for utopia lowers his sights and talks not in terms of a possible model of the ideal but in terms of a satire or critique of the actual. It is often maintained, for example, that descriptions of utopian societies can still serve as vehicles for the criticism or indictment of an existing society – that they can take a satiric part.[20] But this argument must meet the objection derived from the difference that separates the satire from the world that is being satirized. If the satire is to achieve any effect at all, it must be recognizably similar to its object and share with it a ground of common experience; otherwise it will again fail to meet the reproach that it is irrelevant by reason of its adherence to a different time–space continuum. It is noticeable that More is far more effective in exposing the inadequacy of the existent when depicting the actual erstwhile tame sheep who now 'swallow down the very men themselves' than in his presentation of a non-existent good society. The former belongs to the actual whereas the latter belongs nowhere; and what is nowhere cannot speak intelligibly to those who are somewhere.

I have already tried to show the involvement of time in Maimonides's doctrine of the messiah. This is a consequence of the reality principle inculcated by the Bible, which has effectively inhibited all contrary endeavours, or, rather, it has given them a particular twist. Buber points to this when he writes that the Hebrew prophet 'does not confront man with a generally valid image of perfection, with a pantopia or utopia... In his work of realization he is bound to the *topos*, to this place, to this people, because it is the people who must make the beginning.'[21] In other words, it is a particular group of people – the Jews – who face a 'utopian' task, the location of which, however, is a particular territory, a *topos* – the Land of Israel.[22] Both land and people already exists as components of the real and do not require to be discovered, let alone imagined. All the less is it possible to refer to an ideal society in any precise sense. The messianic

---

[20] See, e.g. Dahrendorf, *Essays in the Theory of Society*, p. 118; and Northrop Frye, 'Varieties of literary utopias', in F. E. Manuel (ed.), *Utopias and Utopian Thought*, London, 1973, pp. 25ff.

[21] Buber, *Israel and the World*, pp. 111–12.

[22] See, with qualifications, W. D. Davies, *The Territorial Dimension of Judaism*, Berkeley, Cal., 1982, passim.

figure, for his part, like the prophet, also holds out no ideal (though common to the programme of all is the aspiration to a restored Zion).

The conjunction of these two factors – the pre-existence of a *topos* and an existing agency – have happily limited the scope for utopian imagining. None the less, they have not been altogether sufficient, and some half-a-dozen utopias of Zionist inspiration were composed around the turn of the nineteenth century.[23] This is part of the fateful rapprochement with modernity. I shall consider the most important: Levinsky's *A Journey to the Land of Israel in the Year 5800* (1892) and Herzl's *Old-New Land* (1902).

These are not only the first Jewish utopias but may also be the last. Whereas, in the gentile world, the move from utopia to dystopia took many centuries to accomplish, the same development in the Jewish case was telescoped into less than one. As early as 1984 Benjamin Tammuz published a novella, *Jeremiah's Inn* (*Pundako shel Yerimiyahu*) which depicts a dystopian Land of Israel given over to the coercive rule of militant and obscurantist religious zealots. The same theme was repeated in 1987 in Shmuel Hasfari's drama, *The Last Secular Jew* (*Ha-Ḥiloni ha-aharon*).[24]

To return from dystopia to the utopian days of Levinsky and Herzl: in the former's vision, a Jewish couple sail from Odessa to spend their honeymoon in the Land, which has now become the cultural centre of the whole Jewish people. As the Greek towns once mutually disputed the honour of being Homer's birthplace, so do the Jews of Europe now dispute amongst themselves for the honour of being the birthplace of 'the movement of return'. In the schools, the curriculum is dominated by the study of the Torah.[25] It is health in all its aspects that characterizes the community; mental and physical well-being is fostered by the climate, diet, agricultural way of life, purity of family life, ready availability of medical services and education. There is no longer a profusion of little shopkeepers, 'once almost our second nature, because of our history'. They have returned to lead on the land a natural life;[26] the community is socially healthy in that equality prevails; there is no labour question and no property question, 'for there are no workers and no masters, all are workers and all are masters'.[27] Social health is also manifest in the absence of drunkenness and crime – no

---

[23] These and the others are described in M. Eliav-Feldon, '"If you will it, it is no fairy tale": the first Jewish utopias', *JJS*, xxv (December 1983), no. 2, pp. 85–103.

[24] See the short accounts in *The Observer*, 21 June 1987, and *The Times*, 6 July 1987.

[25] A. L. Levinsky, *Masa l'Eretz Yisrael b'shnat 5800* [CE 2040], Berlin, 1922 (first published 1892), pp. 11, 45.

[26] Ibid., p. 40.

[27] Ibid., p. 49.

hardship, so no crime.[28] There is no great need for military service, as conflict has ceased, not only in the Land but also in Europe, 'from the day that each of the different peoples returned to its own land'. That Europe does, however, remain 'an armed camp' is a consequence of the unresolved conflict between labour and capital. 'In the house of Israel there is nothing but peace and nothing but tranquillity.'[29] Intellectual health is manifest in the profusion of lectures – to which no entrance fee is required, unlike those in Europe – and in the multitude of serious and wholesome publications.[30] The countryside blossoms as never before, with the aid of artificial rain. The Dead Sea has been transformed into a thriving community. 'How great are thy deeds, O man!', exclaims Levinsky.[31]

Herzl's *Old-New Land* is very different. Its chief protagonists are Kingscourt (né Königshoff), a wealthy, anglicized Prussian aristocrat, and a lugubrious young Jewish intellectual of Vienna, Dr Friedrich Löwenberg. After withdrawing to a Pacific island for twenty years, they return in 1923 to a world where Palestine has been transformed into a community devoid of sovereignty but organized in voluntary 'mutualist' associations on the principle of co-operation. Herzl was influenced by Robert Owen, by the Rochdale pioneers of co-operation and by Bellamy's *Looking Backward*. Thus he no longer writes in terms of a Jews' *state* as he had done in the mid-1890s.[32] Constituted in the form of a self-governing enclave within the Ottoman Empire, the inhabitants of Palestine in 1923 – Jew, Christian, Moslem – enjoy life in a polity marked by high technology, publicly owned industries, a mass transport system and noiseless electricity. Irrigation brings bloom to the desert. German opera, French theatre, English open-air sports – these are some of the favoured leisure pursuits. Swiss hoteliers exploit the hot springs of Tiberias as a tourist attraction. Religious tolerance prevails, for religion has been reduced to a private matter and society has no interest in whether men worship the eternal 'in synagogue, church, mosque, or the philharmonic concert'. Women enjoy equality, the suburbs are airy and tree-lined.

Most notable of all, perhaps, the new state has solved the Jewish problem in the world through its removal of Jewish competition. Its learned academies do not foster a national language or culture, rather a cosmopolitan, universalist philosophy, though the *lingua franca* is apparently German. Hebrew the Jews use only for prayer and funeral services. The state has

---

[28] Ibid.

[29] Ibid., p. 50.

[30] Ibid., p. 35.

[31] Ibid., pp. 60–1.

[32] Eliav-Feldon, '"If you will it"', pp. 98–9; see also S. Avineri, 'Ha-Utopiya ha-Zionit shel Herzl', *Kathedra*, no. 40 (1986), pp. 189–200.

no army. Rashid Bey, a Moslem who has been educated in Europe and speaks German, explains to the visitors that there could be no tension with the Jews, by reason of the benefits that they had brought.[33]

In a famous polemic, Ahad Ha'Am, the spokesman of cultural Zionism, derided what he called Herzl's 'imminent days of the messiah' and contrasted it scornfully with Levinsky's earlier work. Whereas the latter was truly concerned with the 'renaissance of Israel', Herzl might be talking about 'the renaissance of Nigeria'.[34]

But this criticism must yield to that other that sees in Herzl's work – also in Levinsky's, for that matter – none of the necessary historical grounding that alone would entitle it to claim credibility. In Herzl's case this is all the more surprising, for his work as diplomat and negotiator showed his sensitivity to the middle-eastern rivalries and interests of the great powers. From that world of conflict to the state of peace no transition is indicated. The work embodies the alienation that spurns the challenge of the existent and can therefore serve neither as inspiration nor as prediction, nor as criticism.

In the same way as Jewish literature is virtually devoid of the utopian genre, so too does Jewish history know of no attempts to establish perfect communities on virgin soil. There can be no such new beginning, *de novo*. The sons cannot escape from the fathers. No Jewish analogies exist to Owen's New Harmony, Fourier's phalanxes, Cabet's Icarean communities or those of the Shakers, Rappites etc. that illuminate the history of North America and whose ephemeral existence testifies to their contrived nature.[35]

The only possible exceptions to this are projected colonies in East Florida (1825) and at Grand Island, in the Niagara river, New York State (1820–5). Of the first, very little is known. It was conceived by Moses Elias Levy, who was born in Morocco *c.*1782, was educated in England and later became a lumber-dealer in Cuba and the Caribbean. He was also engaged in supplying troops. The proposed settlement, for which he won the support of Joseph Crool in London, the messianic thinker and campaigner against Jewish emancipation, was designed as 'a field of action . . . for those who may be trained by a system of education, founded in the noble and great principles of Judaism', as Levy wrote to Isaac Lyon Goldsmid in 1825.

[33] For all the above, see the translation by Lotta Levensohn, republished New York, 1987, with a new introduction by Jacques Kornberg.

[34] *Kol Kitvei Ahad Ha'Am*, 2nd edn, Jerusalem, 1949, pp. 316, 320.

[35] The classic guide to these communities is C. Nordhoff, *The Communistic Societies of the United States*, New York, 1970 (first published 1875). For a more recent account, see Mark Holloway, *Heavens on Earth – Utopian Communities in America 1680–1880*, London, 1951.

This was to be both vocational and religious. But nothing came of Levy's project.[36]

At much the same time, Mordechai Manuel Noah, an American diplomat, journalist, Jacksonian politician and playwright, sought to establish 'Ararat'. This was a colony at Grand Island where the Jews would be prepared and improved for 'that great and final restoration to their ancient heritage which the times so powerfully indicate'.[37] The means of improvement included the abolition of polygamy, encouragement of literacy, and training in agriculture and mechanics.[38] From America and abroad – from rabbis in Hungary, Paris, Bordeaux and elsewhere – came criticism, if not ridicule. In London, chief rabbi Hirschell, whom Noah had nominated as one of the 'commissioners' of the proposed colony, dismissed the scheme out of hand: 'it was to Zion rather than to Niagara that his gaze was turned', Hirschell explained.[39] In Paris, chief rabbi Abraham de Cologna noted that Noah's plan was 'excellent' as a whole: 'but two trifles are wanting: first, the well authenticated proof of the mission and authority of Mr Noah; second, the prophetic text which points out a marsh in North America as the spot for re-assembling the scattered remains of Israel'.[40] In the 1830s, towards the end of his life, Noah turned to the establishment of a 'Judea' in Palestine, possibly under the protection of Britain, that would serve as the harbinger of restoration.[41]

Not even the utopian literature and history of the Jews, in short, offers a counterpart remotely comparable to the utopianism of the gentile world. Even the pseudo-messiah has a genuine *topos*, and this of course generates the very challenges that the utopian evades. Therefore, if on the one hand

---

[36] All the above is based on J. Toury, 'M. E. Levy's plan for a Jewish colony in Florida – 1825', *Michael*, III (1975), pp. 23–33.

[37] Quoted J. D. Sarna, *Jacksonian Jew – the Two Worlds of Mordechai Noah*, New York, 1981, p. 68; see also I. M. Jost, *Geschichte der Israeliten*, X, Berlin, 2nd edn, 1847, pp. 221–36. Noah's colony must of course be distinguished from those secular agricultural colonies founded in the late nineteenth century in Oregon, Colorado, Michigan, Virginia etc. These were intended to normalize the life of Jewish refugees from Russian persecution. (See U. D. Herscher, *Jewish Agricultural Utopias in America, 1880–1910*, Detroit, 1981.)

[38] Ibid.; see also M. Kohler, 'Early American Zionist projects', *Publications of the AJHS*, no. 8 (1900), pp. 97–118; and *Publications of the AJHS*, no. 10 (1902) for some of the interest that Noah's scheme aroused in Europe.

[39] Sarna, *Jacksonian Jew*, p. 73; H. Simons, *Forty Years a Chief Rabbi*, London, 1980, p. 51.

[40] Quoted L. Ruchames, 'Mordecai Manuel Noah and early American Zionism', Proceedings of the Sixth World Congress of Jewish Studies, II, Jerusalem, 1975, pp. 231–2 (Engl. Sec.).

[41] Sarna, *Jacksonian Jew*, pp. 152ff.

reality is not to become an absolute, and on the other the challenge is to be answered, then the answer is to exercise criticism from within the historical realm itself – to use history to attack history. There is, in short, a middle way at the historical level between the antithesis presented by Hegel. 'Rational insight' requires neither the reconciliation with reality nor does the world 'as it should be' necessarily exist only as the result of the individual's opinion.[42]

In terms of this antithesis it is possible to envisage a theoretical criticism couched in the medium of practice. But for this the medium must itself embody certain 'utopian' strivings. This is the responsibility borne by the history of the Jews, as defined by the divine mandate to be 'a light of the nations'.[43] This 'mandate', however, is to be executed within a political world that is common to all nations. The challenge specific to the Jews is to engage in a form of historical activity within the existent that proscribes images of perfection but also rejects reconciliation with the existent. The result is a form of satire, distinct, however, from the illusory satire of the utopian through its anchorage in precisely the same reality as the target of the satire. (It is thus all the less endurable because it is all the more close.) Such satire cannot easily be dismissed as the product of a confrontation between the existent and an imagined state of perfection, for like confronts like.[44]

Only in a sovereign land of Israel can the Isaianic light burn with full brightness. Elsewhere, in the diaspora, the Jews will confront multiple hindrances and the light will burn fitfully, even when not measured by any 'generally valid image of perfection', as Buber pointed out.[45] The Jews of Berlin and London and elsewhere engaged in this enterprise. Theirs was certainly no ideal situation, but it was the only one available to them and therefore the location of their challenge, both to the existent and to 'utopia'.

[42] See above p. 5.

[43] Is. 49:6.

[44] Thus it is not, as Steiner erroneously supposes, 'the (Jewish) insistence of the ideal' (*In Bluebeard's Castle*, London 1974 edn, p. 41) that arouses resentment, but rather the insistence of the real, i.e. the history of the Jews.

[45] See above p. 197.

Glossary

Bet Din (pl. *Batei Din*)   rabbinical court.

Bet HaMedrash   accommodation in synagogue set aside for purposes of study.

Gemarah   see Talmud.

Halakhah (adj. halakhic)   derived from Hebrew *halakh*, 'go' 'walk', used to refer to legal portions of Talmudic and later rabbinic literature.

Ḥevrah (pl. *ḥevrot*)   'society', often used to designate informal group of worshippers.

Kahal   see *kehillah*.

Kehillah (pl. *kehillot*)   legally recognized and authorized Jewish community.

Marrano   Spanish for 'swine'; designation for those converted Jews who continued to maintain certain Jewish practices while living outwardly as Christians.

Mezuzah   rectangular piece of parchment inscribed with certain passages from Scripture (see Dt. 6:9) and, when placed in a case, affixed to a doorpost.

Midrash (pl. *midrashim*)   hermeneutic technique applied to Scripture; result of such application in form of systematic interpretation, arranged verse by verse.

Mishnah   see Talmud.

Oral Law   see Talmud.

Parnass (pl. *parnassim*)   elected leader of a *kehillah* (q.v.).

Pinkas   official record of the activities, decrees, etc. of a *kehillah* (q.v.).

Scheḥitah   ritual slaughter of an animal, without which it is not fit (kosher) as food.

Sha'atnez   literally 'mingled stuff', for example wool and linen, as prohibited in Dt. 22:11.

Talmud   the 'Oral Law' composed of the *Mishnah* (as compiled by R. Judah the Patriarch, *c.*200) and the Gemarah (discussions relative to the Mishnah).

Talmud Torah   elementary school, normally attached to a synagogue and primarily intended for the children of the poor.

Yeshivah   institute for advanced study of the Talmud and related literature.

Yishuv   designation for the Jewish population of Palestine prior to the establishment of Israel.

Abbreviations

A Biblical

Dt.	Deuteronomy
Ex.	Exodus
Ezek.	Ezekiel
Gen.	Genesis
Is.	Isaiah
Jer.	Jeremiah
Lam.	Lamentations
Lev.	Leviticus
Nu.	Numbers
Ps.	Psalms
Zeph.	Zephaniah

B Talmudic

AZ	Avodah Zarah
Ber.	Berakhot
BM	Baba Metziah
Ḥag.	Ḥagigah
Ket.	Ketubot
Kidd.	Kiddushin
Mak.	Makkot
Meg.	Megillah
RH	Rosh Ha-Shanah
San.	Sanhedrin
Shab.	Shabbat
Sukk.	Sukkot
TB	Talmud Babli
Yeb.	Yebamot

C General

AJHS	*American Jewish Historical Society*
AJSR	*Association for Jewish Studies Review*
BCE	Before the Common Era
CCAR	*Central Conference of American Rabbis*
CE	Common Era
EHR	*English Historical Review*
Enc. Jud.	*Encyclopedia Judaica*
HUCA	*Hebrew Union College Annual*
JHSE	Jewish Historical Society of England
JJGL	*Jahrbuch für jüdische Geschichte und Literatur*
JJLG	*Jahrbuch der jüdisch-literarischen Gesellschaft*
JJS	*Jewish Journal of Sociology*
JQR	*Jewish Quarterly Review*
JLA	*Jewish Law Annual*
JPSA	Jewish Publication Society of America
JSS	*Jewish Social Studies*
LBI	Leo Baeck Institute
LBYB	*Leo Baeck Year Book*
M	Mishnah
MGWJ	*Monatsschrift für die Geschichte und Wissenschaft des Judentums*
MJHSE	*Miscellanies of the Jewish Historical Society of England*
MR	Midrash Rabbah
MT	Mishneh Torah
PAAJR	*Proceedings of the American Academy for Jewish Research*
REJ	*Revue des Etudes Juives*
TJHSE	*Transactions of the Jewish Historical Society of England*
ZGJD	*Zeitschrift für die Geschichte der Juden in Deutschland*

Select Bibliography

A Biblical

See list of abbreviations.

B Talmudic Tractates

See list of abbreviations.

C General

1 Rabbinic
2 Communal/Legal
3 Aesthetic
4 Historical
   A Berlin and the German Lands
   B London and England
   C General
5 Messianic and Utopian
6 Philosophical
7 Zionist
8 Memoirs, Diaries, Biography and Letters
9 Documentary
10 Miscellaneous

1   *Rabbinic*

R. Aaron Halevy, *Sepher Ha'Ḥinukh*, ed. R. Ḥayyim Dov Chavel, Jerusalem, 1977.

R. Abraham b. Ḥiyya, *Hegyon Ha'Nefesh*, ed. I. Friedmann, Leipzig, 1860.

R. Abraham Farrissol, *Magen Avraham*, ch. 24, ed. S. Löwinger, *REJ*, NS V (1939).

R. Abraham Isaac Kuk, *Orot*, 3rd edn, Jerusalem, 1963.

Appel, G., *A Philosophy of Mitzvot*, New York, 1975.

Assaf, S., *Batei Ha-Din Ve-sidrehem*, Jerusalem, 1924.

Assaf, S., *B'Ohalei Ya'akov*, repr., Jerusalem, 1943.

R. Azariah de Rossi, *Me'or Eynayim*, 3 vols, ed. David Cassel, repr., Jerusalem, 1970.

Blau, J. (ed.), *Tshuvot Ha'Rambam*, 3 vols, Jerusalem, 1958–61.

Blidstein, G., *Ikronot medini'im le'mishnat ha'Rambam*, Bar Ilan, 1983.

Breuer, M., *Rabbanut Ashkenaz biymei ha'benayim*, Jerusalem, 1976.

Chavel, C. D. (ed.), *Sefer Ha'Mitzvot Le'Ha'Rambam im Hassagot Ha'Ramban*, Jerusalem, 1981.

R. David ibn Abi Zimra, *Magen David*, Amsterdam, 1713.

Efros, I., 'Maimonides' treatise on logic', *PAAJR*, viii (1937–8).

R. Elijah Akiba Rabinowitz, *Tsyon b'Mishpat*, Warsaw, 1899.

R. Ezekiel Landau, *Noda Biyehuda, Mahadura Tinyana*, repr., Jerusalem, 1969.

Faur, Jose, *Golden Doves with Silver Dots*, Indiana, 1986.

Faur, Jose, *Iyunim ba-Mishneh-Torah le-ha-Rambam*, Jerusalem, 1978.

Fraenkel-Goldschmidt, H. (ed.), *Joseph of Rosheim, Sefer Ha-Miknah*, Jerusalem, 1970.

Freehof, S. B., *A Treasury of Responsa*, Philadelphia, 1963.

Guttmann, J. (ed.), Moses ben Maimon, 2 vols, Leipzig, 1908, 1914.

Halkin, A. (ed.), *Crisis and Leadership: Epistles of Maimonides*, Philadelphia, 1985.

Heinemann, I., *Ta'amei Ha-Mitzvot be-sifrut Yisrael*, 2 vols, Jerusalem, 1954, 1956.

Heller-Wilensky, S., *R. Yitzhak Arama u-mishnato*, Jerusalem/Tel Aviv, 1956.

Hirsch, W., *Rabbinic Psychology*, London, 1947.

R. Immanuel Jakobovits, 'Israel, Religion and Politics', *L'Eylah* (Autumn 5741–1980).

R. Immanuel Jakobovits, 'The morality of warfare', *L'Eylah* (Autumn 5743–1983), no.4.

R. Isaac Abrabanel, *Ma'ayenei Ha'Yeshuah*, Stettin, 1860.

R. Isaac Arama, *Akedat Yitzhak*, Pressburg, 1849.

R. Isaac Arama, *Hazot Kashah*, Pressburg, 1849.

R. Israel Isserlein, *Pesakim u-ketavim*, Venice, 1519.

R. Israel Isserlein, *Trumat Ha'Deshen*, repr., Bnei Brak, 1971.

R. Jacob Molin, *Sefer Maharil*, Shklov, 1796.

R. Jacob Sasportas, *Tsitsat Nobel Zvi* (ed. I. Tishby), Jerusalem, 1954.

R. Jacob Weil, *She'elot u-Teshuvot*, Hanau, 1610.

R. Joel Halevy, *Sefer Rabiah*, 3 vols, repr., New York, 1983.

R. Joseph Stadthagen, *Divrei Zikaron*, Amsterdam, 1705.

Judah Halevi, *Kitab Al Khazari*, trans. H. Hirschfield, London/New York, 1905.

R. Judah Loew b. Bezalel, *Derekh Ḥayyim*, repr., London, 1961.

R. Judah Loew b. Bezalel, *Netivot Olam*, repr., London, 1961.

R. Judah Loew b. Bezalel, *Netzach Yisrael*, repr., London, 1960.

R. Judah Loew b. Bezalel, *Tiferet Yisrael*, repr., Jerusalem, 1970.

Kahana, Y.-Z., *Mehkarim be-sifrut ha-teshuvot*, Jerusalem, 1973.

Katz, J., 'L'toldot ha'rabbanut be-motzei y'mei ha'beynayim', in A. -Z. Melamed (ed.), *Sefer Zikaron l'Binyamin de Vries*, Jerusalem, 1969.

Katz, Rabbiner Dr S., 'Von den 613 Gesetzen', *Jeschurun*, II (1915).

Kitve La-rav Yehudah Alkalai, ed. I. Raphael, Jerusalem, 1974, I.

Lichtenberg, A. (ed.), *Kobetz Tshuvot Ha-Rambam*, Leipzig, 1859.

R. Louis Jacobs, *Theology in the Responsa*, London, 1975.

R. Louis Jacobs, 'A. L. Heller's Shev Shema Tata', *Modern Judaism*, I (1981), no. 2.

Marx, A. (trans.), 'The correspondence between the rabbis of Southern France and Maimonides about astrology', *HUCA*, 3 (1926).

R. Meir b. Baruch of Rothenburg, *Sefer Sha'arei Tshuvot*, ed. M. Bloch, 2 vols, Berlin, 1891–2.

R. Meir b. Baruch of Rothenburg, *Tshuvot Psakim u'Minhagim*, ed. Y.Z. Kahana, 2 vols, Jerusalem, 1957, 1960.

R. Menachem Mendel Krochmal, *Tsemach Tsedek*, Lemberg, 1861.

R. Moses Isserles, *Torat Ha'Olah*, ed. D. Elbaum, Tel Aviv, 1983.

Moses Maimonides, *The Guide for the Perplexed*. (I have used the translation by S. Pines, Chicago, 1963.)

R. Moses Minz, *She'elot-u-Tshuvot*, Lemberg, 1851.

R. Moses Schreiber, *Sefer Ḥatam Sofer*, New York, 1958, VI.

Novak, D., *Law and Theology*, 2nd series, New York, 1976.

Novak, D., *Law and Theology in Judaism*, New York, 1974.

Pearl, C., *The Medieval Jewish Mind*, London, 1971.

Ravitsky, A., 'K'fi ko'ah ha'adam – Yemot ha'meshiah be-mishnat ha-Rambam', in Ts. Baras (ed.), *Meshihiyut ve-eskatalogiya*, Jerusalem, 1984.

Robinson, Ira, 'Two letters of Abraham ben Eliezer Halevi', in I. Twersky (ed.), *Studies in Medieval Jewish History and Literature, II*, Cambridge, Mass., 1984.

Safran, A., 'Jewish Time, Sabbatical Time', in J. Sacks (ed.), *Tradition and Transition: Essays presented to Sir Immanuel Jakobovits*, London, 1986.

R. Samuel Jacob Rabinowitz, *Ha-dat ve-ha-leumiyut*, Warsaw, 1900.

Schweid, E., *Ha-Rambam ve-hug hashpa'ato*, Jerusalem, 1973.

Sefer Ha-Ḥinukh, ed. R. Hayyim Dov Chavel, Jerusalem, 1977.

Sefer Ḥassidim, ed. J. Wistinetzki, Berlin, 1891.

Shatz, R., 'Ha-Tfisa ha-mishpatit shel ha-Maharal', *Da'at*, nos 2–3, 1978–9.

Sherwin, Byron, *Mystical Theology and Social Dissent*, London/Toronto, 1982.

R. Shimon b. Anatoli, *Malmad Ha-Talmidim*, Lyck, 1866.

R. Shlomo Zalman Landau and R. Joseph Rabinowitz (eds), *Or la-Yesharim*, Warsaw, 1900.

Simonsohn, S., 'Some disputes on music in the synagogue in pre-reform days', *PAAJR*, 34 (1966).

Ta-Shmah, I., 'The author of *Sefer Ha-Ḥinukh*', *Kiryat Sefer*, 55 (1980), no. 4.

Twersky, I. (ed.), *A Maimonides Reader*, New York, 1972.

Twersky, I., *Introduction to the Code of Maimonides*, Yale University Press, 1980.

Urbach, E. E., *Ḥazal Emunot ve-De'ot*, Jerusalem, 1969.

Vilensky, M. (ed.), *Ḥassidim u-Mitnagdim*, 2 vols, Jerusalem, 1970.

Wurzburger, W., 'Digmei Tafkid ba'manhigut ha'ruḥanit', in Ella Belfer (ed.), *Manhigut Ruḥanit b'Yisrael*, Jerusalem, 1982.

R. Yair Hayyim Bacharach, *Ḥavot Yair*, Frankfurt on Main, 1689.

2   Communal/Legal

Albeck, Sh., *Dinei Mammonot ba'Talmud*, Tel Aviv, 1976.

Cohen, Stuart A., 'The concept of the three Ketarim ("Crowns"): its place in Jewish political thought and its implications for a study of Jewish constitutional history', *AJSR*, ix (1984), no. 1.

Cohn, H., *Human Rights in Jewish Law*, London/New York, 1984.

Elon, M., 'Le-Mahutan shel takanot ha-kahal ba-mishpat ha-ivri', in G. Tedeschi (ed.), *Mehkarei mishpat le-zekher Abraham Rosenthal*, Jerusalem, 1964.

Elon, M., 'On Power and authority', in Elazar D. (ed.), *Kinship and Consent*, Ramat Gan/Philadelphia, 1981.

Elon, M. (ed.), *The Principles of Jewish law*, Jerusalem, 1975.

Falk, Z., *Erkhei Mishpat Ve-Yahadut*, Jerusalem, 1980.

Faur, J., 'Understanding the Covenant', *Tradition*, IX (1968).

Finkelstein, L., *Jewish Self-Government in the Middle Ages*, 2nd printing, New York, 1964.

Frankfort, Henri, 'Kingship under the judgement of God', in M. R. Konvitz (ed.), *Judaism and Human Rights*, New York, 1972.

Funkenstein, A., 'The political theory of Jewish emancipation', in W. Grab (ed.), *Jahrbuch des Instituts für deutsche Geschichte, Beiheft 3*, Tel Aviv, 1979.

Golding, M. P., 'The juridical basis of communal associations in medieval rabbinic legal thought', *JSS*, xxviii (1966), no. 2.

Goodman, L., 'The Biblical laws of diet and sex', in B. Jackson (ed.), *Jewish Law Association Studies II*, Atlanta, 1986.

Goodman, L. E., 'Maimonides' philosophy of law', *JLA*, I (1978).

Graff, G., *Separation of Church and State*, Alabama, 1985.

Handelsman, Y., 'Tmunot be-hanhagat kehillot Yisrael be-Ashkenaz bi'ymei ha-benayim', Ph.D dissertation, University of Tel Aviv, 1980.

Hecht, N. S. and Quint, E. B., 'Exigency jurisdiction under Jewish law', *Dinei Yisrael*, IX (1978–80).

Jackson, E., 'Secular jurisprudence and the philosophy of Jewish law', *JLA*, VI (1987).

Landman, L., *Jewish Law in the Diaspora: Confrontation and Accommodation*, Philadelphia, 1968.

Mendelssohn M., *Jerusalem*, transl. A. Arkush, Hanover/London, 1983.

Morrell, S., 'The constitutional limits of communal government in rabbinic law', *JSS*, xxxiii (1971), nos. 2–3.

Schapira, M., 'Ha'Musag "Tsibur" ba'Mishpat ha'ivri', *Dinei Yisrael*, I (1970).

Schreiber, A., *Jewish Law and Decision-making*, Philadelphia, 1979.

Shilo, S., *Dina d'Malkhuta Dina*, Jerusalem, 1974.

Shohat, E., 'Magamot Politiyot be-sipurei ha'avot', *Tarbitz*, 24 (1955).

Sinclair, D., 'Maimonides and natural law theory', *L'Eylah* (New Year 5747–1986), no. 22.

Strauss, L., 'Quelques remarques sur la science politique de Maimonide et de Farabi', *REJ*, 100 (1936).

Touati, C., 'Grand Sanhédrin et droit rabbinique', in B. Blumenkranz and A. Soboul (eds), *Le Grand Sanhédrin de Napoléon*, Toulouse, 1979.

Trigano, S., 'Le fait politique juif moderne', *Pardès*, VI (1987).

3 Aesthetic

Abrahams, I., 'The Decalogue in art', in *Studies in Jewish Literature in honour of Kaufmann Kohler*, Berlin, 1913.

Adler, Elkan, 'Jewish art', in B. Schindler (ed.), *Occident–Orient*, London, 1936.

Adorno, T., *Aesthetische Theorie*, Frankfurt on Main, 1972.

Altmann, A., 'Zum Wesen der jüdischen Aesthetik', *Jeschurun*, XIV (May–June 1927), nos 5–6.

Bevan, E., *Holy Images*, London, 1940.

Bindschedler, M., *Nietzsche und die poetische Lüge*, Basle, 1954.

Blidstein, G., 'The Tannaim and plastic art: problems and prospects', *Perspectives in Jewish Learning*, V (1973).

Bronner, S. E., 'Between art and utopia: reconsidering the aesthetic theory of Herbert Marcuse', in R. Pippin, A. Feenberg and C. Webel (eds), *Marcuse – Critical Theory and the Promise of Utopia*, London, 1988.

Cohen, Boaz, 'Art in Jewish law', *Judaism* III (Spring 1954), no. 2.

Cohen, H., *Die dramatische Idee in Mozarts Operntexten*, Berlin, 1915.

Craft, R., 'Moses and Aaron in Paris', *New York Review of Books*, 13 December 1973.

Davidowitz, David, *Omanut V'Umanim b'Vatei knesset shel Polin*, Jerusalem, 1982.

Goodenough, E. R., *Jewish Symbolism in Dura*, New York, 1964.

Goux, J.-J., *Les Iconoclastes*, Paris, 1978.

Grotte, A., 'Die Kunst in Judentum und das 2 mosaische Gebot', *Der Morgen*, iv (June 1928), no. 2.

Güdemann, M., 'Das Judentum und die bildenden Künste' (unpublished lecture given at the Jewish Museum, Vienna, 3 January 1898 – typescript, Hebrew University, Jerusalem).

Guttmann, J., *The Jewish Life Cycle*, London, 1987.

Halpérin, I. and Lévitte G. (eds), *Idoles: Données et Débats*, Paris, 1985.

Kahana, Y.-Z., 'Omanut Bet Ha'Knesset be-sifrut ha-halakha', in Kahana, *Mehkarim be-sifrut ha-Tshuvot*, Jerusalem, 1973.

Löw, L., *Beiträge zur Jüdischen Altertumskunde*, Leipzig, 1870.

Murdoch, Iris, *The Fire and the Sun*, Oxford, 1977.

Schwarzschild, S., 'The legal foundations of Jewish aesthetics', *Journal of Aesthetic Education*, IX (January 1975), no. 1.

Scruton, R., *The Aesthetic Understanding*, Manchester, 1983.

Unna, I., 'Asthetische Gesichtspunkte im Religionsgesetz', *Jeschurun* (ed. J. Wohlgemuth), I, (January 1914), no. 1.

Wörner, K. H., *Gotteswort und Magie – die Oper 'Moses und Aron' von Arnold Schönberg*, Heidelberg, 1959.

Zevi, B., 'Ebraismo e concezione spazio-temporale nell'arte', *Rassegna mensile d'Israel*, (June 1974).

4 Historical

A Berlin and the German Lands

Ben-Sasson, H. H., *The Reformation in Contemporary Jewish Eyes*, Jerusalem, 1970.

Breuer, M., 'Emancipation and the rabbis', *Niv Hadmidrashia*, 13–14 (5738/9–1978/9).

Bruford, W. H., *Germany in the Eighteenth Century*, pb. edn, Cambridge, 1965.

Cohen, D., 'Die Entwicklung der Landesrabbinate in den deutschen Territorien bis zur Emanzipation', in A. Haverkamp (ed.), *Zur Geschichte der Juden in Deutschland des späten Mittelalters und der frühen Neuzeit*, Stuttgart, 1981.

Cohen, D., 'Ha'Yehudim ba-provinziyot ha-prussiyot', Proceedings of the Sixth World Congress of Jewish Studies, Jerusalem, 1975, II (Heb. Sec.).

Degani, B.-Z., 'Da'at ha-kahal ha-anti-Yehudit ke'gorem le-gerusham shel ha-yehudim mei-arei Germaniya be-shelhei y'mei ha-beinayim 1440–1530', PhD dissertation, Hebrew University, Jerusalem, 1982.

Eidelberg, S., *Jewish Life in Austria in the 15th Century*, Philadelphia, 1962.

Elbogen, I. and Sterling, E., *Die Geschichte der Juden in Deutschland*, Frankfurt on Main, 1966.

Eliav, M., *Ha-Ḥinukh ha-yehudi be-Germaniya biymei ha-haskalah ve-ha-emanzipaziyah*, Jerusalem, 1961.

Frank, M., *Kehillot Ashkenaz u-vatei dineihen*, Tel Aviv, 1937.

Freimark, P. (ed.), *Juden in Preussen – Juden in Hamburg*, Hamburg, 1983.

Freund, I., *Die Emanzipation der Juden in Berlin*, 2 vols, Berlin 1912.

Friedman, M., 'Mikhtavei Hamlatza le-kabtzanim – "ktavim"', *Michael*, II (1973).

Geiger, L., *Geschichte der Juden in Berlin*, 2 vols, Berlin, 1871.

Glanz, R., *Geschichte des niederen jüdischen Volkes in Deutschland*, New York, 1968.

Gutman, J., *Festschrift zur Feier des hundertjährigen Bestehens der Knabenschule der jüdischen Gemeinde in Berlin*, Berlin, 1926.

Israel, J., 'Central European Jewry during the Thirty Years' War', *Central European History*, xvi (1983), no. 1.

Jersch-Wenzel, S., *Juden und 'Franzosen' in der Wirtschaft des Raumes Berlin/Brandenburg zur Zeit des Merkantilismus*, Berlin, 1978.

Jersch-Wenzel, S., 'The Jews as a "classic" minority in eighteenth and nineteenth century Prussia', *LBYB*, XXVII (1982).

Karriel, J., 'Die Toleranzpolitik Kaiser Josephs II', in W. Grab (ed.), *Deutsche Aufklärung und Judenemanzipation*, Tel Aviv, 1980.

Landshut, E., *Toldot Anshei Ha-Shem u-f'eulatam be-adat Berlin*, Berlin, 1884.

Lassally, O., 'Zur Geschichte der Juden in Landsberg an der Warthe', *MGWJ*, 80 (1936).

R. Liberles, 'Emancipation and the structure of the Jewish community in the nineteenth century', *LBYB*, XXXI (1986).

Marcus, J.R., *Communal Sick-care in the German Ghetto*, Cincinnati, 1947.

Mendelssohn, M., *Gesammelte Schriften*, III, V, Leipzig, 1843–4.

Mendelssohn, Moses, *Gesammelte Schriften*, vii/i, Berlin, 1930.

Padover, S. K., *The Revolutionary Emperor*, 2nd edn, London, 1967.

Pollack, H., *Jewish Folkways in Germanic Lands (1648–1806)*, Cambridge, Mass., 1971.

Priebatsch, F., 'Die Judenpolitik des fürstlichen Absolutismus im 17. und 18. Jahrhundert', *Festschrift für D. Schäfer*, Jena, 1915.

Rawidowicz, S., *Introduction to Moses Mendelssohn: Gesammelte Schriften*, Berlin, 1930.

Rosensweig, B., *Ashkenazi Jewry in Transition*, Ontario, 1975.

Rürup, R., 'Jewish emancipation and bourgeois society', *LBYB*, XV (1969).

Schmidt, H.D., 'The terms of emancipation, 1781–1812', *LBYB*, I (1956).

Schnee, H., *Die Hoffinanz und der moderne Staat*, 6 vols, Berlin, 1953–67.

Schorsch, I., 'The emergence of the modern rabbinate', in W. Mosse, A. Paucker and R. Rürup (eds), *Revolution and Evolution – 1848 in German-Jewish History*, Tübingen, 1981.

Seeliger, H., 'Origins and growth of the Berlin Jewish community', *LBYB*, III (1958).

Shoḥet, A., *Im Ḥilufei Tekufot*, Jerusalem, 1960.

Shpitzer, S., 'Ha-rabbanut ve ha-rabbanim be-drom Germaniya ve-Austriya be-reshit ha-meah ha-15', *Sefer Ha-Shanah*, Bar-Ilan, nos 7–8 (1970).

Shulvass, M., *From East to West*, Detroit, 1971.

Silber, M., 'The historical experience of German Jewry', in J. Katz (ed.), *Toward Modernity, The European Jewish Model*, New Brunswick, 1987.

Silbergleit, H., *Die Bevölkerungs – und Berufsverhältnisse der Juden im deutschen Reich I*, Berlin, 1930.

Sorkin, D., *The Transformation of German Jewry, 1780–1840*, Oxford, 1987.

Stern, M., 'Das Vereinsbuch des Berliner Beth Hamidrasch, 1743–1783', *JJLG*, xxii (1931–2).

Stern, M., *König Ruprecht von der Pfalz in seinen Beziehungen zu den Juden*, Kiel, 1898.

Stern, Moritz, 'Die Niederlassung der Juden in Berlin im Jahre 1671', *ZGJD*, II (1930), no. 2.

Stern, S., *The Court Jew*, Philadelphia, 1950.

Toury, J., 'Der Eintritt der Juden ins deutsche Bürgertum', in H. Liebeschütz and A. Paucker (eds), *Das Judentum in der deutschen Umwelt*, Tübingen, 1977.

Wolbe, E., *Geschichte der Juden in Berlin und in der Mark Brandenburg*, Berlin, 1937.

Zimmer, E., *Harmony and Discord*, New York, 1970.

B   London and England

Alderman, G., *The Federation of Synagogues 1887–1987*, London, 1987.

Apple, R., 'United Synagogue: religious founders and leaders', in S. S. Levin (ed.),

A Century of Anglo-Jewish Life, 1870–1970, London, n.d.

Arared, A. P., *Apprentices of Great Britain, 1710–1773*, with an introduction by R. Barnett, *TJHSE*, XXII (1968–9).

Barnett, A., 'Solomon Bennet: artist, Hebraist, controversialist (1761–1838)', *TJHSE*, XVII (1951–2).

Barnett, A., 'Sussex Hall – the first Anglo-Jewish venture in popular education', *TJHSE*, XIX (1955–9).

Barnett, A., *The Western Synagogue through Two Centuries, 1761–1961*, London, 1961.

Barnett, L. O. (trans.), *El Libro de los Acuerdos*, Oxford, 1931.

Barnett, L. (ed.), *Bevis Marks Records I*, Oxford, 1940.

Barnett, R., 'Dr Jacob de Castro Sarmento and Sephardim in medical practice in 18th century London', *TJHSE*, XXVII (1978–80).

Barnett, R., 'Dr Samuel Nunez Ribeiro and the settlement of Georgia', in *Migration and Settlement – Papers in American Jewish History*, London, 1971.

Barnett, R., 'Mr Pepys's contacts with the Jews of London', *TJHSE*, XXIX (1982–6).

Barnett, R., 'The correspondence of the Mahamad of the Spanish and Portuguese congregation of London during the seventeenth and eighteenth centuries', *TJHSE*, XX (1964).

Beneyahu, M., 'Vikuḥim ba-kehilah ha-sephardit ve-ha-portugesit be-London', *Michael*, X (1986), Heb. Sec.

Bentwich, N., 'More Anglo-Jewish leading cases', *TJHSE*, XVI (1945–51).

Bermant, C., *The Cousinhood – the Anglo-Jewish Gentry*, London, 1971.

Black, E., *The Social Politics of Anglo-Jewry 1880–1920*, Oxford, 1988.

Blumberg, A., 'The British and Prussian consuls at Jerusalem and the strange last will of Rabbi Hirschell', *Zionism*, I (Spring 1980).

Breslauer, W., 'Vergleichende Bemerkungen zur Gestaltung des jüdischen Organisationslebens in Deutschland und England', in H. Tramer (ed.), *In Zwei Welten*, Tel-Aviv, 1962.

Cohen, Stuart, 'Sir Moses Montefiore and Anglo-Jewry', Proceedings of the 9th World Congress of Jewish Studies, Division B, III, Jerusalem, 1986.

Cohn, E. J., 'Eheschliessung in englischen nicht-orthodoxen Synagogen', in *Festschrift zum 60ten Geburtstag von Rabbiner Dr. Lothar Rothschild*, Bern, 1970.

Conway, E. S., 'The origins of the Jewish Orphanage', *TJHSE*, XXII (1970).

Diamond, A. S., 'Problems of the London Sephardi community', *TJHSE*, XXI (1968).

Diamond, A. S., 'The cemetery of the re-settlement', *TJHSE*, XIX (1955–9).

Diamond, A. S., 'The community of the resettlement, 1656–1684: a social survey', *TJHSE*, xxiv (1974).

Duschinsky, C., *The Rabbinate of the Great Synagogue, London, 1756–1842*, repr., London, 1971.

Emanuel, C., *A Century and a Half of Jewish History*, London, 1910.

Endelman, T., 'Communal solidarity among the Jewish elite of Victorian London', *Victorian Studies* (Spring 1985).

Endelman, T., *'The Jews of Georgian England, 1714–1830'*, Philadelphia, 1979.

Finestein, I., 'An aspect of the Jews and English Marriage Law during the emancipation: the prohibited degrees', *JJS*, VII (1965), no. 1.

Finestein, I., 'Anglo-Jewish opinion during the struggle for emancipation', *TJHSE*, XX (1959–61).

Finestein, I., 'Anglo-Jewry and the law of divorce', *Jewish Chronicle*, 19 April 1957.

Finestein, I., *Post-Emancipation Jewry: The Anglo-Jewish Experience* (seventh Sacks lecture), Oxford, 1980.

Finestein, I., 'The uneasy Victorian: Montefiore as communal leader', in Sonia and V. D. Lipman (eds), *The Century of Moses Montefiore*, Oxford, 1985.

Frankel, J., 'Crisis as a factor in modern Jewish politics', in J. Reinharz (ed.), *Living with Antisemitism*, Hanover/London, 1987.

Frankel, J., 'The Russian-Jewish Question and the Board of Deputies' in *Transition and Change in Modern Jewish History – Essays in honor of S. Ettinger*, Jerusalem, 1987.

Fraser, A., *King Charles II*, London, 1979.

Friedlander, M., 'The late chief rabbi Dr N. M. Adler', *JQR*, no. 2 (1889–90).

Gartner, L. P., 'East European Jewish immigrants in England', *TJHSE*, XXIX (1982).

Gartner, L. P., *The Jewish Immigrant in England, 1870–1914*, London, 1960.

Gaster, Moses, *History of the Ancient Synagogue of the Spanish and Portuguese Jews*, London, 1901.

Gilam, A., *The Emancipation of the Jews in England, 1830–1860*, New York/London, 1982.

Goldsmid, F. H., *Arguments Advanced against the Enfranchisement of the Jews*, London, 1831.

Gordon, G. H., 'Blasphemy in English criminal law', *JLA*, V (1985).

Goulston, M., 'The status of the Anglo-Jewish rabbinate, 1840–1914', *JJS*, X (June 1968), no. 1.

Green, G. L., *The Royal Navy and Anglo-Jewry, 1740–1820*, London, 1989.

Haggard, J. (ed.), *Reports of Cases in the Consistory Court of London, I*, London, 1822.

Harris, R. Isidore (ed.), *Jews' College Jubilee Volume*, London, 1906.

Henriques, H. S. Q., *The Jews and the English Law*, Oxford, 1908.

Hyamson, A., *The Sephardim of England*, London, 1951.

Hyamson, A. M., *Jews' College, 1855–1955*, London, 1955.

Hyamson, A. M., *The London Board for Schechita, 1804–1954*, London, 1954.

Jacobs, Joseph, *Studies in Jewish Statistics, Social, Vital and Anthropometric*, London, 1891.

Jewish Board of Guardians, 13th Annual Report, London, 5632–1872; 21st Annual Report, 5640–1880.

Jones, G. Lloyd, *The Discovery of Hebrew in Tudor England*, Manchester, 1983.

Kaplan, J. (ed.), *Shivat ha'Yehudim le-Angliya*, Jerusalem, 1972.

Kaplan, Stanley, 'The Anglicization of the East European Jewish immigrant as seen by the London *Jewish Chronicle*, 1870–1897', *Yivo Annual of Jewish Social Science*, x (1955).

Katz, D., *Philo-Semitism and the Readmission of the Jews to England*, Oxford, 1982.

Laski, N., *The laws and Charities of the Spanish and Portuguese Jews Congregation of London*, London, 1952.

Laws of the Great Synagogue Revised, London, 5623–1863.

Lehmann, Ruth, *The Library – A History*, London, 2nd rev. edn, 1967 – 5727.

Levin, S. S., 'The origins of the Jews' Free School', *TJHSE*, XIX (1955–9).

Levine, Rev. E., *The History of the New West End Synagogue, 1879–1929*, Aldershot, 1929.

Levy, A. B., *The 200-year-old New Synagogue, 1760–1960*, London, 1960.

Liberles, R., 'The Jews and their bill: Jewish motivations in the controversy of 1753', *Jewish History (Haifa)*, II (1987), no. 2.

Lipman, V. D., *A Century of Social Service, 1859–1959*, London, 1959.

Lipman, V. D., 'Jewish settlement in the East End of London, 1840–1940', in A. Newman (ed.), *The Jewish East End, 1840–1939*, London, 1981.

Lipman, V. D., 'Synagogal organization in Anglo-Jewry, *JJS*, I–II (1959–60).

Lipman, V. D., 'The age of emancipation, 1815–1880', in V. D. Lipman (ed.), *Three Centuries of Anglo-Jewish History*, Cambridge, 1961.

Lipman, V. D., 'The Anglo-Jewish community in Victorian society', in D. Noy and I. Ben-Ami (eds), *Studies in the Cultural Life of the Jews in England*, Jerusalem, 1975.

Lipman, V.D., *The Social History of the Jews in England, 1850–1950*, London, 1954.

Lipman, V.D., 'Trends in Anglo-Jewish occupations', *JJS*, II (1960).

London Missionary Society, Thirteenth Report, London, 1807.

McKeon, M., 'Sabbatai Sevi in England', *AJSR*, II (1977).

Magnus, Laurie, *The Jewish Board of Guardians and the Men who Made It*, London, 1909.

Margoliouth, Rev. Moses, *The History of the Jews in Great Britain, III*, London, 1851.

Marly, Diana de, 'Sir Solomon de Medina's textile warehouse', *THJSE*, XXVII (1982).

Mayhew, H., *London Labour and the London Poor*, 2 vols, London, 1851.

Meirovich, H., 'Ashkenazic reactions to the conversionists, 1800–1850', *TJHSE*, XXVI (1979).

Meisels, I. S., 'The Jewish Congregation of Portsmouth (1766–1842)', *TJHSE*, VI (1907).

Mills, J., *The British Jews*, London, 1853.

Minute Books of the Board of Deputies of British Jews, nos 1–6, 11 (1760–1850, 1871–8).

Newman, A., *The Board of Deputies of British Jews, 1760–1985*, London, 1987.

Newman, A., *The United Synagogue, 1870–1970*, London, 1976.

Ornstein, P., *Historical Sketch of the Beth HaMidrash*, London, 1905.

Osterman, N., 'The controversy over the proposed re-admission of the Jews to England (1655)', *JSS*, III (1941).

Patinkin, D., 'Mercantilism and the readmission of the Jews to England,', *JSS*, viii (1946).

Perry, N., 'Anglo-Jewry, the law, religious conviction and self-interest (1655–1753)', *Journal of European Studies*, XIV (1984).

Perry, N., 'La chute d'une famille sefardie', *Dix-huitième siècle*, XIII (1981).

Perry, T.W., *Public Opinion, Propaganda and Politics in 18th Century England*, Cambridge, Mass., 1962.

Picciotto, J., *Sketches of Anglo-Jewish History*, rev. and ed. I. Finestein, London, 1956.

Pollins, H., *A History of the Jewish Working Men's Club and Institute, 1874–1912*, Oxford, 1981.

Pollins, H., 'Jews on strike', *Jewish Chronicle*, 4 January 1974.

Pollins, H., *The Economic History of the Jews in England*, London/Toronto, 1982.

Quinn, P. L., 'The Jewish schooling systems of London, 1656–1956', PhD diss., University of London, 1958.

Rabb, T.K., 'The stirrings of the 1590s and the return of the Jews to England', *TJHSE*, XXVI (1974–8).

Rabinowicz, O., 'Sir Solomon de Medina', *JHSE*, (1974).

Ravid, B., '"How profitable the Nation of the Jews are": the Humble Addresses of Menasseh b. Israel and the *Discorso* of Simone Luzzatto', in J. Reinharz and D. Swetchinski (eds), *Essays in Jewish Intellectual History in honor of Alexander Altmann*, Durham, N. Carolina, 1982.

Report of the Committee appointed on the subject of parliamentary grants for education to Jewish schools, London, 1852.

Roth, C., *A History of the Jews in England*, 3rd edn, Oxford, 1978.

Roth, C. (ed.), *Anglo-Jewish letters, 1158 – 1917*, London, 1938.

Roth, C., 'Educational abuses and reforms in Hanoverian England', in *M.M. Kaplan Jubilee Volume* (Heb. Sec.), New York, 1953.

Roth, C., *Essays and Portraits in Anglo-Jewish History*, Philadelphia, 1962.

Roth, C., *The Great Synagogue, London, 1690–1940*, London, 1950.

Roth, C., 'The lesser London synagogues of the 18th century', *MJHSE*, III (1937).

Routledge, R., 'The legal status of the Jews in England, 1190–1790', *Journal of Legal History*, V (1982), no. 2.

Rubens, A., 'Portrait of Anglo-Jewry, 1656–1836', *TJHSE*, XIX (1960).

Rumney, J., 'The economic and social development of the Jews in England, 1730–1860', PhD diss., London, 1933.

Salaman, R., 'Whither Lucien Wolf's Anglo-Jewish community?' *JHSE*, London, 1954.

Samuel, E.R., 'The first fifty years', in V.D. Lipman (ed.), *Three Centuries of Anglo-Jewish History*, Cambridge, 1961.

Samuel, W., 'The first London synagogue of the re-settlement', *TJHSE*, X (1921–3).

Saraiva, A.J., 'Antonio Vieira, Menasseh b. Israel et le cinquième empire', *Studia Rosenthaliana*, VI (1972).

Schechter, S., *Studies in Judaism*, 2nd series, repr., Philadelphia, 1945.

Schorsch, I., 'From messianism to realpolitik: Menasseh b. Israel and the readmission of the Jews to England', *PAAJR*, xlv (1978).

Scult, M., 'English missions to the Jews', *JSS*, XXXV (1973), no. 1.

Sharot, S., 'Religious change in native orthodoxy in London, 1870–1914', *JJS*, XV (1973), no. 1, p. 58.

Simons, H., *Forty Years a Chief Rabbi*, London, 1980.

Singer, S., 'Orthodox Judaism in early Victorian London, 1840–1858', PhD thesis, Yeshiva University, New York, 1981.

Singer, Steven, 'The Anglo-Jewish ministry in early Victorian London', *Modern Judaism*, V (Oct. 1985), no. 3.

Sisson, C.J., 'A colony of Jews in Shakespeare's London', *Essays and Studies by Members of the English Association*, xxiii (1938).

Solomons, Israel, 'Lord George Gordon's conversion to Judaism', *TJHSE*, VII (1911–14).

Stein, S., 'Some Ashkenazi charities in London', *TJHSE*, XX (1964).

Stein, S., *The Beginnings of Hebrew Studies at University College*, London, 1952.

Van Oven, Joshua, *Letters on the Present State of the Jewish Poor in the Metropolis*, London, 1802.

Weinberg, Dr A., *Portsmouth Jewry, 1730s–1980s*, London, n.d.

White, J., 'Jewish Landlords, Jewish tenants: an aspect of class struggle within the Jewish East End, 1881–1914', in A. Newman (ed.), *The Jewish East End, 1840–1939*, London, 1981.

White, J., *Rothschild Buildings*, London, 1980.

Whitehill, G.H., 'Introduction to Bevis Marks Records, III', *JHSE* (1973).

Wilensky, M., 'The royalist position concerning the re-admission of Jews to England', *JQR*, XLI (1950–1).

Williams, Bill, *The Making of Manchester Jewry, 1740–1875*, Manchester, 1976.

Wolf, L., 'Cromwell's Jewish Intelligencers', in Cecil Roth (ed.), *Essays in Jewish History*, London, 1934.

Wolf, L., 'Crypto-Jews under the Commonwealth', *TJHSE*, I (1895).

Wolf, L., 'Status of the Jews in England after the re-settlement', *TJHSE*, IV (1899–1901).

Wolf, L., 'The origin of the Neve Zedek', in C. Roth (ed.), *Essays in Jewish History*, London, 1934.

Yogev, G., *Diamonds and Coral*, Leicester, 1978.

Zimmels, R. Jacob, 'Psakim u-Tshuvot mi-bet dino shel R. Shlomo bar Zvi [Rabbi Solomon Hirschell]', in *Essays presented to Chief Rabbi Israel Brodie*, London, 1967 (Heb. Sec.).

C   General

R. Abraham Farrissol, *Iggeret Orhot Olam*, Venice, 1586.

Adler, Elkan (ed.), *Jewish Travellers*, London, 1930.

Arkin, M., *'Aspects of Jewish Economic History'*, Philadelphia, 1975.

Ben-Sasson, H.-H., *Trial and Achievement*, Jerusalem, 1974.

Bloom, H., *Economic Activities of the Jews of Amsterdam*, repr., New York, 1969.

Chazan, R., *Medieval Jewry in Northern France*, Baltimore/London, 1973.

Ettinger, Sh., 'The beginnings of the change in the attitude of European society towards the Jews', *Scripta Hierosolymitana*, VII (1961).

Graupe, H.M., *Die Entstehung des modernen Judentums*, Hamburg, 1969.

Hertzberg, A., *The French Enlightenment and the Jews*, New York/London, 1968.

Hyman, L., *The Jews of Ireland*, London/Jerusalem, 1972.

Jost, I.M., *Geschichte der Israeliten*, X, Berlin, 2nd edn, 1847.

Kochan, L., *The Jew and his History*, London, 1977.

Schwarzfuchs, S., 'Les nations Juives de France', *Dix-Huitième Siècle*, 13 (1981).
Schwarzfuchs, S., *Napoleon, the Jews and the Sanhedrin*, London, 1979.
Vogelstein, H. and Rieger, P., *Geschichte der Juden in Rom, II*, Berlin, 1895.
Weinryb, B.D., *The Jews of Poland*, Philadelphia, 1973.

5   Messianic and Utopian

Aescoly, A.Z. and Even-Shmuel, Y., (eds), *Ha-Tenuot ha-meshihiyot be-Yisrael*, Jerusalem, 1956.
Aran, G., 'A mystic-messianic interpretation of modern Israeli history', *Studies in Contemporary Jewry*, IV (1988).
Breuer, M., 'Ha-Diyun beshalosh ha-shevuot be-dorot ha-aharonim', in *Ge'ulah u-medina*, Jerusalem, 1979.
Buve, P. Sergius, 'Utopie als Kritik', in *Säkularisation und Utopie – Ebracher Studien*, Stuttgart, 1967.
Casper, B., 'Reshit Zemichat Ge'ulatenu', in Jonathan Sacks (ed.), *Tradition and Transition: Essays presented to Chief Rabbi Sir Immanuel Jakobovits*, London, 1986.
Cohen, G.D., 'Messianic postures of Ashkenazim and Sephardim', *LBI*, New York, 1967.
Crool, Joseph, *The Fifth Empire*, London, 1829.
Crool, Joseph, *The Last Generation*, London, 1829.
Duveau, G., *Sociologie de l'Utopie*, Paris, 1961.
Elam, Yigal, 'Gush Emunim – false messianism', *Jerusalem Quarterly*, no. 1 (Fall 1976).
Eliav-Feldon, M., '"If you will it, it is no fairy tale": the first Jewish utopias', *JJS*, xxv (December 1983), no. 2.
Frye, Northrop, 'Varieties of literary utopias', in F.E. Manuel (ed.), *Utopias and Utopian Thought*, London, 1973.
Funkenstein, A., 'Maimonides: political theory and realistic messianism', *Miscellanea Medievalia*, xi (1977).
Furter, P., 'Utopie et Marxisme selon Ernst Bloch', *Archives de la Sociologie de la Religion* (1966).
Gekle, H., *Wunsch und Wirklichkeit*, Frankfurt on Main, 1986.
Graetz, M., 'Ha-Meshihiyut ha-hilonit ba-meah ha-tesha-esreh kederekh shiva la-yahadut', in Ts. Baras (ed.), *Meshihiyut ve-eskatalogiya*, Jerusalem, 1984.
Graus, F., 'Social utopias in the Middle Ages', *Past and Present*, no. 38 (December, 1967).
Hacker, J., 'Links between Spanish Jewry and Palestine, 1391–1492', in R. Cohen (ed.), *Vision and Conflict in the Holy Land*, Jerusalem, 1985.
Hexter, J.H., *More's Utopia – the Biography of an Idea*, New York, 1965.
Higger, M., *The Jewish Utopia*, Baltimore, 1932.
Holloway, Mark, *Heavens on Earth – Utopian Communities in America 1680–1880*, London, 1951.
Hundert, G.D., 'No messiahs in paradise', *Viewpoints*, II (1980), no. 2.
Kasher, M.M., *Ha-Tekufah ha-gedolah*, Jerusalem, 1972.

Kaufmann, D., 'Azriel b. Solomon Dayiena et la seconde intervention de David Reubeni en Italie', *REJ*, 30 (1895).

Kraemer, J., 'On Maimonides' messianic posture', in I. Twersky (ed.), *Studies in Medieval Jewish History, II,* Cambridge, Mass., 1984.

Levinsky, A.L., *Masa l'Eretz Yisrael b'shnat 5800* [CE 2040] Berlin, 1922, (first published 1892).

Mannheim, K., *Ideology and Utopia*, pb. edn, Engl. trans., London, 1960.

Manuel, F.E. and F.P., *Utopian Thought in the Western World*, Oxford, 1979.

Morgenstern, A., *Meshihiyut ve-yishuv Eretz-Yisrael*, Jerusalem, 1985.

Myers, Jody, 'Attitudes towards a resumption of sacrificial worship in the nineteenth century', *Modern Judaism*, vii (February 1987), no. 1.

Neusner, J., *The Messiah in Context*, Philadelphia, 1984.

Nordhoff, C., *The Communistic Societies of the United States*, New York, 1970 (first published 1875).

Novak, D., 'Maimonides's concept of the messiah', *Journal of Religious Studies*, ix (1982), no. 2.

Passmore, J., *The Perfectibility of Man*, pb. edn, London, 1972.

Polak, F.L., 'Utopia and cultural renewal', in F.E. Manuel (ed.), *Utopias and Utopian Thought*, London, 1973.

Rosenberg, Shalom, 'Exile and redemption in Jewish thought in the sixteenth century', in B. Cooperman (ed.), *Jewish Thought in the Sixteenth Century*, Harvard, 1983.

Salmon, J., 'Meshihiyut masortit u-leumiyut modernit', *Kivunim*, xxi (1983).

Schapira, J., *Bishvilei Ha-Geulah*, 2 vols, Tel Aviv, 1947.

Schein, Sylvia, 'An unknown messianic movement in thirteenth century Italy: Cesena 1297', *Italia*, V (1985), 1–2.

Scholem, G., 'Die Metamorphose des häretischen Messianismus der Sabbatianer in religiösen Nihilismus im 18. Jahrhundert', in *Zeugnisse – Theodor W. Adorno zum 60. Geburtstag*, Frankfurt on Main, 1963.

Scholem, G., 'Jacob Frank and the Frankists', *Enc. Jud.*, VII, cols 55–72, Jerusalem, 1971.

Scholem, G., 'Redemption through sin', in G. Scholem, *The Messianic Idea in Judaism*, London, 1971.

Schwarzschild, S., 'A note on the nature of ideal society – a rabbinic study', in A.H. Strauss and H.F. Reissner (eds), *Festchrift for Curt Silbermann*, New York, 1969.

Shapira, Anita, 'Zionism and political messianism', in *Totalitarian Democracy and After – International Colloquim in memory of Jacob Talmon*, Jerusalem, 1984.

Sharot, S., 'Jewish millenarianism: a comparison of medieval communities', *Comparative Studies in Society and History*, XXII (1980).

Sharot, S., *Messianism, Mysticism and Magic*, Chapel Hill, North Carolina, 1982.

Shatz, R., review of I. Tishby, *Tsitsat Nobel Zvi*, *Behinot*, X (1956).

Shatz, R., 'Kavim l'demuta shel ha'hitor'rut ha'politit-meshihit l'achar gerush Sefarad', *Da'at*, XI (summer 1983).

Silver, A.H., *A History of Messianic Speculation in Israel*, repr., Gloucester, Mass., 1978.

Taubes, J., 'The price of messianism', Proceedings of the 8th World Congress of Jewish Studies, Division C, Jerusalem, 1982.

Tishby, I., *Meshihiyut b'dor gerushei Sefarad u'Portugal*, Jerusalem, 1985.

Tishby, I., *Netivei Emuna u-minut*, Jerusalem, 1964.

Wacholder, B.Z., *Messianism and Mishnah*, Cincinnati, 1979.

Waxman, Chaim, 'Messianism, Zionism and Israel', *Modern Judaism*, VII (1987), no. 2.

Werblowsky, R.J.Z., 'Crises of messianism', *Judaism*, VII (Spring 1958), no. 2.

Wilson, B., *Magic and the Millennium*, London, 1973.

Wischnitzer, R., *The Messianic Theme in the Paintings of the Dura Synagogues*, Chicago, 1948.

Yerushalmi, Y.H., 'Messianic impulses in Joseph ha-Kohen', in B. Cooperman (ed.), *Jewish Thought in the Sixteenth Century*, Cambridge, Mass., 1983.

Zeitlin, S., 'The Essenes and messianic expectations', in L. Landman (ed.), *Messianism in the Talmudic Era*, New York, 1979.

6 Philosophical

Baeck, Leo, *God and Man in Judaism*, Engl. trans., London, 1958.

Bloch, E., *Das Prinzip Hoffnung*, 2 vols, Frankfurt on Main, 1959.

Bloch, E., *Subjekt-Objekt*, enlarged edition, Frankfurt on Main, 1962.

Buber, M., *Israel and the World*, New York, 1948.

Cohen, Hermann, *Religion der Vernunft aus den Quellen des Judentums*, repr., Wiesbaden, 1978.

Culler, J., *On Deconstruction – Theory and Criticism after Structuralism*, London, 1987.

Dahrendorf, R., *Essays in the Theory of Society*, London, 1968.

Dubnow, S., *Nationalism and History*, ed., K.S. Pinson, Philadelphia, 1958.

Eisen, A., *Galut*, Indiana University Press, 1986.

Fackenheim, E., *To Mend the World*, New York, 1982.

Feuerbach, L., *Das Wesen des Christentums*, 2 vols, Berlin, 1956.

Formstecher, Dr S., *Die Religion des Geistes*, Frankfurt on Main, 1841.

Fox, M. (ed.), *Modern Jewish Ethics*, Ohio, 1975.

Graupe, H., 'Steinheim und Kant', *LBYB*, V (1960).

Halamish, M. and Schwarz, M. (eds), *Hitgalut, Emuna, Tvuna*, Ramat-Gan, 1976.

Handelman, Susan, *The Slayers of Moses*, Albany, New York, 1982.

Hegel, G.W.F., *Grundlinien der Philosophie des Rechts*, Hamburg edn, 1962.

Hirsch, Samuel, *Die Religionsphilosophie der Juden*, Leipzig, 1842.

Horkheimer, M., *Die Sehnsucht nach dem ganz Anderen*, Hamburg, 1970.

Hudson, W., *The Marxist Philosophy of Ernst Bloch*, London, 1983.

Jonas, H., 'Jewish and Christian Elements in Philosophy', in Jonas, *Philosophical Essays*, repr., Chicago, 1980.

Kohler, K., *Grundriss einer systematischen Theologie des Judentums auf geschichtlicher Grundlage*, Leipzig, 1910.

Langer, S., *Philosophy in a New Key*, Mentor edn, New York, 1952.

Lazarus, M., *Die Ethik des Judentums*, Frankfurt on Main, 1904.

Leibowitz, I., *Emunah, Historiya ve-arakhim*, Jerusalem, 1982.

Lévinas, E., *Difficile Liberté*, Paris, 1963.
Lévinas, E., *Du Sacré au Saint*, Paris, 1977.
Lévinas, E., *La Conscience Juive*, Paris, 1963.
Loewe, R. (ed.), *Studies in Rationalism, Judaism and Universalism*, London, 1966.
Löwith, K., *Wissen, Glaube und Skepsis*, 2nd edn, Göttingen, 1962.
Lukacs, G., *Geschichte und Klassenbewusstsein*, Berlin, 1923.
Marcuse, H., *Counter-Revolution and Revolt*, London, 1972.
Néher, A., 'Vision du temps et de l'histoire dans la culture juive', in *Les Cultures et le Temps*, Paris, 1975.
Nozick, R., *Anarchy, State and Utopia*, Oxford, 1974.
Plato, *Dialogues, III, The Republic*, trans. B. Jowett, Oxford, 1931.
Quinton, A. (ed.), *Political Philosophy*, Oxford, 1968.
Ravitsky, A., 'Ha-Tsefui ve-ha-Reshut ha-netuna', in Col. Har'even (ed.), *Yisrael le'krat ha-me'ah ha-21*, Jerusalem, 1984.
Reichmann, E.G., 'Max Horkheimer the Jew – critical theory and beyond', *LBYB*, XIX (1974).
Ricoeur, P., *Lectures on Ideology and Utopia*, New York, 1986.
Shear-Yashuv, A., *The Theology of Salomon Ludwig Steinheim*, Leiden, 1986.
Strauss, L., *What is Political Philosophy?*, Westport, 1973.
Unseld, S. (ed.), *Ernst Bloch zu ehren*, Frankfurt on Main, 1965.

7 Zionist

Ahad Ha'Am, *Kol Kitvei*, 2nd edn, Jerusalem, 1949.
Aran, G., 'The roots of Gush Emunim', *Studies in Contemporary Jewry, II*, Indiana University Press, 1986.
Avineri, S., 'Ha-Utopiya ha-Zionit shel Herzl', *Kathedra*, no. 40 (1986).
Ben-Horin, S.R., *Ḥamishim Shnot Tsiyonut*, Jerusalem, 1946.
Don-Yehiya, E., 'Religious leaders in the political arena: the case of Israel', *Middle Eastern Studies*, xx (1984), no. 2.
Don-Yehiya, E. and Liebman, C., 'The symbol system of Zionist socialism: an aspect of Israeli civil religion', *Modern Judaism*, I (1981), no. 2.
Herzl, T., *Old-New Land*, trans. Lotta Levensohn, republished New York, 1987, with a new introduction by Jacques Kornberg.
Hess, M., *Rom und Jerusalem*, repr., Tel Aviv, 1935.
Kalischer, Z.H., *Drishat Ziyon*, ed. I. Klausner, Jerusalem, 1964. (First published 1863.)
Katz, J., *Le'umiyut Yehudit*, Jerusalem, 1979.
Klausner, I., *Be-Darkhei Zion*, Jerusalem, 1978.
Kohler, M., *Early American Zionist Projects*, Publications of the AJHS, no. 8, 1900.
Leibowitz, I., 'State and religion', *Tradition* xii (1972), nos. 3–4.
Luz, Ehud, 'The moral price of sovereignty', *Modern Judaism*, vii (1987), no. 1.
Nehorai, M., 'The state of Israel in the teachings of Rav Kook', *Da'at*, nos 2–3, (1978–9).
Rubinstein, Amnon, *Mi-Herzl ad Gush Emunim*, Tel Aviv, 1980.
Ruchames, L., 'Mordecai Manuel Noah and early American Zionism', Proceedings

of the Sixth World Congress of Jewish Studies, II, Jerusalem, 1975 (Engl. Sec.).

Shilhav, J., 'Interpretation and misinterpretation of Jewish territorialism', in D. Newman (ed.), *The Impact of Gush Emunim*, London/Sydney, 1985.

Tal, U., 'The land and the state of Israel in Israeli religious life', Proceedings of the Rabbinical Assembly of America (76th Annual Convention), xxxviii (1976).

Tal, U., 'The nationalism of Gush Emunim in historical perspective', *Forum* (Jerusalem) (Fall/Winter 1979), no. 36.

Tal, U., 'Totalitarian democratic hermeneutics and policies in modern Jewish religious nationalism', in *Totalitarian Democracy and After – International Colloquim in memory of Jacob Talmon*, Jerusalem, 1984.

Toury, J., 'M.E. Levy's plan for a Jewish colony in Florida – 1825', *Michael*, III (1975).

8 Memoirs, Diaries, Biography and Letters

R. Abraham Kuk, *Hazon Ha-Geulah*, Jerusalem, 1941.

R. Abraham Kuk, *Igrot Ha-Ra'ayah*, Jerusalem, 1943–65, III.

Altmann, A., *Moses Mendelssohn*, London, 1973.

Avineri, S., *Moses Hess: Prophet of Communism and Zionism*, London/New York, 1985.

Bloch, Ch., 'Theodor Herzl and Joseph S. Bloch', *Herzl Year Book, I*, New York, 1958.

Cohen, Arthur A., 'Martin Buber and Judaism', *LBYB*, XXV (1980).

Dinari, Y.A., *Hakhmei Ashkenaz be-shilhei y'mei-ha'benayim*, Jerusalem, 1984.

Freudenthal, M., 'R. Michel Chasid und die Sabbatianer', *MGWJ*, 76, NS 40 (1932).

Herzl, T., *Diaries*, IV, Engl. trans., New York/London, 1960.

Hyamson, A.M., *David Salomons*, London, 1939.

Maimon, S., *Geschichte des eigenen Lebens*, Schocken edn, Berlin, 1935.

Marcus, J.R., *Israel Jacobson*, Cincinnati, 1972.

Marcus, J.R., 'Shed a tear for a transport', in Sh. Yeivin (ed.), *Studies in Jewish History presented to Raphael Mahler*, Merhavia, 1974, (Engl. Sec.).

Michaelis, D., 'The Ephraim family', *LBYB*, XXI (1976).

Montefiore, M., *Diaries*, ed. Louis Loewe, 2 vols, London, 1890.

Ruderman, D., *The World of a Renaissance Jew*, Cincinnati, 1981.

Sarna, J.D., *Jacksonian Jew – the Two Worlds of Mordechai Noah*, New York, 1981.

Scholem, G., 'Baruchiah – Rosh ha-Shabbataim be-Salonika', *Zion*, VI (1941).

Scholem, G., *Sabbatai Zvi – The Mystical Messiah*, Engl. trans., London, 1973.

Stern, M., 'Der Oberlandesälteste Jacob Moses', *Mitteilungen des Gesamtarchivs der deutschen Juden*, vi (1926).

Stern, M., 'Die Anfänge von Hirschel Loebels Berliner Rabbinat', *Jeschurun*, xvii (1930).

Stern, M., 'Meyer Simon Weyl, Der letzte Kurbrandenburgische Landrabbiner', *Jeschurun*, xiii (1926).

Stern, M., 'Salomon Kajjem Kaddisch, der erste kurbrandenburgische Landrabbiner', *Jeschurun*, VI (1919).

Yuval, I.J., *Ḥakhamim be-doram*, Jerusalem, 1989.

9   Documentary

'Aus dem ältesten Protokollbuch der Portugiesisch-Jüdischen Gemeinde in Hamburg', trans. J. Cassuto from the original Portuguese, since destroyed, *JJLG*, X (1913).
Dinur, B.-Z., *Yisrael Ba'Golah*, vol. II, pt 3, Jerusalem, 1968.
Druyanov, A., *Ktavim le-toldot Ḥibbat Ziyon*, Tel Aviv, 1925, II.
Hertzberg, A. (ed.), *The Zionist Idea*, Philadelphia, 1960.
Marcus, J.R., *The Jew in the Medieval World: A Source Book, 315–1791*, New York, 1965.
Meisl, J. (ed.), *Pinkas kehillat Berlin*, Jerusalem, 1962.
Stern, Selma, *Der Preussische Staat und die Juden*, 7 vols, Tübingen, 1962–75.
Transactions of the Parisian Sanhedrin, trans. D. Tama, New York/London, 1985.

10   Miscellaneous

Borochov, B., *Nationalism and the Class Struggle*, Engl. trans., Westport, 1973.
Carmell, A., Das Judentum und der Umweltschutz, in *25 Jahre Jüdische Schule Zurich*, Jerusalem, 1980.
Davies, W.D., *The Territorial Dimension of Judaism*, Berkeley, Cal., 1982.
Finbert, E.-J. (ed.), *Aspects du Génie d'Israel*, Paris, 1950.
Steinschneider, M., *Allgemeine Einleitung in die jüdische Litteratur des Mittelalters*, Jerusalem, 1938.
Zunz, L., *Gesammelte Schriften, III*, Berlin, 1876.

Index

228   *Index*